second edition

CLASSROOM MANAGEMENT

Methods and Techniques for Elementary and Secondary Teachers

Johanna Kasin Lemlech

University of Southern California

Longman

New York & London

Classroom Management, Second Edition

Longman Inc., 95 Church Street, White Plains, N. Y. 10601

Associated companies:
Longman Group Ltd., London
Longman Cheshire Pty., Melbourne
Longman Paul Pty., Auckland
Copp Clark Pitman, Toronto
Pitman Publishing Inc., New York

Lemlech, Johanna. Pp. 13, 58, and adapted pp. 211–213 from *Handbook for Successful Urban Teaching*, Harper & Row, 1977. Reprinted by permission.

Executive editor: Raymond T. O'Connell
Production editor: Robert M. Goodman
Text design: Carol Basen
Cover design: Joseph DePinho
Cover illustration/photo: National Education Association
Production supervisor: Pamela Teisler

Library of Congress Cataloging in Publication Data

Lemlech, Johanna Kasin.
   Classroom management.

   Bibliography: p. 325
   Includes indexes.
   1. Classroom management—United States.
I. Title.
LB3013.L455   1988   371.1'02   87-16934

ISBN 0-582-28667-0

88   89   90   91   92   93   9   8   7   6   5   4   3   2   1

Contents

Preface

Knowledge of good classroom management is so basic to sound professional practice that it should be considered an essential element of a teacher's professional literacy. The way in which the teacher manages the classroom affects the teacher's instructional expertise. Several recent research studies of teacher effectiveness have noted that the classrooms of successful teachers look almost like magic shows because students seem to change activities and move about so smoothly, almost automatically. In these classrooms the teachers have mastered specific techniques for planning an optimal number of meaningful activities, for anticipating potential problems, and for creating an enriched, inviting environment. The students in these classrooms appear to know what is expected of them; they seem satisfied with their own progress, and they know what to do when they need assistance. The formula for success seems to be teachers who, while monitoring the students' progress and anticipating learning or behavioral problems, are able to provide meaningful options matched to students' learning needs.

The goal of this book is to assist elementary and secondary teachers with their classroom preparation by describing classroom management procedures and by suggesting ways to work with students and other adults to create learning environments and to develop effective classroom instructional practices. Examples of suggested practices are fictitious; however, all of the suggestions, ideas, checklists, and exhibits included within the text have been verified with experienced teachers and by classroom research studies of effective teachers.

Teachers are leaders who influence students; as such, they need self-confidence, self-respect, status, and control of themselves and their environment. The teacher's professional responsibilities include human relations skills for working with students and coordinating the activities of other adults within the classroom. When teachers feel comfortable with their personal preparatory efforts such as lesson planning, arranging the instructional environment, and preparing record-keeping devices, they are able to consider those other dimensions of teacher behavior that affect their leadership role and their interactions with students and other adults.

The text is organized to progress from a focus on the meaning of classroom management in Chapter 1 to the management of group behavior in Chapters 2 and 3. Chapter 4 provides information about ways to evaluate students' progress. Chapters 5 and 6 focus on instructional skills and ways to improve instruction through knowledge of specific classroom management techniques. Chapter 7 looks at the classroom environment and how environmental settings affect academic activities. Chapter 8 reconsiders certain teaching techniques and suggests ways to refine teacher behaviors affecting learning. Chapter 9 provides suggestions for teacher-parent conferences. Chapters 10 and 11 focus on the collegial and leadership responsibilities of teachers and ways to improve professional performance.

In the Appendix are ideas for learning centers for elementary classrooms, some of the ideas are also appropriate for the development of learning packets for middle school and junior high school classrooms.

This book suggests a number of methodological approaches, record-keeping devices, and organizational routines along with suggested teaching behaviors. It is intended as a resource for the beginning teacher as well as for the practicing professional. The book was motivated in part by my own fifteen years of teaching in the public schools and by the questions about classroom management that were raised by my students at the university. The examples are derived from my own experiences in the schools and from sound research studies in elementary and secondary classrooms. I hope that the practices suggested here will be helpful to you as you plan and implement your own program.

Acknowledgments

I am indebted to a number of people who have contributed significantly to this book: Bernard Lemlech for a husband's patience and encouragement; Raymond O'Connell, editor, for his enthusiastic monitoring and support; Michael Stieger for photographic work; Margery Lemlech for artwork; Donna Stieger for teaching vignettes; and Shirley Levine and her faculty at the Heschel School for observation experiences.

To Bernie

CHAPTER 1

Teacher Behavior

> How can we judge the worth of a society?...If the children and
> youth of a nation are afforded opportunity to develop their
> capacities to the fullest, if they are given the knowledge to
> understand the world and the wisdom to change it, then the
> prospects for the future are bright.
>
> Urie Bronfenbrenner, *Two Worlds of Childhood* (New
> York: Russell Sage Foundation, 1970), p. 1.

CHAPTER HIGHLIGHTS

Teacher's role

Three teachers anticipate needs (elementary and secondary)

Definition of classroom management

Modeling

Key teacher behaviors

Maintaining good student behavior

Managing typical classroom problems

Classroom management textbooks typically address themselves to the
teacher's role as disciplinarian. Some of these textbooks point out the
many roles of the teacher, which range from counselor to book-keeper
to policeman, and then with funny stories and cartoon figures, they
implore the beginning teacher to "start out mean and hard," "don't
crack a smile the first week," and "be vigilant." However, in this textbook, it is presumed that there is only one role for which a teacher is
employed: the instructional role. The teacher is expected to fulfill this
role. This role demands specific knowledge and skill competencies,
such as knowledge of subject matter and skills for diagnosing learning
problems, prescribing objectives, providing assistance, reinforcing
needs, assessing competence, and reteaching. The teacher's instructional tasks are aimed at helping individuals learn. But to be successful
in carrying out the functions of instruction, the teacher needs to deal
with the social system of the classroom, and this involves classroom
management and organization functions. The link between instruction

and management is critical to success in the classroom. When teachers plan instructional processes, they must consider the ways in which students differ; teaching for learning must be directed at the individual student, but management involves consideration of how groups work together in a defined environment. For this reason the text is organized to discuss, first, individual student behavior, and then the management of group behavior. The two chapters on instruction (Chapters 5 and 6) will address the management tasks embedded within certain teaching strategies and learning experiences. Other chapters will provide information about the classroom environment, accountability measures, planning for substitute teachers, and relations with parents and other adults. The text concludes with ways to improve personal performance. Before beginning the first section of this chapter, see if you can define classroom management. ("Classroom management is...")

WHAT IS CLASSROOM MANAGEMENT?

◆ *(Julie Kramer is an elementary teacher.)*
    The summer was almost over, and Julie Kramer, who teaches in a traditional nine-month school, was sitting at the breakfast table with a thoughtful expression on her face. Her family exchanged knowing smiles, recognizing that reflective look; Julie was thinking about teaching.
    "Julie, you've been teaching for seven years now. Why do you worry so much about a new class?"
    "I'm not really worried, Herb, but I have many things to prepare. You can't just walk into a classroom the day school opens and expect things to take care of themselves."
    "What do you prepare, Mom? Give us a for instance!"
    "Maintenance chores are performed during the summer in schools that do not maintain a year-round program. This means that tables are polished, walls and floors scrubbed. All the furniture will be stacked in the middle of the room. I've got to decide how I want to arrange the furniture for my new class. To make that decision, I have to think about grouping, classroom interaction, and the special learning centers I want in my room. I need to think about access to textbooks and the other instructional materials that I use and about traffic patterns in the classroom."
    "Why is that so difficult?"
    "Well, what would happen if I decided to move our kitchen table closer to the refrigerator?"
    "That's easy. We would have trouble walking into the kitchen and the table would be in the path of the sink and the stove."
    "OK, what would happen if I moved our table up against the wall?"
    "We would all have to sit on one side and we couldn't see each other when we wanted to talk."
    "That's right, Craig, and the same things happen in classrooms. You need to consider walking patterns, exits, classroom rules, discussion circles, reading groups; all of the normal daily routines and activities."

"Why don't you just arrange your classroom the same way each year?"

"Many teachers do. But I find that when I teach a new grade level or think about different children, I have different needs in my classroom that require new arrangements to improve classroom life."

◆   *(Stewart Jackson is a high school history teacher.)*

Stewart Jackson unconsciously whistled a tuneless melody as he polished his shoes. "Yep, gotta do some unit planning," he thought to himself. "Got to go visit the 'teacher' store. Time to get a move on!"

Stewart began to make a list of what he would buy and what needed to be refurbished to prepare for his first teaching position. His "buy" list included pictures for the bulletin boards, map duplicating masters, a simulation, and a resource kit.

"But my real problem," he thought to himself, "is developing some resource units. I'm not going to get caught in the trap of having to rely totally on the students' textbooks. Textbooks are going to be a resource, not a bible!"

◆   *(Midge Brady is an elementary teacher in a year-round school.)*

"Three weeks off and spring vacation will give me time to really get prepared," Midge Brady thought. "By golly, I'm going to really keep track of the kids this time. When I have a parent conference, I'm going to be so prepared I'll be able to refer to my records and say some specific things about learning progress. Let's see now, I need to record oral participation, group work, homework assignments, peer tutoring, reading skills, mathematics concepts, social studies...." Midge began drawing charts, making diagrams, and listing skills for the information she sought about each child's progress.

Although these three teachers are fictitious, they are similar to many of the teachers who teach in elementary and secondary schools in the United States. Julie Kramer, Stewart Jackson, and Midge Brady recognized the need for advance preparation before entering the classroom door or beginning the new school year. Julie was concerned about classroom interaction and the classroom environment. Stewart Jackson was thinking about instructional materials and the need to prepare resource units to facilitate lesson planning. Midge was determined to organize record-keeping devices to report and monitor learning progress. Each of these preplanning components increases the likelihood that the teacher will feel confident, comfortable, and on top of the situation in the classroom.

Classroom management is the orchestration of classroom life: **planning curriculum, organizing procedures and resources, arranging the environment to maximize efficiency, monitoring student progress, anticipating potential problems.** The classrooms of successful teachers often look like magic shows because, in elementary classrooms, students seem to glide from one activity to the next; and in secondary classrooms, the students appear totally involved and responsive to the task at hand. The teachers' behavior appears effortless and slick. In these classrooms the teachers have mastered specific techniques for planning an optimal number of meaningful activities, for anticipating potential problems, and for creating an enriched, inviting environment. The students in these classrooms appear to know what is expected of them; they seem satisfied with their own progress, and they know what to do when they need assistance. The successful formula seems to be teachers who, while monitoring the students' progress and anticipating learning or behavioral problems, are able to provide meaningful options matched to students' learning needs. Brief examples of positive and negative classroom management skills follow to demonstrate the definition used in this text.

RESEARCH AND READINGS

Kounin, Jacob S. (1970). *Discipline and group management in classrooms*. New York: Holt, Rinehart & Winston, p. 63.

Kounin defines successful classroom management as "producing a high rate of work involvement and a low rate of deviancy in academic settings."

Duke, Daniel L. (Ed.). (1982). *Helping teachers manage classrooms*. Alexandria, VA: Association for Supervision and Curriculum Development, p. vii.

Duke described classroom management as "the provisions and procedures necessary to establish and maintain an environment in which instruction and learning can occur."

◆   Mr. Smith teaches algebra. As the period begins, he waits at the door and greets the students. He hands each student a practice assignment. The students store their belongings under the desks and immediately begin work. Mr. Smith walks around the class observing students as they think through the problem. As students complete the assignment, they look up at the chalkboard to verify their understanding. When most of the students have completed the practice assignment, Mr. Smith allows the students to question him about the problem. This leads to his presentation for the period.

After the presentation the students once again work a sample problem. This time working with a partner, they discuss the problem. Whole-class discussion of the problem follows. The period ends with the teacher complimenting the students' work and giving them an assignment for the next day.

Ms. Howard teaches next door to Mr. Smith. She also teaches algebra. When her students come into class, she begins to search for lecture notes. She asks a student, "What were we working on yesterday?" She frowns at several students hoping to get them quiet; ultimately she shouts at them. She finally begins to lecture, but a number of students are not paying attention. Ms. Howard gives the students an assignment and becomes angry when a student asks how to do it. She insists on quiet. The students leave class grumbling.

Observers in these two classrooms would notice some very obvious differences. In Mr. Smith's classroom it is obvious that the teacher preplanned (1) the practice assignment, (2) the lecture presentation, (3) the work assignment after the lecture, (4) the homework assignment. The classroom appears to be well managed. The students in Mr. Smith's classroom apparently knew the procedures for work and participation. This is illustrated by the fact that they immediately stored their belongings and started work on their practice assignment; they anticipated being able to question the teacher about the practice work; they were accustomed to working with a partner. Mr. Smith closely monitored his students' understanding by walking around the classroom and observing them as they worked and through his question and discussion strategies. Mr. Smith avoided problems because his timing was appropriate; the transition from one strategy to the next was barely discernible. The students appear to be satisfied and involved at all times during the class. The students seem to know what is expected of them; they cooperate with each other and with the teacher. Disruptive behavior is not in evidence.

Now let's think about Mr. Smith's neighbor, Ms. Howard. In her class the students do not go right to work because the teacher cannot even remember what the group was working on during the previous class. This gives the students time and opportunity to get involved in disruptive and non-school-related activity. We know that Ms. Howard did not preplan her lesson. When Ms. Howard begins her lecture, she has difficulty keeping the students quiet and focused; it is apparent that the students are not involved. The lack of student involvement may be the result of a lecture that is inappropriate, too difficult, or dull. Ms. Howard appears to be unaware of her students' learning needs, and she has not planned an appropriate activity. The students' behavior may be the consequence of an accumulation of experiences in this classroom in which appropriate routines have not been developed. There is considerable evidence that Ms. Howard's classroom is poorly managed.

RESEARCH AND READINGS

Brooks, Douglas M. (1985). The first day of school. *Educational Leadership*, 42(8), 76–78.

Experienced junior high math and science teachers on the first day of school begin classes in a businesslike manner, minimize the lag time between activities, and maintain eye contact with the entire class.

These findings are consistent with the behavior of experienced elementary teachers on the first day of school.

EFFECTIVE CLASSROOM MANAGEMENT

Some classroom problems represent unexpected happenings: Johnny left his arithmetic book at home and is unable to do his seatwork; gym clothes were left in a locker that was broken into; it has suddenly begun to rain, and the children cannot go outside for physical education; Brad and Sue are having an argument; the film that you were expecting did not arrive; the achievement tests are for the wrong grade level, and you now have two hours of classroom time to fill. These realities of classroom life necessitate managerial and teaching skills that go beyond typical lesson planning. The teacher needs not only a "bag of tricks" for the unplanned time that suddenly materializes but also group process skills—for working with students and other adults—and management techniques—for dealing with people, equipment, supplies, actions, and inaction.

The key to successful classroom management is preplanning. It is not enough for the teacher to engage in lesson planning. To be successful, the teacher must also think about avoiding common classroom occurrences that motivate misbehavior. The best-planned lesson will fail if the teacher forgot to provide appropriate instructions, or to give resource information, or to decide what to do with finished papers. Each of these pitfalls can motivate inappropriate classroom behavior that will make the difference between productive and nonproductive learning.

Studies of classroom management have differentiated between effective teachers and ineffective ones. Effective classroom managers remember to:

1. Set classroom routines and standards and communicate these to students.
2. Monitor compliance of standards and rules by teaching and reinforcing them, helping students to accept and understand them.
3. Preplan instruction, anticipating students' needs for materials, assistance, and movement.
4. Develop accountability systems to keep track of students' progress and develop students' self-control and self-evaluative skills.
5. Analyze tasks and learning experiences to anticipate time allotment, involvement, and task constraints.

Modeling

The student teaching experience is based on modeling theory, as are medical internships and apprenticeship programs. Teachers learn new skills and refine existing skills by working with colleagues who "model" the desired skill. In classrooms a whole group of students can be influenced by teacher behavior. Kounin (1970) found that when a teacher disciplines a student in the presence of other students, there is a "ripple" effect. The impact of an angry desist can embarrass and produce emotional conflict for students witnessing the interaction. Adolescents are particularly vulnerable to the influence of peers.

Just as misbehavior can be contagious, so can appropriate social behavior. Early studies by Bandura and associates (1961, 1963) have indicated that children begin imitating others' behavior during the preschool years. Character education in the United States was always considered to be the job of the family and the church; however, in recent years there has been growing acceptance and understanding of the responsibility of all adults in school and in the home to participate in directing the human development and socialization of children.

Appropriate classroom behavior can be encouraged by using what we know about modeling. The adage about doing what I say not what I do is pertinent to the theory of modeling. If the model performs an act in a certain way but instructs others to do it differently, the model's performance will be imitated, not the lip service instruction. If students observe that their teacher is disrespectful to or uncooperative with others, they are not likely to imitate cooperative and respectful behavior.

Modeling requires two phases for success: acquisition of the desired behavior and performance of the desired behavior. Bronfenbrenner (1970) distinguished between ignorance of an appropriate behavioral pattern and lack of motivation to perform the pattern. If the desired behavior is within the behavioral repertoire of the student, yet it is not performed, then the problem is motivational, not acquisitional. Therefore the treatment must deal with making the desired behavior more attractive and socially rewarding.

RESEARCH AND READINGS

Bronfenbrenner, Urie (1970). *Two worlds of childhood*. New York: Russell Sage Foundation, p. 133.
   "The most 'contagious' models for the child are likely to be those who are the major souces of support and control in his environment; namely, his parents, playmates, and older children and adults who play a prominent role in his everyday life."

Three factors affect the modeling process (Bronfenbrenner, 1970): the characteristics of the subject, the characteristics of the act to be performed, and the characteristics of the model. The person to be influenced must be able, physically and mentally, to perform the desired behavior and be motivated to perform it. If the subject is disinterested, then responsiveness will be limited; thus the problem for the model is to arouse interest in the desired act.

In terms of the desired behavioral pattern, if it is complex, then the pattern should be taught in a step-by-step fashion so that success is assured. The model should communicate what is to be learned and give assurance (praise) when it has been accomplished. To illustrate:

> Goal: Pass the ball to a teammate in basketball
>   Step 1: Teach ball-passing skills.
>   Step 2: Provide time for students to observe others using desired skills during an actual game or use a movie or television game for observation.
>   Step 3: Provide game practice using the skill.

The characteristics of the model constitute the most important factor affecting the modeling process. Bronfenbrenner identified seven properties of the model that affect the process and that are of particular interest in a study of classroom management.

1. If students perceive the teacher as an individual possessing "competence, status, and control over resources" (p. 132), then the teacher will be more effective.

2. As model, the teacher or peer will be more effective if perceived by the subject as someone of importance to him or her personally.

3. The most influential models will be those who play major roles in the life of the subject, affecting the support and control of the subject's environment. These may be classmates, parents, older peers, teachers.

4. If the subject perceives the model as being like him- or herself, then the power of the model will increase. This often makes peer teaching very effective.

5. If the child can see several examples of the desired behavior by different models, the effect will be more powerful. For instance, if students were to observe professional basketball players playing good team ball and practicing unselfish ball-passing behavior, it would be more effective than the teacher lecturing about the desired behavior.

6. Since group conformity needs are strong, if the model can exhibit a behavior conspicuous to the student's family or aspired group, performance of the behavior will be more likely.

7. Performance of the desired behavior (rather than acquisition) is more likely if the subject sees that the consequences of the behavior are self-fulfilling for the model. If the model achieves undesirable effects as a consequence of the behavior, then it decreases the likelihood of similar behavior by the subject.

When modeling is combined with reinforcement theory, desired effects can be maximized. Praising appropriate behavior is an example of the use of both theories. However, if the teacher praises behavior that is not optimally appropriate or provides feedback to some children and not to others, then the students do not perceive the teacher as an effective model. The characteristics of the model, properties 1, 4, 5, and 7 in the patterns of behavior, would be in jeopardy.

Bandura (1977, pp. 22–29) identified four components governing learning through modeling. The procedures he identified are as follows:

1. *Attentional processes.* Using attentional processes, the learner perceives modeled behavior. Modeled behavior varies in effectiveness depending on the attractiveness of the model or the interest aroused by the model (for instance, a pro football or pro baseball player).

2. *Retention processes.* Modeled behavior must be remembered by the learner in order to be performed. Observational learning is dependent on visual imagery and verbal coding. The learner retrieves visual images of behavior for future performance. During early childhood years, visual imagery is particularly important. (The three-year-old may remember the swagger of the bad guy on TV and the way in which he drew his gun and prepared to fire.) The teenager visualizes the "cool" performance of a "big wheel" with a cigarette in the mouth. Verbal coding of the observed behavior occurs when the learner converts visual information into a code for delayed use. (The three-year-old may remember for future performance how to say, "Bang-bang, I got you!") Before coming into the kitchen to show Mommy what he has learned, the three-year-old may mentally rehearse what he has learned. The teen visualizes how she or he will look with the cigarette. Mental rehearsal improves the performance.

3. *Motor reproduction processes.* The learner converts symbolic representation into actions by performing the modeled behavior. If the learner has acquired the behavioral skill required by the act, then he or she will reproduce the behavior accurately. If skills are lacking, then repeated modeling and practice will be required. Skills are rarely performed perfectly without practice and feedback.

4. *Motivational processes.* If the three-year-old sees the bad guy punished, he will be less likely to be influenced by the performance; however, if the modeled behavior is effective and rewarding for the model, then modeling the behavior will be favored by the learner.

Bandura (1977, p. 29) cautions that "the failure of an observer to match the behavior of a model may result from any of the following reasons: not observing the relevant activities, inadequately coding modeled events for memory representation, failing to retain what was learned, physical inability to perform, or experiencing insufficient incentives."

Using Modeling in Classroom Management

The effects of modeling are more evident when students are confronted with a new situation. The story told below by a friend's sixth-grade daughter is typical of the many classroom incidents that occur frequently because teachers virtually ask for them—or model them.

◆   Our class isn't usually like this, but she [the substitute] was acting so nasty and saying such stupid things. Jimmy dropped his pencil and the substitute teacher said, "Ha, Ha! That's very funny; I hope you're enjoying yourself."

Jimmy didn't mean to drop his pencil the first time, but he sort of looked around and winked, and we all followed his lead and dropped our pencils.

We hadn't thought of doing anything else, but then she said, "Well, now that you've had a pencil drop, I suppose you're going to have a book drop."

So-o-o everyone just kind of looked at each other, and lots of kids just started dropping their books on the floor.

The substitute teacher was not only predicting group misbehavior, she was directing it through her own sarcastic interaction with Jimmy and the class. When students do not know what to expect from an adult or a new situation, they are more likely to imitate behavior. In this case they observed a frustrated and impatient teacher who had misunderstood a student. The class sympathized with Jimmy who they felt was mistreated; they made the inference that this was not a friendly teacher, and so in a sense they imitated the teacher's own sarcastic behavior by doing precisely what she said to do.

Peer relationships are a critical element in the socialization process, but schools often operate as if students only interact with adults. This is an adult-centric view of life. In some classrooms teachers spend an inordinate amount of energy attempting to prevent student-to-student interaction. Yet peer relationships contribute to both socialization and social and cognitive development. Johnson and Johnson (1983) report that students' interaction facilitates the learning of attitudes, values, skills, and information not typically obtainable from adults. Through interaction students imitate each other's behavior. Using peers as models, students receive reinforcement and direct learning. Peer models shape social behavior, attitudes, and perspectives. Interaction with peers may provide opportunities for learning prosocial behavior. Johnson and Johnson (1983, pp. 128–129) suggest that peer relationships be structured by teachers to promote constructive goals:

1. Plan situations in which students will work together to achieve a common goal.
2. Focus on group product rather than individual products.
3. Teach interpersonal skills (group skills).
4. Structure the situation so that students have responsibilities for the success of the group and each other.
5. Encourage support, acceptance, concern, and commitment by all members of the group.
6. Hold members of the group accountable for group actions; members are responsible to and for each other.
7. Ensure that students are successful in their group work.

Suggestions for beginning and managing group work will be found in Chapter 2.

Good student behavior can be developed and maintained by fostering cooperative behaviors and by modeling appropriate behavior through teacher-student interactions. A number of key teacher behaviors will be discussed.

Consistency and equity

Mr. Hannibal rarely gives Paul time to respond during a classroom discussion. The consequence of this behavior is that Paul does not try to respond when he is called upon, and his classmates become more eager to compete for Paul's response time.

TEACHER: Paul, can you tell us why the Netsilik Eskimos migrate?
  PAUL: Um-mmm-mmm...
  MABEL: Mr. Hannibal, Mr. Hannibal, I know.
  JEAN: [Waving her hand in the air] It's because they're...
TEACHER: Well, all right, Mabel, you tell us.

Another version of the same discussion could have sounded this way:

TEACHER: Paul, can you tell us why the Netsilik Eskimos migrate? [Long pause]
TEACHER: Paul, do you recall some reasons why animals migrate?
  PAUL: Why, yes. Animals migrate when they need food or if the weather isn't right for them. Oh, I remember, the Netsiliks migrate...

In the second sequence the teacher waited for Paul to respond. After several seconds the teacher gave Paul a content clue that helped him to recall what he knew about migration and to compare animal and human migration patterns.

Analysis of the two instructional patterns provides several bits of information that are appropriate for discussion. Mr. Hannibal waited several seconds before giving Paul a content clue; research by Rowe (1974) indicated that most teachers wait only one second before calling on another student or else they answer the question themselves. Yet students' participation, interaction, involvement, and creativeness increase when teachers, using the technique of teacher silence, wait several seconds (three to five) before providing additional clues or calling on another student. Wallen (1966) discovered that cognitive achievement also increases when teachers accept students' statements by using, extending, summarizing, or clarifying them.

Still to be discussed is what happens in a classroom when a teacher selectively provides some students with content clues or is silent for a period of time to allow them time to reflect but cuts off other students consistently. Indirectly, the teacher's behavior toward the second group can affect (a) the students' motivation to respond; (b) their self-concept, based on the teacher's nonverbal lack of acceptance; and (c) the students' level of aspiration. In the first sequence, Mr. Hannibal's behavior encouraged impatience and lack of reflectiveness in the other children.

This discussion focuses on the instructional implications of inconsistency. It is important to recognize that whenever teachers are inconsistent in their responses to students, ultimately it affects classroom behavior. Suppose that Mr. Hannibal expects students to work quietly without talking to neighbors while doing practice assignments, but that there is a favored group of students who are able to communicate with each other without being penalized. The obvious inconsistency will affect the behavior of other students. Inconsistency occurs when teachers interpret classroom rules differentially or provide inequitable cues or responses to students. Tables 1.1 and 1.2 provide checklists to monitor your classroom behavior.

Table 1.1. Checklist for Elementary Awareness-Consistency

1. Without looking at your roll book, can you name all the children in your classroom?
2. If you were unable to name all of the children, whom did you forget? Do these forgotten children have any characteristic in common?
3. Can you name the children who always contribute to a discussion?
4. Can you name the children who rarely contribute to a discussion?
5. What efforts can you make to encourage children to contribute to a discussion?*
6. Your students have turned in work papers or projects. Identify some ways that you can demonstrate awareness to your students.*
7. When an individual's performance varies from the student's typical work, what do you do?*

8. Do you spend more time with some children than with others? Do you have an instructional purpose for doing so?

9. Do you remember to praise good performance based on individual differences? (Do only certain children get praised?)

10. Do you repeat directions, when requested, for all children?

11. Do you tend to "close out" certain children with discouraging responses?

---

* Some possible suggestions:

5. Make a habit of calling on many children, not a certain few. Give each child the same amount of time to respond (5 seconds). *l. l*

6. Talk to each student personally when you return the work; write a personal statement to each child; return the work promptly; discuss the importance and relevance of the work to ongoing activities.

7. Talk to the child individually; inquire if the child is "satisfied" with personal progress; express concern.

Table 1.2. Checklist for Secondary Awareness-Consistency

1. Use your roll book and select one group (class) of students. Can you remember something about each of the students? If you cannot remember something specific about each student, the next time you meet the class, see if the students you forgot have a common characteristic.

2. Using the same class of students, can you name the students who always contribute to a discussion?

3. Which students rarely contribute to a discussion?

4. What efforts can you make to encourage students to contribute to a discussion?*

5. Your students turn in work papers, homework, and projects. Identify some ways that you can demonstrate awareness to your students.*

6. When an individual's performance varies from the student's typical work, what do you do?*

7. Do you spend more time with some students than with others? Do you have an instructional purpose for doing so?

8. Do you remember to praise good performance based on individual differences? (Do only certain students get praised?)

9. Do you repeat directions, when requested, for all students?

10. Do you tend to "close out" certain students with discouraging responses?

---

* Some possible suggestions:

4. Call on students even if they do not volunteer. Encourage students to talk to each other rather than to you. Be noncommittal in your response and refer the question to others for further discussion. Give each student the same amount of time to respond.

5. Talk to each student personally when you return the work; write a personal statement to each student; return the work promptly and discuss the importance and relevance of the work to ongoing activities in the classroom.

6. Express concern about the student's performance to him or her personally; ask the student to explain the inconsistent performance.

Clarity

Principals frequently tell of visiting classrooms and asking students, "What are you supposed to be doing?" and the students too often responding, "We don't know." The principals are not telling tales and the students are not dumb. What then is the problem? Fuzzy and imprecise language is the villain. Students want and need to know what, how, and why. In order to perform individually or in a group assignment, students must understand what they are supposed to do (Table 1.3, p. 14). Most classroom activities require some degree of structuring in terms of the goal, time limitation, who is to do what, quality requirements, and the use of materials.

If teachers use imprecise language ("Boys and girls, make a time line beginning when your parents were children.") or give an assignment without verifying that the children understand it, misbehavior and confusion are the invariable consequences. Kounin (1970) verified that student behavior is affected by the clarity of the language teachers use to give directions to students before they begin work.

A related problem is the use of textbooks in social studies and science for reading assignments. Subject matter textbooks are more difficult than basal reading textbooks for students. If the assignment is to be productive, then materials must be introduced to organize the reading so that students understand the author's purpose, to define unfamiliar concepts, and perhaps to suggest an outline for gathering data and answering questions. Ausubel (1963) suggested the need for advance organizers to structure what is to be learned.

Problems also occur during classroom discussion because class members are unsure of the purpose of the discussion or because the teacher, as the discussion leader, does not ask questions effectively. For students to take part in a classroom discussion, the purpose of the discussion must be understood; questions must elicit responses from

---

Table 1.3. Checklist for Giving Directions and Assignments

1. Establish eye contact. (Ask students to look at you.)
2. Scan class to verify that students are not performing another task. (Remind students to put everything out of their hands like pencils, books, blocks, etc.)
3. Lower your voice to make students focus on what you are saying.
4. Speak clearly.
5. Give concise directions.
6. Verify student understanding through one or more of the following:
   a. Ask one or more students to repeat directions.
   b. Ask if anyone has a question.
   c. Monitor students' initial efforts if they are to perform a task.
7. Rephrase directions if students do not understand.

many students; questions must be interesting and motivating; questions must be clearly stated so the listeners know what is being asked.

Giving directions that are precise and clearly stated takes practice. A good way to check on the clarity of your directions is to ask several students to repeat the instructions for an assignment. Then be prepared to sit back in shock as you discover the different perceptions the students have about what you thought you stated so clearly!

USE SECRET STORY & GO AROUND THE ROOM !

Acceptance and respect

For students to feel accepted, the teacher must communicate interactive cues verbally or nonverbally. For instance, when a student looks up with an agonized expression while taking an examination, the teacher could walk over and pat the youngster on the shoulder, thereby communicating understanding. Or the teacher might encourage continuation of the task through eye contact and a nod to the student. The teacher in these two examples is saying, "I understand how you feel." The teacher may not necessarily agree with the student that the examination is difficult, but this has nothing to do with accepting the student's feelings.

For some time teachers have recognized that when students feel good about themselves, they are able to perform better in the classroom. A student's feelings of self-worth and self-esteem depend on the degree to which the child is aware of others' acceptance. A student's recognition of acceptance in the classroom by peers and teacher is related to practices that affect the self-concept. When teachers allow students to make decisions that affect them personally, they are letting the students know that there is trust in their joint relationship. When teachers communicate to students the acceptable boundaries for classroom behavior and proceed to carry through with the implementation of behavioral guidelines, then students have rational means by which to interpret personal actions. When a teacher plans for successful student performance, the students feel responsible to follow through, and they interpret the teacher's expectation as an affirmation of respect.

Sometimes a personal comment to a student will communicate teacher interest in the student as an individual. Similarly, during class or group discussions, some teachers consciously coordinate and extend students' ideas into statements or questions and ask others to reflect and share their ideas. In this instance the teacher is demonstrating, "I listened." The teacher is also modeling listening behavior that students will learn to imitate.

Accepting students' feelings and attitudes cannot be faked. The teacher's verbal or nonverbal body language betrays personal reactions to students. If the teacher pays no attention to inappropriate behavior or a student's failing performance, it is tantamount to indifference. Instead of ignoring the student's failure or misbehavior, the teacher can quietly confide to the student, "I expect you to do better," or, "How can I help you?" With this type of interaction, the student learns that the teacher sees, listens, and cares; the teacher is affirming the importance of the student.

Praise

Wittrock (1986) identifies two functions of praise in the classroom. First, praise can be used to motivate and reinforce appropriate behavior. For example, Juan completed ten math problems and each was correct. In the past Juan had never completed more than five, and usually these had been done in a haphazard manner. Juan deserves some praise and encouragement to continue his effort. If the praise is given appropriately, not only will it serve to reinforce his own feelings of success but it will motivate others to produce. To accomplish this the praise must be situation specific. "Juan worked hard in math today and it really paid off. His paper is correct, and neat too. I know you can keep up the good work, Juan." To reinforce appropriate behavior, praise should be natural; it should be used frequently for all students; it should be used discriminatively and conditionally. Note that Juan's teacher attributed his accomplishment to effort and implied that he will be successful in the future if he continues to put forth effort.

The second function of praise is to provide students with information. Praise is used to alert students that a classmate has performed (modeled) appropriately. Perhaps the student receiving the praise has read a passage in the textbook with expression; by praising the student, the teacher provides the listeners with insight about the teacher's expectation for performance. Research on students' thought processes suggests that this second function of praise may be much more important in the classroom than using praise to encourage performance.

Firmness

Kounin (1970) described the firmness dimension of more effective teachers as an "I mean it" factor. In his study of kindergarten children he found that firmness motivated conformity in children witnessing a teacher's firm behavior, whereas a teacher who treated children roughly or angrily produced disruptive behavior and emotionally upset children. Students' reactions to firmness appear to be consistent in both elementary and secondary education. It appears that a teacher cannot be firm without also being alert to students' needs, aware of developmental progress, and precise in language habits. Each of these dimensions adds to and facilitates the teacher's success with students, and each is dependent on the others in order to achieve good classroom management.

There are two important principles related to firmness that should be considered: Firm teacher behavior is related to the establishment of rational, enforceable rules; rules must be interpreted and enforced equitably for all children. Firmness is often communicated to students in the form of the teacher's expectations for student behavior and student accomplishments. Rule-setting will be discussed in Chapter 2.

Flexibility and adjusting to students' needs

Teacher responsiveness to unexpected happenings is another way in which behavior is modeled for students. For example, a sixth-grade teacher discovered that his students did not understand the division of fractions. Since he had taught it earlier in the semester, he thought his students just needed to be reminded about the process of inverting the divisor. When he had several students demonstrate problems on the chalkboard, he suddenly realized that they really had a basic learning problem. Instead of attempting to go on with the introduction of a new concept, he asked all of the students to work out a division problem on their papers. He checked their work individually and quickly divided the class into two groups. He introduced the new concept to the students who understood the division of fractions, and then went to the cupboard and found some plastic models for the other students to work with so he could review the problem.

This teacher adjusted to a learning problem that suddenly emerged. He was prepared for it in the sense that he had classroom equipment that allowed him to use a multisensory approach to teaching mathematics. He was aware of the need to use a different strategy to reteach the subject. He diagnosed the problem and prescribed a new teaching objective. The teacher did not continue his original plan once he became cognizant of the new need; he adjusted work activities to student needs.

The development of flexibility in the use of teaching strategies can be the teacher's greatest asset. When confronted with a learning problem, teachers are forced to make some instant decisions concerning their teaching approach, the students' learning style, a new objective, work activity, use of materials, and time allotment. When teachers are unwilling to adjust their plans, they court disaster because if students are confused they will not stay on task, and this is when teachers have classroom management problems.

Unexpected events during the school day are also normal in the course of teaching. For instance, just as you are about to clinch a learning experience, the fire bells begin to ring. Or equipment breaks down and spoils the lesson. Visitors, assemblies, the loudspeaker in the classroom, special personnel, all may represent unplanned happenings that require flexibility and adjustment.

Good classroom managers are consistent and equitable in the treatment of student behavior; they provide clear instructions; they are respectful of students (thereby generating respect from students); they provide encouragement and meaningful praise; they are rational and consistent in maintaining standards; and they adjust to both students' needs and unplanned school events. These behaviors promote positive teacher-student relationships and help students appreciate the teacher as model.

Additional Ways to Maintain Good Student Behavior

Individualizing and Personalizing Instruction

A lockstep system for classroom instruction can be frustrating to both teachers and students. Instead of trying to keep all students at the same level for efficient presentation of instruction, a teacher should make learning a step-by-step process so that students experience continuous progress. When teachers individualize classroom teaching, they are able to focus on the learning tasks needed, progressively, for each individual. This process entails monitoring student progress with checklists and objectives, prescribing objectives, reinforcing needs, and evaluating growth.

Individualizing instruction increases private contact between teacher and students, and thus rapport and understanding are developed in greater depth. The teacher uses ideas and suggestions that are meaningful to the individual student. The student becomes aware that he or she is important to the teacher and as a result begins to take charge of personal programming and progress. The student becomes a seeking individual, asking for assistance when needed. Responsibility for learning develops. However, it is important to remember that all instruction should not be individualized. Social literacy is dependent on group activities.

Some of the basic planning decisions for individualizing and personalizing instruction include:

Assessing each student's learning level
Developing an appropriate learning objective continuum
Planning a learning experience continuum
Developing a feedback system
Evaluating progress

Mobility: Teacher and Students

Looking back into history at the old schoolmaster and schoolmarm, we note that the teacher sat at a high desk in the front of the room during a great deal of the school day. (The teacher's switches to help maintain order were kept behind the desk.) Interaction among students was uncommon and considered unnecessary, and the development of rap-

You Must Move around the room

port with students was not a professional goal. Schoolrooms, teaching objectives, and the teaching process were different in those days (Lemlech & Marks, 1976). Today, most teachers consistently move around their classrooms, assisting students, noting progress, and maintaining attention.

One of the simplest means of maintaining discipline in the classroom is by physical presence. Wandering around the classroom, the teacher can inspect work, put a hand on a child's shoulder, smile, point to an error, applaud effort through hand gestures or facial expression. These nonverbal acts reinforce appropriate classroom behavior and serve to tell students that the teacher is interested, aware, and working. Moving about the classroom, the teacher implements many of the previously discussed modeling behaviors.

Teachers feel good moving about the classroom because they feel in control of events. The teacher is more alert and students are forced to maintain alertness. However, students also need to move about. Physical activity improves attention and keenness. Learning experiences in the classroom should be varied so that students have periods of quiet work and of more active work where they are allowed to get up, move to a learning center, work and talk with others. Sometimes merely getting up to choose a textbook—reinforcement activity—or to put an assignment in a special place relieves the monotony of sitting. Many classroom problems are prevented by planning movement to get the fidgets out. The aware teacher recognizes an imminent attack of the fidgets before it occurs and flexibly plans it away. (This would be a good time to review the teaching episode about Mr. Smith and his algebra class (p. 4). Note the pacing of instruction and the way in which Mr. Smith monitored students' progress.)

Monitoring Progress and Behavior

Effective teachers continuously evaluate learning by the use of observational techniques as they move about their classrooms, by scanning students' faces for signs of confusion or boredom, by conferring with students individually and in small groups, by using checklists to record progress, by testing, and by assisting students to self-evaluate.

There are three monitoring functions that affect classroom management:

1. Checking students' understanding of assignment instructions and of work in progress.
2. Verifying short- and long-term accomplishments.
3. Checking up on student behavior.

Each will be discussed separately.

If students misunderstand what they are supposed to accomplish or are confused about directions, they will disturb others as they attempt to get information from their peers about their assignment. A good way to prevent this is to verify that students understand the assignment before you turn them loose to begin work. This can be accomplished by asking a student to repeat what is to be accomplished. Another way is to ask students if they have any questions about the assignment. It is also a good idea before you get involved with an individual student or another task that you walk around the room as students begin their work and verify that they are proceeding correctly. If you discover that the students do not appear to understand their task, stop them. Ask everyone to put their pencils down and look up at you. Then move to the chalkboard or a central location and rephrase and explain the task once again. Then verify that the students understand. If necessary have a student demonstrate what is to be accomplished. For some tasks it may be a good idea to have the whole group or class perform one problem or portion of the assignment; then verify understanding before expecting the students to work individually.

About midway through an assignment it is also a good idea to verify that students understand what they are working on and are not performing their task in a robot fashion. Whereas students of high ability will typically ask for assistance when they are confused, low-ability students are likely to accept confusion as natural and continue performing the task, perhaps incorrectly, whether it makes sense or not (Anderson, 1984).

It is extremely important that teachers monitor students' accomplishments. This simply means that after students have performed a task, it should be corrected. For some assignments there should be a system that helps students self-evaluate their work. Some work tasks should be corrected as a group and some only by the teacher. Whatever the system, students need feedback. It is the feedback that helps students improve their performance and lets them know that you are aware of their progress.

When students are given assignments of long duration, it is important that teachers provide a time when students report their progress. In junior and senior high school there might be a system in which students turn in their notes or an outline of their work so that the teacher can assess progress toward the goal. These checkpoints may be graded or just marked in some way to let the students know that you have verified their progress.

Monitoring conduct is one of the most important tasks that a teacher needs to learn to be an effective classroom manager. At all levels of education the teacher needs to prove that he or she is "withit." "Withitness" is a term used by Kounin (1970) that basically means that the teacher is aware of what is happening. Some teachers seem to have built-in antennae that tell them when a student is about to misbehave;

other teachers need to develop those instincts. The withit teacher spots a potential troublemaker and proceeds to quietly go and stand next to the student (or give him or her the evil eye). If this is done without alerting the rest of the class, the misbehavior will not spread; the teacher has successfully squashed it before it happened or took hold of others.

Student conduct is also related to the duration, pace, and rhythm of instruction. Monitoring students' progress and interest in assignments is necessary to determine whether or not a lesson is progressing appropriately. This will be discussed further as we consider teacher timing, another behavior that affects classroom management.

Timing

Mr. Warner seemed to have some kind of inner antennae. Observing his students, he could detect tiredness or satiation with a presentation or an ongoing activity. He was able to achieve a high rate of work from his students because he seemed to know instinctively when to sustain or to terminate a work or play activity. The following example will illustrate:

◆   The fourth graders were doing group research. One group used a filmstrip and tape recorder. A second group had a teacher-prepared information sheet to read. A third group used some assigned textbooks, and the fourth group was using topographic maps of California.

The children were studying about work opportunities in California. Mr. Warner had motivated the research with a story about a family that had migrated to California and would soon be seeking work.

Mr. Warner checked each group as it worked. Sometimes he assisted by reading a word for an individual or by answering questions. After about 15 minutes, he noticed that the group with the filmstrip had finished, and the children were beginning to raise their voices. He scanned the other groups and realized that the group with the information sheet and the group with the maps would be finished soon, but that the group with the textbooks was lagging far behind.

Quickly, he decided to suggest to the three groups that they write a statement summarizing their findings. Next he walked over to the textbook group and began asking them some leading questions to expedite their search.

Looking at his watch, Mr. Warner realized that the motivation and research had consumed 20 minutes. Time for evaluation, he thought to himself. So, standing in a central location, he asked each group to turn their chairs so they could see one another. Each group contributed to the evaluation, and several times children questioned other groups.

As the discussion began to taper off, Mr. Warner said, "Boys and girls, you have really learned a great deal about California's industries and agriculture. Tomorrow we will continue our story and find out what the Brooks family decided to do. Now let's have Bob's group put their books away and go to their regular seats."

Each group was called upon to clean up, and Mr. Warner congratulated the students for their speedy performance. Then he picked up his guitar and began to strum. As he did so, he nodded to the class and they began to sing.

Timing is essential to effective teaching. Knowing when to quicken the pace or to change activities to prevent restlessness, satiation, or misbehavior appears to be almost instinctive in some teachers, while others have to develop it. Erickson and Mohatt (1982) studied participation by Indian students in two classrooms on an Odawa Indian Reserve in Northern Ontario. They found that the tempo of interaction differed in the two classrooms, one of which was taught by an Indian teacher, the other by a non-Indian teacher. The Indian teacher maintained a steady flow of interaction, while the cadence of interaction controlled by the non-Indian teacher was staccato. The researchers concluded that the rhythm maintained by the Indian teacher was consonant with the culture of the students, and as a consequence this teacher was more successful in sustaining student involvement.

MANAGING PROBLEM SITUATIONS

Some Typical Classroom Problems

Elementary and secondary students often have different problems in the classroom, so many of these comments will be specific to the group involved; however, since there is a great deal of overlap and similarity in handling inappropriate behavior, you will find it valuable to read through all of the examples. It is important to remember that when students behave inappropriately, the behavior must be dealt with promptly to avoid escalation. The way in which you deal with special problems will affect both the errant student and the rest of the class, so you must be calm and rational in your approach.

The Incessant Interrupter

There are a variety of reasons why some students habitually interrupt instructions or discussions. Obvious causes include the student's need to seek attention and appreciation. (Perhaps the student rarely has anyone listening to him or her at home.) Other causes may be inattention to group instructions, extreme competitiveness, nervousness, insecurity, or impulsiveness. The teacher may have to deal with the actual cause of the undesired behavior, but usually this can occur only during an individual interaction with the student.

To curtail the problem, some teachers are successful using the following techniques:

1. Try a nonverbal gesture. Shake your head at the offender; catch the subject's eye and gesture with your hand to "hold off" a moment; gain eye contact and then hold one finger to your lips.

2. Use a direct statement such as "Richard is speaking now" or (for young elementary students) "It's Mary's turn." These statements should be made in a noncommittal, unemotional tone of voice.

3. Focus on the interruption. Sometimes the incessant interrupter can be helped by peers if you stop and ask the whole class, "How can we help Mabel so that she can remember to wait her turn to speak?" (This works in elementary grades but not secondary.) In junior high you might ask the group, "How does it feel to be interrupted all the time?"

4. If the students are working in small groups and the interrupter is monopolizing the conversation, give the interrupter a job. Appoint him or her the group recorder or secretary to take notes on the discussion and then report to the class during the evaluation.

Vindictiveness, Rudeness, and Defiance

Through actions or statements, the vindictive, defiant student is begging for help. However, giving help or attempting to analyze what went wrong while the student is putting on a performance for the rest of the class is not only an impossible task but downright silly. The real need is to defuse the situation and end the "showtime." Therefore, you as the teacher must focus on two acts simultaneously: getting the class back to work and quieting the student or separating the student from the classroom.

First, give the class an assignment if they do not already have one. If they have a work assignment, then remind them, "OK, gang, you have more than enough to keep you busy. Let's continue our work now." This will let the class know that you are confident you can handle the situation and that you have not lost your cool. It is important to do this because defiant statements or vindictive actions frighten everyone, and the class will be worried about what will happen next.

The next step is to deal with the student causing the problem without expressing personal anger. This is difficult because defiant or rude expressions are aimed at the teacher. Obviously, there is personal involvement; in some way, the interaction between teacher and student has gone wrong. But your calmness in this situation will reassure not only the class but the student as well. If the student can be talked into taking his classroom seat and appears to be more composed, then you can talk to the student after class or later in the day. "Martin, we both realize that you are feeling upset. We will talk about it later when we are both cool." This acknowledges to the student that there is mutual involvement and that you are concerned about his behavior. Since you have not responded in anger, the student will be somewhat mollified that his alarming behavior did not go too far and that you are maintaining an adult role. Maintenance of adult composure sobers the problem student as well as the class.

If Martin's act occurred far from his classroom seat, it may be impossible to have him walk to it. In this instance slowly walk over to the student, being extremely careful that the defiant student and the rest of the class are aware that you have no intention of touching the student. Open the classroom door and suggest to the student, "Martin, compose yourself outside. I will talk with you in a moment."

Once the situation is defused and classroom activity is continuing normally, the teacher must carry out the promise of a private conversation. This should be a fact-finding session in which the teacher listens to the student's interpretation of what happened and why. Very likely the problem did not begin in the classroom but is a reflection of the student's problems at home or on the campus or playground. Students do not blow up in the classroom if they feel that the teacher is uninvolved. Gather information, then respond by suggesting ways for mutual understanding in the future. At this point the teacher must decide whether more than one conference will alleviate the problem or whether the student needs help from someone other than the teacher.

Many schools have policies dealing with rude classroom behavior. You may want to remind the student of that policy as well as any classroom rules the student may have broken. If the student was extremely disrespectful, you may want to refer the student to the discipline officer at your school. When this action is taken, it should be understood by the student that he or she will not be allowed back in the classroom unless there is agreement about appropriate classroom behavior.

Nonaccountability

In almost every classroom there is a student who refuses to work, is described as unresponsive, or appears to lack responsibility. For a variety of reasons this student seems to be unable to set personal goals and carry through with them. One can presume that this student may be lacking in self-confidence, assertiveness, responsibility, and so on. This student needs to be monitored frequently by the teacher. It is important to deal with this problem before the student is too far behind to make up the work. During a private conversation with the student, the teacher must determine whether the problem has to do with inability to perform the work; if this is the case, then it is necessary to provide the student with assistance. However, if the problem is lack of motivation and lack of responsibility, then the teacher and student should set small, easily achieved goals. When a task is completed, the student should receive credit; in elementary grades the teacher might make a fuss about it and really congratulate the student. The student should be helped to immediately set a new goal that will also be easily achieved. A chart or record book may be designed so that as tasks are performed and success is demonstrated, the student can keep track of progress toward goals.

It is important in situations like this to let parents or guardians in on the problem. Parent conferences (Chapter 8) should be scheduled regularly to develop consistent school-home procedures for assisting the student. During the beginning stage of "treatment" it may be wise to focus on in-school accountability and try to avoid homework. A confrontation with the student about accountability with homework will not be beneficial at this time. If, however, it is the homework that is the problem, then make sure that the assignment is short, that it is checked promptly each day, and that parents are apprised of the treatment.

During private talks with the student, discuss how every individual is accountable. Give examples of the ways in which teachers must be accountable. Ask the student to give examples of how others (coaches, parents, peers, community workers) are responsible, interdependent, and accountable. Also remember that teachers cannot solve all classroom problems. The nonaccountable student may need the attention of the school counselor or school physician.

The Classroom Bully

Although the classroom bully is often a loner, insecure students may gravitate to the bully for protection, recognition, or attention. The bully is seeking classroom status, and the best way to deal with the situation is to give this individual some personal responsibility. Again, this is a problem that requires teacher-student conferencing to discuss the student's problem. If the student can be helped to face the motivation for his or her bullying actions, the problem will be alleviated very simply.

If bullying tactics are the consequence of real anger, then the student's aggressiveness requires a number of interrelated measures. First, the student needs a system whereby he or she can become composed. Next, the student should be helped to understand the causes of angry feelings and ways in which to deal with them, other than by hitting or fighting. If there are certain situations that always make the student blow up, then these should be discussed, with the teacher suggesting how to avoid them. As the student practices new ways of behaving, the teacher can reinforce changes by encouraging and praising the student. If there is another student that the bully really admires, it may be possible to pair them in activities so that the deviant individual learns to model appropriate behavior from the admired peer.

Aggressive behavior in the junior high school classroom may take the form of name calling or general disrespect for other students. If this occurs the offending student should be immediately told that this is unacceptable. If it continues the student should be penalized by the classroom teacher or sent to the school office for discipline.

Conclusions about Managing Problem Situations

Some classroom problems are inevitable; however, teachers who consistently have management problems have probably failed to anticipate student needs and interests and the needs that arise as a consequence of the learning environment. Classroom management encompasses more than the management of students' behavior. As noted at the beginning of the chapter, classroom management is the anticipation of potential problems.

The rigid disciplinarian would deal with classroom behavioral problems by punishing undesired behavior, but this leads to disrespect for the individual being punished and diminishes the student's self-respect. With a loss of self-respect, the student also loses the ability to initiate and direct personal activities. In fact, the student becomes "other-directed." The punishment syndrome for dealing with behavioral problems inevitably poses the question of how to choose appropriate punishment and leads to unavoidable teacher threats and scoldings.

Discipline and punishment do not need to be synonymous. Students, parents, and teachers all desire disciplined classrooms. Parents at times express almost nostalgic concern about classroom discipline, and teachers fear the lack of it! The effective classroom teacher anticipates potential problems and preplans key activities to prevent problems. If all students in the classroom help to set rules and are knowledgeable of the guidelines for maintaining rules, discipline can be consistent and equitable. Student self-direction and responsibility can be encouraged. The degree to which standards, goals, and ideals are fulfilled depends on a challenging environment, commitment to academic standards, modeling, and evaluation.

CASE STUDY PROBLEMS

[Note to Readers: Some case study problems will be followed by the notation (E) or (S) to indicate that the problem pertains to elementary or secondary teachers. Most of the case study problems are not grade specific. Some of the problems will have suggestions for possible responses; however, in most cases you will need to refer to the chapter for information.]

1. Neatness.   Mary Beth rarely finishes an assignment. She is friendly, courteous, and excessively neat. She appears to begin assignments at the same time the other students do, but midway through the allotted time period, she will be searching for a new pencil, meticulously erasing an error, starting over, or thinking about her work. Suggest some ways to help Mary Beth and some accountability measures to monitor her progress.

Suggestions: Mary Beth's problem probably relates to something that happens in the home; a parent conference would be a good idea. However, in the meantime start Mary Beth with a short assignment and watch her to make sure she finishes it. Congratulate her for completing the assignment and suggest that she make a chart to keep track of how well she does in completing assignments. Explain to Mary Beth that while neatness is important, it is also important to demonstrate understanding of content. Use this strategy for several days before you put Mary Beth back on the regular assignment.

2. Clarity.   Mr. Bell prides himself on being organized, yet he consistently seems to have classroom management problems. His students complain that he is boring. Mr. Bell always groups his students and provides different assignments for each group. The following is an example of Mr. Bell's directions to one group in his classroom.

"All right, listen carefully. Your assignment is on the board over in the left corner. Before you start, be sure to write your name at the top of your paper on the right side. Remember to copy your questions and then write your answer. Be sure you write in complete sentences. Do not look at your neighbor's work. Be sure to use pencil so that you can erase if you need to. You will have about 20 minutes to do your work. We will exchange papers. When you check someone else's work you will be asked to write your name on the paper at the lower left. All right, take out your books and go to work."

Suggestions: Mr. Bell has provided both standards for the form of the work and information about work requirements; however, if he has a particular form that he desires on his work assignments, it should be communicated to the whole class and be a set standard that does not have to be repeated each time he gives an assignment.

Note that Mr. Bell confuses the students with too many specifics. (Your assignment is on the "left" side of the board; write your name on the "right" top of the paper; write your name on the "left" bottom on the paper when correcting it.)

We do not know what subject Mr. Bell is teaching, but assuming it is not handwriting practice, it does not make a great deal of sense to have the students copy the questions and then write their answers in complete sentences. This makes the assignment "busy work." Mr. Bell has not communicated to the students the purpose of the assignment or its importance. Without this information students lack motivation and a way to link what they are to do with what they have been doing (curriculum continuity).

Mr. Bell has not determined whether or not students understand the directions and the content assignment. We assume that the board assignment provides students with a page number in a specific book.

Finally, Mr. Bell has not told the students what they should do if they complete their assignment early. It appears that Mr. Bell has not considered student motivation; key aspects of lesson organization have not been provided; he is not aware of students' needs; nor does he monitor student understanding.

3. Firmness.   "I've told you repeatedly that I will not allow students to get out of their seats during work time. Why can't you remember? Why don't you understand that I mean it?"

Identify several problems that this teacher is having, why they have occurred, and what can be done about them.

4. Ripple Effect.   Ms. Brown was directing a discussion with her class, and most students were participating. However, two students were conducting their own discussion in whispered voices, and Ms. Brown had a feeling it would soon escalate. In a loud voice Ms. Brown reprimanded the offending students. The whole class stared at her, and she realized she would not be able to get the same interest and involvement in the discussion again.

What should Ms. Brown have done to (1) stop the private discussion? (2) motivate student involvement in the discussion? (3) help the students recognize their discourtesy?

QUESTIONS

1. What kinds of classroom situations should teachers anticipate to prevent classroom management problems?
2. Discuss the role of praise in the modeling process. Under what circumstances is praise inappropriate?
3. Why is timing an essential teacher skill for classroom management?
4. What are some ways teachers sometimes treat students differentially? How does this affect students?
5. Suggest ways teachers can communicate acceptance and respect.

CHAPTER 2

Managing Group Behavior
Beginning the School Year

CREATING GROUPNESS

To foster cooperative, responsible, and independent behavior in students, teachers learn to manage group behavior in a manner that creates an accepting interactive environment. A variety of techniques is needed to enable the teacher to be effective in the management of classroom groups. For instance, it is necessary to perform planning tasks with groups of students; implementation tactics are important; teaching cooperative work skills within groups requires special attention; evaluating goal achievement requires insight and understanding. These teaching skills are all interdependent and are basic to classroom management and effective classroom instruction. Joyce and Harootunian (1967) called these kinds of tasks "interpersonal skills."

This chapter will focus on how teachers begin to establish appropriate standards and procedures as well as group cooperation, responsibility, and interdependence at the beginning of a semester. The first three weeks of school are considered critical by most experienced teachers. It is during this period that the teacher must establish an effective classroom environment that promotes student learning.

A new teacher or a teacher working with a new class of students does not begin to group students as soon as they walk in the door. Students coming together in a classroom for the first time are similar to a crowd collected together to see a stage show: They cannot be considered a group. Although the students, like the playgoers, have something in common, neither group has what is known as *groupness*. Groupness, or what some human relations specialists call *oneness*, can only occur when a relationship has been developed among the group's varied individuals. Even though some of the students in the class may have been together in previous semesters (or classes), the very fact that their environment and teacher have changed creates a new set of variables that affect the students' prior interdependence and interrelationship.

GETTING ACQUAINTED

Teachers develop oneness in different ways. On the first day of school an eighth-grade teacher told her class that they were going to play a game called Passing a Face. The teacher explained that the person beginning the game would make a face at the person sitting next to him or her. That person would accept the face, try to change one aspect of it, and then pass it on to the next person. The game would end when the last person accepted the face and turned to the person who began the game. The game was to be performed without talking. The teacher divided the class into three groups and asked the students to arrange their desks so that they could see each other. The teacher chose a student in each group to begin the game. The teacher joined one of the groups. In no time at all, the students were chuckling. After all of the students had experienced passing a face, the teacher evaluated by asking the groups: "How did the game make you feel?" "How else do you think this game could be played?" "What was difficult about the game?" "What did you like best?"

This teacher successfully broke the ice and diminished the natural uneasiness that students have when they begin the semester with a new teacher and new classmates. As students share a common experience and chuckle together, they develop positive peer relationships. The teacher was able to laugh with them and take pleasure in the activity. She concluded the activity by saying, "We needed a get acquainted activity; now it is time for you to find out what this course is about and what your teacher expects of you."

A sixth-grade teacher develops oneness by having students write a class song. The song is written at the beginning of the school year and becomes the class theme song. Sixth graders enjoy the "king of the castle" system in elementary schools, and the theme song seems appropriate to develop their class feeling. The gradual growth of a sense of belonging and of caring about one another is a critical component in groupness.

Another example is a physical activity, used by a second-grade teacher. (This activity has been used successfully at the college and senior high level.) The class is divided into four groups, and each group holds hands in a circle. Group 1 and group 3 are told to make any shape or movement with their bodies that they desire, but that their ultimate position must be maintained and that they must each touch another person in some way. Groups 2 and 4 are to observe until groups 1 and 3 are ready. Then groups 2 and 4 are to fill in unused space. Group 2 works with the unused space of group 1 and group 4 works with group 3. These two groups are to assume body positions around, within, and under the other two groups, and they too are to touch their own group members.

After this has been accomplished, the teacher gives the signal, and groups 1 and 3 are to escape without touching groups 2 and 4. After escaping, they are to be resourceful and make a new shape around, within, or under groups 2 and 4. This activity can be continued for any length of time.

The evaluation focuses on the following: In what ways did you have to depend on your classmates? How does it feel to depend on others? How did you use your classmates' ideas and develop your own ideas? What body skills did this game require? How did it feel to change spaces with your body?

Activities that require group cooperation, responsibility, dependence on one another, and group discovery facilitate the awareness and the feelings dimensions required for the development of group solidarity and oneness.

RESEARCH AND READINGS

King, Nancy (1975). *Giving form to feeling*. New York: Drama Book Specialists.

   This book provides a creative resource for group activities similar to the activities suggested in this section.

The adult audience for college football games and other sports events attests to our lifelong need to belong, to identify with, and to care about a special group or a time of life. In some inner-city schools principals have found that if a sense of caring can be developed within students and their parents, vandalism and other crimes decrease. In several Los Angeles elementary schools, principals begin the school day by appearing on the playground with a loudspeaker and demanding of the children, "Name the best school in Los Angeles." The students respond in unison with the name of their school. Corny? Perhaps, but also extremely effective in creating a sense of belonging and caring.

Children's group experiences affect their ideas about appropriate social roles, values, and attitudes. Group membership teaches conformity, responsibility, and leadership and affects ego development. Peer group involvement is an important reference for the individual; therefore, it must be understood and planned carefully by the teacher.

GROUP CHARACTERISTICS

Sociologists have provided useful information about the characteristics and behavior of groups. All groups need structure, and the classroom is no exception. In a formal sense the teacher is the leader of the classroom group, and the students identify with their teacher, their peers, and their school. Members of the group (classroom) assume specific roles. Some students become leaders; others, participants and observers. Although this is a normal characteristic of group behavior, it is the teacher's responsibility to develop leadership capabilities and responsibility in all students. For this reason flexible grouping patterns assume increased importance in the classroom.

All groups need rules (norms). When rules are accepted by the members of a group because the rules are important in terms of personal values, then groups function efficiently and successfully. The development of classroom rules must be a joint endeavor of students and teacher. If rules are imposed and are meaningless to group members, they will not be obeyed.

Successful groups also need a means by which to communicate problems, interests, and information important to group members. If students do not feel free to communicate their feelings to teacher and classmates, they will not learn to perceive the viewpoints and feelings of others, and moral development, diversity, and individuality will suffer.

Rule making is more critical at the elementary level than in secondary education because secondary students have been "socialized." The following excerpt illustrates how a first-grade teacher teaches the need for rules and structure to youngsters during the first week of a new semester:

♦   I divide my class into five groups and give each group an activity. For the first four groups I tell them where to work and how to proceed. For the fifth group I just hand them their materials and leave them sitting on the rug. The first four groups are highly motivated and work happily, but the fifth group begins to disturb others. It isn't long before I have to stop the entire class to find out what is the matter. I allow the fifth group to tell their story about what happened, and then I call on all of the children to evaluate the cause. Pretty soon the children place the blame on me for not providing the same guidance by telling the fifth group who the leader was, what the rules were, and where to work. I accept the blame, and the children have learned an important concept about working in groups.

In summary, all groups need a defined structure that includes knowing who is in charge. Groups need to accept a system of rules that govern members' behavior, and groups need to articulate their objectives, develop procedures, and communicate their problems. Elementary teachers probably have more interactions with students in small groups and on a one-to-one basis than in a large group; however, secondary teachers should be aware (as well as elementary teachers) that students' individual responses to the teacher, whether they are being taught in a large or a small group, affect the teacher's overall actions. Since interactions are reciprocal, affecting one another, it is important that teachers study their own teaching style to improve the social climate of the classroom and the learning performance of students.

RESEARCH AND READINGS

Slavin, R. E. (1980). Cooperative learning. *Review of Educational Research,* *50*(2), 315–342.

    Cooperative teamwork has a positive effect on achievement when instruction is well conceived and students are accountable for performance.

Thelen, Herbert A. (1954). *Dynamics of Groups at Work.* Chicago: University of Chicago Press.

Now that you are thinking about group activities to help students become acquainted and the characteristics of groups, it is time to consider the decisions teachers must make when they begin the school year or prepare for instruction with a new class of students. These decisions involve arranging the room environment, planning the instructional program, and organizing procedures and resources. The planning process will involve the anticipation of potential problems. If you go back and review the definition of classroom management, you will note that almost all of the components used in the definition are considered in planning for the beginning of school. To assist you, three checklists [for both elementary and secondary level (Tables 2.1 and 2.2)]

Table 2.1. Checklist before School Starts—Elementary

Preparation of Room Environment	Plans Completed (+)	Plans Not Completed (−)
Arrange tables/desks for students (Do you have enough?)		
Provide area for teacher-directed instruction (near chalkboard)		
Consider traffic lanes (Is there easy access to exits, directed instruction area, and centers? Do any of your students require special consideration because of a handicapping condition?)		
Provide area for learning centers		
Provide area for library books, texts, references		
Arrange bulletin boards (Consider content areas and students' interests.)		
Survey equipment in room (chart rack, chart box, etc.) (Obtain needed equipment.)		
Consider storage facilities for kits, PE equipment, AV, realia, pictures, manipulatives, teacher resource materials, art supplies, paper, pencils, etc.		

Organization of Procedures and Resources	Plans Completed (+)	Plans Not Completed (−)
Obtain textbooks and workbooks (Do you have enough for each student? Did you remember your teacher's editions?)		
Obtain supplies (paper, pencils, art materials, tagboard, etc.)		
Obtain class list of students (if available)		
Obtain cumulative records and health records (if available)		
Check bell schedule (When is recess?, lunch?, dismissal?)		
Check exits to be used by your classroom		
Check playground areas to be used by your class for play and recess (Do you need to obtain play equipment for your class?)		

Table 2.1. *(Continued)*

Organization of Procedures and Resources	*Plans Completed (+)*	*Plans Not Completed (−)*
Check lavatory facilities to be used by your class		
Check school rules needed during first week of school		
Check your school duties during first week of school		
Check out area to be used by your class during a fire drill (Which exit will you use? Verify your procedures.)		
Prepare a helper chart (Pocket charts work well.)		
Prepare a temporary seating chart		
Prepare stand-up name cards or name tags		
Prepare a daily schedule		
Do you know how to contact the office if you require assistance?		

Instructional Planning	*Plans Completed (+)*	*Plans Not Completed (−)*
Have you planned to introduce yourself to the students?		
Have you planned a get acquainted activity for students?		
Have you planned a motivating presentation to tell students about their work with you this semester?		
Have you thought about the room standards you will need to communicate to students during or before content instruction?		
Have you planned content and activity blocks with time allotments for the entire school day?		
Have you planned and prepared follow-up seatwork as needed for instruction?		
Have you planned additional challenging work for fast workers?		
Have you planned extra activities to serve as "sponges" for unplanned time?		

Table 2.2. Checklist before School Starts—Secondary

Preparation of Room Environment	Plans Completed (+)	Plans Not Completed (−)
Arrange tables/desks (Do you have enough?)		
Consider traffic lanes (Do you have easy access to supplies and exits? Have you considered handicapped students?)		
Provide area for small groups or learning centers if used		
Provide area for texts and references		
Arrange bulletin boards. (Consider subject field and students' interests.)		
Survey equipment in room (chart rack, map rack, AV, etc.)		
Consider storage facilities for kits, AV, realia, teacher resource materials, paper, pencils, etc.		

Organization of Procedures and Resources	Plans Completed (+)	Plans Not Completed (−)
Obtain textbooks and other materials (Do you have sufficient numbers? Did you remember your teacher's editions?)		
Obtain supplies (paper, pencils, bulletin board paper, etc.)		
Obtain class lists, if available		
Check academic records and health records of students, if possible		
Check bell schedule (Will it be different during the first week of classes?)		
Check recess, lunch, and dismissal times		
Check exits for dismissal and for fire drills (Do you know school procedures and where you are to stand with your class?)		
Check lavatory facilities for students		
Check school rules for absence, tardiness, hall passes		

Table 2.2. *(Continued)*

Organization of Procedures and Resources	*Plans Completed (+)*	*Plans Not Completed (−)*
Check your school duties for first week of school		
Prepare temporary seating charts for each period (Fill in students' names if you have class rosters for junior high school; leave blank for senior high school.)		
Prepare a time schedule of activities to be used during each period		
Prepare handouts for students [outline of content, assignments, homework procedures (syllabus), etc.]		
Prepare a system for distributing and checking out textbooks to students (Record book number and match student names.)		

Instructional Planning	*Plans Completed (+)*	*Plans Not Completed (−)*
Have you planned to introduce yourself to students?		
Have you planned a get acquainted activity for students?		
Will you call roll or have students fill out an information card about themselves?		
Have you planned to introduce your course syllabus, course requirements, grading procedures to students?		
Have you thought about the behavior standards you will expect of your students? (How will you communicate these?)		
Have you prepared a content presentation and activity?		
Have you planned time allotments for each activity during the class periods?		
Have you prepared worksheets if needed for the activities?		
Have you planned a homework assignment, if needed?		

have been designed to help you verify your classroom preparation, organization of procedures and resources, and instructional planning.

CLASSROOM ENVIRONMENT

Sometime before the first day of the semester go to your school and check out the school schedule. Remember that your grade level may determine the time of recess, lunch, and dismissal. If classes have been organized, obtain a list of your students (elementary) or lists of class periods (secondary). Elementary teachers can also obtain cumulative records (student's academic history) and health cards (student's personal health record). Secondary teachers may need to check with grade-level counselors to view their students' records.

Now check out your classroom. Your tables, chairs, and desk arrangement may not be to your liking or even appropriate for your students and your teaching style. Note room accessories: audiovisual equipment, chart racks, map rack, bookcases, round tables, display tables, aquarium, and so on. Check storage facilities (cupboards, shelves, closets) and supplies (for teacher and students).

Before you begin to move furniture, make decisions about your instructional program. Remember that the classroom environment should support the instructional program. (The environment should *not* determine the program.) Your instructional program is determined by your students' needs and abilities. For example, the cumulative record will tell you what reading texts elementary students have completed. (In some schools reading and math records will be prepared separately for the new teacher to use.) The health record can be used to find out which students have physical conditions that will affect their seating location.

In elementary classrooms it is a good idea to make a tentative seating chart for the first day of class. This chart should not be too "handsome" because class reorganization during the first week is common. It is also a good idea to prepare tagboard stand-up cards for the table tops to have students write their names. (In first grade you will need to prepare the name cards if students are to have a permanent seat assignment.) You may also desire name tags for the students to wear to help you identify them on the playground. Anticipate that you may have unexpected students on the first day of school.

For middle schools and junior high schools you may also want to prepare a seating chart ahead of time. Typically at these levels you will seat students alphabetically and make necessary changes as you become acquainted with the students.

In senior high school it is a good idea to have students select their own place in the classroom. You might remind the students, however, that they are responsible for selecting a place where they can work. Then during the first class meeting distribute a seating chart and have the students write in their own names in the appropriate spot.

We will deal more specifically with the classroom environment in Chapter 7. Let us now consider instructional planning for the first few days of the semester. This discussion will differ from the in-depth discussion of planning, assessing, and grouping for instruction provided by the focus on instructional management skills in Chapters 4 and 5.

PLANNING INSTRUCTION FOR THE BEGINNING OF SCHOOL

Your major problems on the first day of school include: (1) getting acquainted with your students, (2) communicating your expectations (while alleviating their concerns), and (3) establishing a friendly but businesslike environment for work. Let us look at the tasks involved in each of these three components.

Getting Acquainted

Getting acquainted with your students helps you to identify individuals for communication and classroom management purposes. The first task is to learn names; this is why it is important to establish a seating chart as soon as possible. You will find that it makes a big difference if you can call a student by name and thereby impede misbehavior. Knowing students' names also establishes a more personal relationship, and this is another factor that promotes good behavior. Groupness, discussed at the beginning of the chapter, establishes both peer relationships and teacher-student relationships; once group feelings are established, it is much harder for students to break school and classroom rules. Finally, it is important to resolve student uneasiness. Quite often the student has heard about the reputation of certain teachers and may be very concerned about how he or she will be perceived as a member of the group.

Communicating Expectations and Alleviating Student Concerns

Students are interested in learning about what you have planned for the semester. You may also want to learn about their expectations for learning. Some teachers like to ask students what they expect to learn this semester (or in this course). Students' preconceptions are useful for planning purposes. If you choose to hear about what your students expect, you may want to jot their ideas on the chalkboard; then proceed to communicate some substantive information and clarify students' misconceptions about the course/semester. Remember, the information you provide will be passed on to parents and friends. Concentrate on making your presentation interesting and motivating. If you are planning field trips, tell them about it. If there will be guest speakers (secondary), inform them. You want students to look forward to what is to come because the first day or two in class are concerned with organizing details that may be somewhat disappointing to students.

Also, you need to communicate your philosophy both about the subject field and about teaching, in general. If you are a secondary teacher, will you be having group projects? Oral reports? Will you mostly be lecturing? Group discussions? What about the students' written work, what are your expectations here—term papers? Cooperative projects? How will students be evaluated? This is a good time to pass out your course outlines, assignments, readings, and so on. If you are an elementary teacher you can still let students know about your philosophy of teaching by telling them a little bit about whether they will be working in small groups, at learning centers, about group projects, art work, or dramatic work. Also, how do you feel about students' finishing their work assignments, or walking around the room, getting a drink, and so on? *Set the stage!*

Establish a Friendly, Businesslike Environment

This is your most important task on the first day of school. You want to communicate that you like teaching and you like students, and that you are a friendly, concerned adult; however, the classroom is a work environment, and students need to know that work is to be expected in an orderly environment. You initiated expectations of work when you assigned (or had students select) seat locations. In elementary classrooms you should assign special monitor (helper) responsibilities. Try to provide every student with a special task to perform. If that is impossible, let the students know that monitors will be changed regularly and everyone will have an opportunity to perform the favored tasks.

As you begin to communicate procedures and work tasks also focus on the room standards with which you can live. For example, encourage students to ask questions if they do not understand you, but insist that all students listen to both the question and your response. You do this through the following management procedures:

1. Mabel raised her hand and asked whether they were supposed to go to their seats when they first arrived in the morning or whether they should sit on the rug. Or, in a secondary classroom, Tom asked whether they should begin the work on the chalkboard when the bell rang or wait for instructions.

   2. You notice that several students are not listening. In a quiet voice ask the students to look at you. Wait until they do so. If you need to, walk over to the student(s) who is (are) talking and stand there. When you have attention, ask the students if they all heard the question. Have it repeated by Mabel or Tom. Then respond. Next, tell the students that you expect students to be courteous to their classmates and listen to their questions as well as to the responses. (Don't make a big deal of it, but communicate your firmness.)

Keep Students Involved

On the first day of class keep students involved. Don't let time hang heavy! Remember that if students have nothing to do they can always make mischief. Select learning experiences that are interesting but not too complicated and ones at which students will experience success and closure. You want students to feel secure, optimistic, and enthusiastic about you and the class.

   As you provide content activities, communicate, and have students generate, class standards and procedures. For example, you have just given the students a math assignment to perform. Ask them what they think would be a good idea for getting personal assistance from the teacher, if they have a problem, without disturbing their friends (or not alerting their classmates that they need help). Elicit from them that they will raise their hand shoulder high and wait for eye contact from you. Then they are expected to wait until you are free and able to come over to their desks to provide assistance. (If you have a better system, communicate it at this time.)

   During the first week of school when you are focusing on class standards and procedures, it is a good idea to make presentations to the whole class to ensure that everyone hears the same thing at the same time. You will probably be more successful with whole class activities at this time. Now let's rejoin our fictitious teachers and see what kinds of content activities they provide and what rules and procedures they teach on the first day of school.

Teaching Application—Midge Brady's Classroom—Primary Grades

◆   8:30–8:40 A.M.: Greetings, Introductions, Lunch Count, Name Tags

As the students arrived, Midge directed them to the cloak room to store sweaters and lunches. She immediately selected one youngster to take her place and she went to the rug area in front of the chalkboard. She beckoned the children to sit down in front of her.

When they were all there, she smiled and introduced herself. She took out a box of stick-on name tags and as she called a student's name she gave him or her the name tag and asked the child to tell something about himself or herself. [Typically the statement was "I like to..."] Once or twice she had to say, "Just a minute, boys and girls, whose turn is it to talk?" [Roberto's] "What should we do when someone is talking to us?" [Look at the person and listen.]

Next Midge asked the students, "How many are going to the cafeteria today?" [7] Midge selected two of the cafeteria youngsters to take the count to the cafeteria. [She selected two, so they could find their way together!]

8:40–9:00 A.M.: Room Environment, Language, and Science

Now, Midge asked the students to look around the room and tell her what was interesting to them. They identified the various centers and the bulletin boards. She helped them read the captions on the bulletin board displays. One student asked when they could use the centers and Midge asked the class when they thought they could work at the centers. The students responded with "free time" and "when our work is done." Midge agreed and said that sometimes they would be assigned to work at a center, but what do you think will be important to remember when you work at a center? ["To not disturb others." "To work quietly."] Finally, one student asked, "What's in the cage at the science center?"

"I thought you'd never ask." Now Midge brought out Harry the Hamster. She asked if anyone could read his name, and one student [named Harry!] was able to read it. After a short discussion about hamsters, she said, "Let's write a story about Harry." This was their story.

> Harry has large cheek pouches.
> Harry has a short hairy tail.
> Harry eats corn and oats and lettuce and carrots and kibble.
> Harry lives in Room 12.

After school Midge would write the story on tagboard for the students' first experience story.

9:00–9:05 A.M.: Seat Assignments

Midge took out the stand-up name tags and arranged them on one table at a time. As she finished a table, she called the students' names and asked them to take their places. [She purposefully called on a small group of students at a time so that the move would be orderly.]

9:05–9:25 A.M.: Art

When all the students were seated, she placed some large boxes of crayons on the table and passed each child a piece of paper. She asked the students to draw a picture about Harry the Hamster and Harry's friends.

While the students were drawing, Midge observed their work and also made a list of needed room helpers on the board. Later, she would ask for volunteers and insert name cards and monitor jobs in the pocket chart she had prepared for that purpose.

9:25–9:40 A.M.: Recess Preparation and School and Classroom Standards

Students were told to pass in papers and "show me that you are ready to take a walk and go to recess." When crayons were back in boxes and students were looking at her expectantly, Midge asked the students, "Which door do you think we should use to go to the playground?" [Back door] "How should we walk to the door so that we don't cause a traffic jam?" [To the front and then to the door] "Let's have Table 2 demonstrate for us." [They don't do a good job.] Midge sent them back to their table and called on a different group to demonstrate. In this way she emphasized that she expected a quiet and orderly exit.

Now she told the students that she would take them to the right lavatories for them to use. She encouraged the students to go to the bathroom and to get a drink of water. "I am going to wait for you today and take you to our play area on the playground."

9:40–10:00 A.M.: Recess

Midge distributed some balls and set up several games for the students. She told them that they were to line up in front of their room at the end of recess (when the bell rang).

10:00–10:20 A.M.: Discussion of Room Standards and Preparation for Reading

Midge once again brought the students to the rug area and asked them about their recess activities. She talked to them about school rules and began a discussion of room standards. She identified the following problem areas for discussion:

- Putting work down when the teacher has something to share
- Responding to the dimmed light signal which will indicate that the teacher needs to talk to them
- Respecting classmates' right to work
- Respecting others' belongings
- Maintaining a clean and neat environment
- Walking in the classroom
- Using quiet voices when you need to talk to a friend
- Listening to others' ideas
- Use of the pencil sharpener and the drinking fountain
- Sharing equipment, games, books

Some of these group-living problems had already been discussed, and Midge checked a list as they talked about each one. For example, they had talked about walking in the classroom before recess, and she had introduced the dimming of the lights when the students were drawing their hamster pictures.

10:20–11:00 A.M.: Reading

With some basic understanding about room standards, Midge felt the students were ready for reading groups. She had planned some very easy review work which would help her get acquainted with the students' ability levels. She introduced a listening center to the students and explained how the students would listen to a story and then follow directions for their follow-up work. She identified the students who were to go to the listening center and got them started. Next she handed out some simple follow-up work to be performed by another group of students at their desks. Finally she summoned a third group of students to carry their chairs to the area in front of the chalkboard for directed instruction.

The reading lesson would be of a review nature. She would use the pocket chart to introduce key words in the story. While the students read silently, she would be able to monitor the work of the students at the listening center and those involved at their desks.

She planned to be very alert to students' behavior during this work period. She would emphasize (1) how students could obtain assistance if they needed it, (2) quiet work voices, (3) walking in the classroom, (4) consideration of others, and (5) completion of work tasks. Although the reading time would be short on the first day, she planned to work with all three groups because she wanted to get acquainted with the students' work and wanted them to learn group work standards so they would know how to carry their chairs up to the reading group and move to a learning center as well as perform seatwork at their desks.

At the end of the reading period, Midge displayed large newsprint charts for students to look at to correct their seatwork and their work at the listening center. Then the students were taught to pass their papers in for the teacher to keep.

11:00–11:20 A.M.: Physical Education

Midge talked about how sometime this week they were sure to have a fire drill. She asked the students if they knew how to recognize a fire drill. They talked about the signal of the bells and what their responsibility would be. Midge explained that if the fire bell sounded they would need to get in line very quietly and wait for her directions. She told them that they would practice getting in line, and, when they went out on the playground, she would show them where they were to stand with her during a fire drill.

Once again Midge emphasized with the students how to line up at the door; this time the purpose was to go outside for a practice fire drill and for physical education. She would also use this time to allow the students to go to the lavatories and to get drinks. She had planned to introduce the apparatus to them and the safety standards they would need to know to play on the apparatus safely. Because she wanted the students to be active and get the wiggles out, she worked with half of the class on the apparatus at a time and had the other half play dodge ball.

11:20–11:35 A.M.: Music

After physical education Midge brought the students to the rug area and sat down in front of them and began to sing using her autoharp. She taught one new song and reviewed several old favorites of the students.

11:35–11:40 A.M.: Preparation for Lunch

Midge explained to the students that she was going to take them to the lunch area to show them where they were to sit to eat lunches. She gave directions to the students eating in the cafeteria and to those who were going home for lunch. Then she excused small groups of students at a time to go to the cloak room for lunches, sweaters, and to line up at the door. [The students had already learned to do this quietly!]

11:40 A.M.–12:40 P.M.: Lunch   *Discuss*

12:40–12:55 P.M.: Literature (Storytime)

Midge had the students sit at their desks, and she suggested that some of them might want to put their heads down and rest while she read a story to them. She liked to do this after lunch because of its calming effect.

12:55–1:10 P.M.: Handwriting and Spelling

Midge planned to introduce several spelling words and encourage the students to think about their manuscript writing. She was combining the two subjects because she wanted to do as much as possible on the first day even though a great deal of time was spent on helping the students get a good start in the classroom.

1:15–1:45 P.M.: Mathematics

Using the flannel board, Midge introduced an arithmetic story. She had several students demonstrate using both the flannel board and the chalkboard. Then she introduced how she wanted the students to write a heading on the paper with their name and how to fold the paper for their work. She gave them crayons once again and had them practice the number story using squares on their paper. As they worked, she observed and provided assistance. She also made notes to herself about which students appeared to have difficulty with the math concepts. When the students finished, Midge praised how well they had worked on the assignment. She asked students to share their work and told them that they would be working on number stories again tomorrow. The students passed their papers to the front of the room, and Midge collected them.

1:45–2:00 P.M.: Review of Room Standards, Recap of "What We Have Learned"

Midge reviewed with the children some of the key standards that had been developed during the day. She planned to write these on a chart for review purposes the next day. Then she asked them what have we learned today? She elicited the language and science story about the hamster, the drawing activity, reading, listening activity, physical education, music, handwriting, spelling, mathematics, and the story she had read to them. The students responded with the actual activities [dodge ball]; she helped them attach subject field names to the activities. Her purpose was to refresh their memories so that when parents or others asked them what they had done at school on their first day, they would be able to respond in a positive manner. She told them that she had enjoyed her first day with them and hoped that they too had enjoyed school. "You did so many things really well. Be sure to tell your parents about the work you completed today." Once again the students lined up at the door, and Midge led them off the school grounds.

Highlights of Midge Brady's First Day
- Gradual introduction of procedures and rules as they were needed for learning and school activities
- School orientation by taking students to lavatories and recess area; emphasis on which lavatories to use and playground area to play on; led students to lunch and cafeteria area; talked about and demonstrated fire drill procedures; led students off of school grounds at dismissal time.

- Academic work orientation by teaching substantive content on the first day of school so that students would have something of importance to talk about to parents and friends; emphasis on businesslike work environment; emphasis on school success.

Teaching Application—Julie Kramer's Classroom—Upper Grades (Elementary, Middle School)

◆ 8:30–9:00 A.M.: Greetings, Introductions, Lunch Count, Seat Assignments

Julie Kramer's students knew what to expect on the first day of school. They automatically stored their possessions in the cloak room and took seats waiting for their classmates and teacher to formally begin school. As students arrived, they joyfully waved high fives and exchanged greetings. When it appeared that all of the students were in seats, Julie went to the front of the room and waited for the students to quiet down and look at her. She welcomed them and said she wanted to tell them a little bit about herself and about their studies in this classroom, but first, "Let's say the Pledge of Allegiance." She gestured to one student and asked him to lead them.

When the students had again settled, she talked briefly about her expectations for the semester and how she believes that the class is a "team" and how a team can accomplish great things together when all the individuals help each other. She discussed what she called her "rules to live by." Her list included:

- Walk in the classroom
- Talk in the classroom quietly
- Do not disturb friends
- Raise your hand for help or "catch my eye"
- Respect others' rights

Next Julie assigned seats to the students and asked them to write their names on the tagboard she had provided to stand up on their desk tops "so that I can get acquainted with you quickly." She passed out a box of crayons for each student and pencils for this purpose. She also gave each student a dictionary notebook for spelling words they needed help on. She intended to pass out texts for each subject as they were needed throughout the day.

Julie called attention to the science and social studies centers and bulletin boards. [What do the bulletin boards tell you about what we will be studying?] Then she told the students that they were to play a game to help get better acquainted with each other. She proceeded to give directions for the body movement and cooperative group activity.

9:00–9:45 A.M.: Reading

Using the reading lists she had received with her class list, Julie planned review activities for three reading groups, although she had a hunch that she might want to use four groups when she got settled. She discussed her procedures of having one group at a time in the front of the room with her and the other two groups working at their desks. Once again she went over several standards she expected of the students. [Do not disturb others; be courteous; raise your hand if you need help.] She pointed out the bookcases where library books were stored and introduced several of them to interest the students. She also called attention to some reading activities to develop vocabulary and comprehension. She said that one group at a time should select library books to read and use the reading activities as well. She demonstrated how each activity had a self-check feature. She also called attention to where papers could be obtained and stored upon completion. She explained that while one group read books and used the reading work activities, another group would be doing a specific follow-up reading activity. She passed out a dittoed worksheet to these students and told them that when it was their turn to come to the front of the room to read with her, they would correct their papers. Next she helped the group she would work with first to bring their chairs to the front of the room.

Reading on the first day would really be very short, but long enough to develop standards for work and help students realize that they were going to have to settle down for academic tasks right from the start. For the two groups who did follow-up seatwork after their reading group, she provided newsprint charts with their answers so that they could correct their own work immediately. [For the group that performed the follow-up tasks first, they corrected papers in the reading group before beginning direct instruction.]

9:45—10:00 A.M.: Preparation for Recess

Julie explained to the students that she had selected team assignments for them for physical education; however, after they were better acquainted, she would allow them to select their own teams. She set up the teams and identified four captains. She explained about the playground area assignments. She reminded them to use the lavatories facing the playground and "don't forget to get a drink." She called on one team at a time to get in line and then took them to the playground to identify their play area.

10:00—10:20 A.M.: Recess

10:20—10:30 A.M.: Discussion of Recess, Fire Drill

After recess the students were directed to take their seats, and Julie asked them about any team problems or recess-related concerns. Then she discussed fire drill procedures. "I expect you to line up quietly at the door; I will indicate to you which table should go to the door first; then we will immediately walk to our designated spot on the playground. If by some chance you are not in the classroom when the bell rings for a fire drill, you should proceed directly to our place on the playground." Then Julie drew a diagram on the board to indicate their spot.

10:30—11:00 A.M.: Language Arts

Julie utilized the synectics strategy to introduce creative writing. Students worked individually after the group participation to complete this assignment. Then students shared their stories. These were collected for Julie to review. While students worked individually, Julie circulated and provided spelling assistance when requested. Spelling words were written into the spelling notebook provided to each student.

11:00—11:30 A.M.: Social Studies

Julie handed out a blank map of the world and asked the students to see if they could identify the nations of the world on their blank map. "Use pencil and write lightly in case you are wrong; don't be afraid to guess." Students were slightly outraged. "We can't do this." "Well, why not?" asked Julie. After a discussion about why it was important to know where countries are located, Julie pulled down a wall map of the world. She explained that quite frequently maps placed the British Isles in the center because the first mapmakers lived in England, and they believed that England was the center of the world. She called on different students to come up to the wall map and identify different countries. Then she provided time for the students at their desks to write in the names of the countries. Each country was written on the board to help students with spelling.

Julie explained that the class would begin their social studies studying about world geography. She urged them to "take good care of your map and keep it in the desk until we work on them again tomorrow."

11:30–11:50 A.M.: Spelling

Julie passed out spelling books and a spelling folder to each student. She explained that they would be working on one unit each week, but that there would also be special spelling words that related to social studies, science, and health. Because this was the first day of the week, they would take a pre-test. She explained the procedures for each day of the week. After the pre-test, which was self-corrected, she taught the students the spelling procedures to help them study. While they began their initial study period, she circulated and observed their work.

11:50 A.M.–12:00 NOON: Preparation for Lunch

Students were directed to clean their desk top by putting all work inside desks. Then Julie talked about lunch area and cafeteria rules. She reminded students to visit the bathroom and get drinks before coming back to class. [She did allow students to get drinks in class as long as they were quiet about it!] Then she asked for an orderly line at the door and led the way to the lunch area and the cafeteria.

12:00–1:00 P.M.: Lunch

Students have 30 minutes to eat lunch and 30 minutes for play activities.

1:00–1:10 P.M.: Literature

Julie selected a fairly long book to begin with the students. She explained that she liked to read aloud and hoped that they would enjoy this time each day as a short period to relax and listen to a story. By reading aloud interesting stories, she hoped to set a pattern that would encourage students to come in from lunch and settle down to listen or read independently. Julie anticipated that this period would also be used for students to read silently with their own selected fiction book when she was not reading aloud.

1:10–1:50 P.M.: Mathematics

Julie's study of the academic records of her students indicated that they should probably work in two math groups, but to verify their placement she decided on a diagnostic test. As students completed their work, she handed them a dittoed sheet that had funny math story problems to work. When all the students were through, they talked about what she would learn about the students from the diagnostic test and how it helps a teacher become better acquainted with students. They also shared the math story problems and demonstrated some of them with concrete objects.

1:50–2:15 P.M.: Physical Education

Julie explained that they would have various physical education units just like in other subject fields. However, on this first day she decided that they would just utilize their teams and have two teams playing baseball and two teams playing volleyball. She intended to observe the teams to make sure that the teams were balanced appropriately.

2:15–2:30 P.M.: Recap of Day, Preparation for Dismissal

Before coming back to the classroom, Julie allowed time for students to get drinks on the playground; then she walked leisurely with the students back to the classroom and told them to take their seats to discuss the events of the day. She told them that tomorrow we need to select people for school and class responsibilities (office monitor, helpers in the kindergarten rooms, equipment monitors, etc.). She also told them that they had done a good job on their first day in this classroom and she wondered if "they could think about what they had learned today."

The students identified the location task to identify the countries of the world on a blank world map; they recalled comparing two objects to develop a direct analogy (synectics strategy) in order to write creatively; then they mentioned reading and spelling. But best of all was recess, lunch, and PE! Julie helped to fit the content fields with the activities so that students were aware of the subjects they had encountered throughout the day.

Next Julie asked them, "What have you learned about me and the way you need to work in this room?" She elicited from the students the various standards she had developed throughout the day, and in this way she reinforced them for tomorrow. She reminded the students about the appropriate exit from the school grounds; tomorrow we shall begin with reading and we shall begin our homework schedule. [To this the students sighed.] "You did a good job today; I'm real pleased with you." At precisely 2:30 P.M. Julie directed an orderly dismissal table by table to obtain their belongings from the cloak room and to leave the room. [Since this was a sixth-grade class, Julie did not have the students line up for dismissal.]

Highlights of Julie Kramer's First Day

- Students were provided with straightforward information concerning rules and procedures in the classroom. This demonstrated the teacher's consideration of the maturity of the students.
- Although it is likely that the majority of the students were not new to the school, the teacher took time to talk about lunch and cafeteria rules and orient the students to playground regulations and fire drill procedures.
- Academic content was taught on the first day of school and the teacher made a point of having the students recall the activities, and she summarized the content areas.

Teaching Application—Stewart Jackson's First Day of School—Secondary

◆   8:00–8:06 A.M.: Greetings

Stewart Jackson stood at the door of his classroom to greet the students when they arrived. He made a point of looking directly at each student and nodding or smiling.

As students arrived, he handed each a dittoed sheet that asked the student for his or her opinion about freedom of the press. The opinionnaire had ten questions, and the student tabulated his or her response on a table of reactions. He also told each student to select a place to sit.

Stewart had planned about 6 minutes for this activity. The planned time would allow students who were still not sure of their schedule to make it to class before he began formal introductions.

8:06–8:26 A.M.: Focus on the Academic, Focus on Student Concerns

When Stewart felt sure that all of the students had arrived, he asked them to put pencils down and give him their attention. He commented that he hoped they had selected a seat where they would be comfortable in this classroom. Then he passed out a course syllabus that described what would be covered in the course, how grades would be established, long-term assignments, and homework. He directed the students to each topic and spoke seriously about each aspect of the course. He encouraged students to ask questions about the syllabus and the course requirements.

Stewart asked the students if they had some expectations about their semester in this course. Once again he encouraged students to talk about what they anticipated. Next he talked about his expectations. He explained that each class period would be a combination of student activities, individual and small group, lecture, and discussion. He said that he had few class rules, but lots of expectations. For example, he expected that students would arrive on time to class, and "I will do the same." "I expect that when I am talking, you will give me complete attention. I will do the same for you." "I expect that when assignments are due, you will hand them in on time, and I will correct them in a timely manner and return them to you." "In short, I expect courtesy *from* you, and I will be courteous *to* you."

8:26–8:32 A.M.: Procedures

Stewart passed out a seating chart and asked students to fill in their names. He also passed out a 3 × 5 card and asked the students to write in their full name, grade level, and home room number. While the students were filling in the seating chart and the information card, he passed out the books and had students sign for them.

8:32–8:44 A.M.: Lecture

Stewart wanted to provide a somewhat "upbeat" lecture on the first day to excite the students. He began by telling them that he had asked their opinion about freedom of the press to help them be aware that our opinions influence our judgments about people and events. He talked about newsmen, newspapers, photographers, and television reporters. When he concluded, he selected two students to collect and tabulate the questionnaire about freedom of the press.

8:44–8:50 A.M.: Discussion

Stewart had planned the questions he would ask of the students to get a good discussion going. He believed in using a question pattern that would propel a discussion from the identification of issues and facts to consideration of values and in-depth critical thinking. He attempted to get all of the students to participate.

8:50–8:54 A.M.: Recap

Stewart suggested that the students read the front page of the newspaper in preparation for tomorrow's class meeting. He promised that they would have the results of the class opinions about freedom of the press. He commented that he thought they were good thinkers and he looked forward to working with them this semester.

Highlights of Stewart Jackson's First Day

- The teacher set the tone of the class by focusing on the academic syllabus, long-term assignments, and homework.
- The teacher did not spend a great deal of time talking about behavioral standards; nor did he pass out a list of rules. However, he communicated in no uncertain terms that he expected respectful, courteous behavior in his class.
- Business procedures were kept at a minimum. Students filled out the seating chart, signed for textbooks, and provided the teacher with an information card about themselves.
- Academic content was certainly the focus through the opening introductory assignment, the lecture, discussion, and homework assignment.

PLANNING FOR THE FIRST DAY

Pedagogy does not provide a magical list of "do's and don'ts" for the first day with a new group of students. One needs to use common sense. If you are teaching middle school or junior high school, suggestions provided for "upper elementary" are appropriate in most cases for you. High school students need much less guidance concerning school rules and procedures than young elementary students. However, all students need their uncertainties about a new teacher alleviated; they want to know what is expected of them, and they want to know what is important to their teacher. In reading the above case studies it is important to realize that every teacher has a distinct style of teaching. What works for one teacher may not for another. Stewart Jackson obviously felt no need to spend time playing a get acquainted game in a senior-high-school class, but this does not mean that it would have been inappropriate to do so. Let us consider some of the key components that our three teachers dealt with on their first day of the semester.

Beginnings

In different ways each of our three teachers welcomed the students and established themselves with the students through verbal and nonverbal means. It is important that students know something about you and that you find a way to learn something about each student. Get acquainted activities and introductions are appropriate.

It is extremely important that you spend time introducing course content or grade-level content so that students can recognize the intellectual side of schooling. The focus on content should be motivating so that students will have something to look forward to. Communicate to students your love of subject matter. If you have planned field trips or interesting activities, tell the students about it.

Rules and Expectations

To achieve the goals of American education, it is not appropriate to shape students into docile and passive beings. Schools are extremely regimented by bells, schedules, standardized tests, promotion standards, and so on. We cannot help students become critical thinkers if we forbid individuality and control all aspects of school life. This means that teachers must achieve a balance between dominating and routinizing classroom life and promoting active, participatory, responsible citizens.

Achieving that perfect balance probably depends on teacher expectations. Students can recognize when teachers have high expectations through the appropriateness of classroom standards and the energy and vigor with which a teacher describes the academic and intellectual tasks to be accomplished.

Standards and expectations should be clearly identified. During the first day, and in fact, the first three weeks, teachers should be extremely alert to consistency and equity in reinforcing standards of performance.

RESEARCH AND READINGS

Boyer, Ernest L. (1983). *High school—A report on secondary education in America.* New York: Harper & Row, p. 149.

"Much of what the teacher must do to succeed in teaching is a matter of common sense—careful planning for each lesson, educational goals for each day's work, pacing and timing, love of the subject matter, and respect for the students. Clarity in procedures, discipline in carrying through, and the careful measurement of accomplishments are essential elements in the formula for success."

Unplanned Events

Although teachers always need to be prepared for the unexpected, this is particularly true during the first week of classes. An unexpected surge in enrollment may cause a major shift in your class population. In secondary classrooms where students select their own classes, it is not uncommon for students to still be shifting and changing schedules throughout the first week of classes.

Other unexpected events may include sudden announcements or equipment that is not available or does not work, special teachers for music, art, or physical education who are suddenly unavailable. All of these events require quick thinking and perhaps special activities to fill unplanned time. (Some teachers call these activities "sponges.")

These special activities should be meaningful, not just a time filler. Vocabulary development through puzzle activities works well. Alphabetizing first-, second-, and third letter discrimination is appropriate for middle and upper elementary students. Reading library books is always desirable. Math and science story problems can be intriguing. Of course, if you are available to direct the activity then it is possible to present a special music lesson, or a game, or even read to the children. At the secondary level it is usually possible for students to read out of their textbook until you are ready to work with them. (Remember that suggestions for upper elementary grades are usually appropriate for middle school and junior high students.)

Activities

Most teachers and certainly most students think of classroom life in terms of the activities engaged in during the school day. Our fictitious teachers helped students recognize the content fields associated with the activities; however, when teachers plan a program incorporating "time," they most typically are planning activities. Gump (1982) defines activity as "a bounded segment of classroom time characterized by an identifiable focal content or concern and a pattern or program of action." What students are doing within an activity has an effect on classroom management. Some activities are extremely motivating, while others are quite conventional. Motivating activities may require more energy from both teacher and students and behavior may need to be considered; whereas conventional, routinized activities may have a defined direction and require little or no consideration of behavior. Thus it is important as teachers preplan activities for the first week of school to be cognizant of the level of student involvement and the management requirements of specific activities.

Dismissal

Whether you are teaching lower elementary grades or senior high school, it is important that you tell students that they must wait until you dismiss them at the end of the period/school day. Explain that there may be special announcements that you save until the end of the day/ period or there may be a homework assignment that you will tell them about at that time. It can be extremely dangerous if students make a dive for the door when they hear the dismissal bell. For this reason it is a good idea to dismiss small groups of students at a time whether you have them line up at the door or merely walk out on their own. Establish a dismissal routine so that students know to clean up, leave things orderly, and are ready to listen to you at dismissal time. The recap of the day's (or period's) events should be an important part of the dismissal process.

Review the day or Class

TEACHING HINT

During the First Day of School:

1. Maintain a quick pace of activities.
2. Praise students for participation.
3. Remind students of the importance of time.
4. Pause (in mid-sentence, if necessary) for silence to get students' attention. (Do not give directions while students are talking.)

"You talk I will listen — I'll talk you listen"

CASE STUDY PROBLEMS

1. Bathrooms (E).   Young children need to visit the bathroom frequently. Although recess was not long ago, a child has asked to leave the room. What system will you establish to allow students to leave class for this purpose without disturbing others? How will you ensure that only one student leaves at a time?

2. Nurse's office (E).   Benjy cut his hand on the aquarium. He should visit the nurse. You cannot leave the room. What procedures will you follow?

3. Leaving the room (S).   You want to send six students to the library. Will they need hall passes? How will you monitor their activity?

4. Transitions.   Transitions between activities or between subjects can be costly in terms of time. You have discovered that you waste about 20 minutes a day. How can you minimize transition time? Consider the distribution and collection of materials, papers, and books, and clean-up activity. Think about ways to motivate a smooth transition.

5. Attention signals.   You are providing instruction to a small group of students; it is time to change groups. How will you signal the next group that it is their turn? What behavioral expectations do you have, and will you communicate to students, related to the movement of groups in your classroom?

6. Obtaining assistance.   You are teaching a small group of students; the rest of the students are working individually. Sam needs help; how can he obtain your assistance without disturbing the entire classroom?

7. Obtaining assistance (S).   You always begin class as soon as the tardy bell rings and have planned activities until it is time for dismissal. Suppose that a student has been absent; when can he or she talk with you and obtain your assistance?

QUESTIONS

1. Why is it important to create groupness? Suggest some ways to accomplish it.
2. Since all groups need rules, should teachers make the rules and impose them? Why?
3. Plan some opening day activities at the grade level you are or will be teaching.
4. Plan an opening day's schedule at the grade level you are or will be teaching.
5. Why should teachers take time to remind students about what they have studied in the course of the school day?

CHAPTER 3

Managing Group Behavior
Grouping for Better Teaching

In Chapter 2 the focus was on the management of the whole-class group and ways that teachers work with the whole class to foster group responsibility, cooperation, and caring. In this chapter we shall examine the purposes for working with students in both the large (whole) group and in small groups and the teacher's management tasks. Chapter 5 provides specific information about how to begin small-group instruction.

FLEXIBLE GROUPING: WHY IS IT IMPORTANT?

Traditionally, both educators and psychologists considered the interaction between teacher and student as the most important relationship for teaching and learning. As a consequence most teachers learned to focus on whole-class, large-group instruction. During the 1970s, instructional research detected differences in goal outcomes between large- and small-group instruction. Mosston and Ashworth (1985) comment that the consequence of this research was that many teachers began to view instruction on a "versus" basis. "A model or idea is presented versus all others (group instruction vs. individualized instruction, affective vs. cognitive, rote vs. discovery, direct vs. indirect teaching)" (p. 31).

The perspective presented in this text on classroom management is that both large- and small-group instruction are necessary for effective teaching and for learning. To determine the appropriate grouping for instruction teachers need to think about (1) what is to be taught (content and purpose), (2) who is to be taught, and (3) the context for instruction (environmental conditions). Both large- and small-group instruction need to be integrated to teach skills and to teach thinking. Each approach requires different management processes that will be discussed in this chapter.

When students are perceived as individuals rather than as members of a specific group, the change to flexible grouping is an easy step. Grouping becomes a strategic device in order to individualize instruction or to normalize instruction, and students are no longer stereotyped or manipulated to fit a group mold. Subgrouping may be a more realistic organizational pattern within the classroom, with subgroups changing from day to day and composed of two to five students. Peer tutoring and the use of learning centers also enable the teacher to subgroup efficiently. If other adults are involved in the classroom or if two or three teachers are able to team up for the teaching of skill subjects, flexible grouping is enhanced. Record-keeping devices, such as checklists, provide a system to monitor student progress in skills, thereby providing teacher and student with information that can be used for instructional advantage.

There are two purposes for grouping in the classroom: individualization of instruction and socialization. To individualize instruction, successful teachers often group students homogeneously for the purpose of teaching a specific concept or skill. For socialization purposes heterogeneous groups are formed to promote interaction among students. Each of these purposes will be discussed in terms of classroom management and of interpersonal skills for working with students.

INDIVIDUALIZATION

Since teaching the whole class often means that the teacher is instructing a quasi-average individual, both the high and the low achievers are dissatisfied. To reduce the range of achievement and the necessity to teach to a fictitious average student, teachers group students to facilitate instruction and to meet individual needs. Maynard Brown's classroom provides an example.

◆   Mr. Brown was teaching reading. Nine students were sitting in a semicircle in front of him. Each child was given a sheet of paper with some sketches of the story that they had read on the previous day. The children were told to number the pictures in the order of the story's sequence of events. Seven of the children did it quickly; two were unable to arrange the pictures in order. The teacher assigned the two children, Bill and Suzy, to a listening post to listen to a simple story. Next the teacher used a flannel board with flannel cutouts to retell the story to the two children. Then the two children were asked to arrange the events of the story.

While Bill and Suzy were at the listening post, Maynard Brown instructed the other seven children. Their needs indicated that they were ready to identify cause-and-effect statements in their reading books. Mr. Brown gave them the instruction they needed and then divided them into two-, two-, and three-student clusters. Each cluster worked together to identify cause-and-effect statements. When Mr. Brown finished his flannel board lesson, Bill and Suzy were assigned a reinforcement activity, and he evaluated the work of the three clusters of students. On this particular day Bill and Suzy received more time and attention than did the seven other children. Maynard Brown's management skills included working with several groups simultaneously and manipulating time and content. His personal skills included treating each student as an individual.

Jean Scaparelli teaches English in a junior high school. She has just returned test papers to her students. "OK, folks, don't get upset. Some of you didn't do as well as you probably expected. Consider this test as an introduction to writing thesis statements. Some of you need more practice, and I will help you today."

"For those of you who feel satisfied with your test results, you may go on and read the selection from Hawthorne's *The House of the Seven Gables*. The rest of us will work in teams and get some help writing provocative thesis statements." Ms. Scaparelli then suggested that the students turn to some essays in their literature book, and she had them work with a partner to identify the authors' thesis statements. She monitored their work and provided feedback. Then she gave them some topics and once again had them work with a partner, this time to write thesis statements. After about 25 minutes she declared, "You're all experts now. Good work. OK, begin work on the Hawthorne selection and if you need help raise your hand and I'll come around."

Personalizing Instruction

In Mr. Brown's class Bill and Suzy felt that Mr. Brown cared about them, as evidenced by his personal instruction. The other members of the class also realized Mr. Brown's regard because they were not held back as a consequence of the skill needs of two individuals. Instead, they learned to appreciate their own growth and their teacher's technical skills. They were secure in the knowledge that when they needed individual assistance they too would receive the benefit of Mr. Brown's personal instruction. Similarly, the junior-high-school students were not subjected to dull and repetitive teaching because some of the students needed extra practice and reinforcement. Ms. Scaparelli provided for individual needs and grouped students flexibly to accomplish it.

Manipulating Time and Content

Teachers in self-contained classrooms have two distinct advantages over departmentalized classroom teachers. In the self-contained classroom teachers can decide on a daily basis which students have special instructional needs; the teacher can manipulate both the length of time expended with individuals or groups and what is to be taught. Jed and Mabel may need extra personal instruction on Monday, but Bill and Suzy can receive some special help on Tuesday. A specific reading skill can be introduced during reading and expanded upon later in the day during social studies. In this way the teacher can avoid fragmented teaching, integrate conceptual learning, and save time.

However, teachers in departmentalized settings can also manage individualized instruction. By planning sequential learning experiences that allow additional practice for students having learning problems yet provide expanded and enrichment activities for students ready to progress, teachers can accommodate the natural heterogeneity that occurs in all classrooms.

Guidelines for Managing Individualized Instruction

1. Analyze present ability level.
2. Plan a program to personalize instruction; set goals. Group students according to skill needs. Individualize for one-to-one instruction. Choose appropriate instructional materials and equipment.
3. Plan reinforcement activities and enrichment to meet individual needs.
4. Evaluate student performance and educational plan.

Student-Directed Instruction

Up to this point individualizing instruction has been considered from the standpoint of more efficient teaching. Sometimes this is called *precision teaching*. In the discussion it has been assumed that the teacher makes the decision for individualizing instruction on a one-to-one basis or by grouping students for similar teaching objectives. But sometimes students make instructional planning decisions. Some students, particularly secondary students, may feel that they can learn more efficiently alone. Some students may prefer to plan their own learning and to take responsibility for it. Learner assertiveness and independence are appropriate teaching/learning goals; therefore, if students are able to plan appropriately and to implement a learning strategy, they should be encouraged to do so. As the teacher plans with the student, reservations to be considered should include ego needs and cooperative work skills involved in group behavior. During a private conference with the student, the teacher should ask questions to assess the student's readiness for self-direction.

Ego-Satisfying Readiness Questions

1. What will you try to accomplish? (Can the student set realistic goals?)
2. What is your plan? (How will the student accomplish the goals?)
3. What materials will you use?
4. What will you do if you discover that you need help?
5. After you accomplish your goal (be precise), what will you do next?

Group-Satisfying Questions

1. Do you prefer to work alone? Why?
2. In what ways is working alone easier?
3. In what ways is working with others easier?
4. What problems do you have when you work with others?
5. Do you like to participate in a group? In what ways?
6. Do you like to help others? How?
7. Do you like others to assist you? In what ways?
8. Do you feel uncomfortable about asking for assistance? Why?
9. Do you feel uncomfortable about using others' ideas? Why?

There are many other questions the teacher could ask to determine the student's need and readiness for self-direction. Even secondary students may not be psychologically ready to direct their own program of studies. The purpose of asking the student questions is to elicit information about the student in order to plan an instructional program that is appropriate for the individual. All students should have opportunities for self-direction, but self-directed activity time is not to be interpreted as a period when the teacher is absolved from preplanning. A great deal of classroom structuring is required to manage individualized activities in terms of providing space, materials, equipment, conference time, and accountability measures.

SOCIALIZATION   *Good*

The second purpose for grouping students is to promote behavior associated with diversity, individuality, cooperation, rationality, responsibility, and respectfulness. Grouping students changes interaction patterns in the classroom from focusing on teacher-to-student instruction to student-to-student instruction; responsibility for success also begins to shift from total teacher responsibility to student participation and responsibility. Small-group work forces student involvement in planning, participation, and evaluation.

Johnson (1980, p. 125) cites a number of consequences and correlates of peer relationships:

1. Contributes to the socialization of values, attitudes, competencies, and ways of perceiving the world.
2. Predicts future psychological health.
3. Teaches social competencies, thereby reducing social isolation.
4. Affects the likelihood of potential problem behaviors in adolescence, such as the use of drugs.
5. Provides the context in which students learn to master aggressive impulses.
6. Contributes to the development of sex role identity.
7. Facilitates ability to perceive others' viewpoints (movement from egocentric to sociocentric behavior).
8. Affects achievement motivation and educational aspiration.

Students may be organized in groups at any grade level and for almost any subject or activity: science experiments, role playing, simulations, research, group planning, discussions, art projects, conflict-decision making, tutorials, story- or playwriting. The earlier discussion about group characteristics pointed out the need for group cohesiveness and group interaction. To develop the feeling of groupness, the teacher must organize the group work for a specific purpose, and that organization should continue until the mission is accomplished. Some educators believe that group work is more productive when students choose their own group members or when groups are organized around the common interests of the group members. However, since grouping should be only for the duration of a specific task, it may be wise to experiment with student-organized groups and teacher-chosen groups. The advantages of the teacher exercising judgment may outweigh other considerations. For instance, the teacher can consider female-male ratios, leadership capabilities, extroverts and introverts, readers and nonreaders—in short, all of the interactional needs of a heterogeneous group, in order to promote peer group learning.

Skills

Students learn social participation skills in group activities. Working together, students assume a variety of roles as they plan and problem solve. The roles include expediter, arbitrator, negotiator, evaluator, researcher, and so on. Performing these roles, students learn to perform many of the following skills related to social participation:

> Cooperate with others in a participatory situation.
> Observe and share observations; express own viewpoint.
> Listen to others' viewpoints and experiences.
> Suggest resources.
> Plan individual and group research.
> Assist others; accept assistance; accept responsibility.
> Develop individual and group plans, tasks, and actions.
> Conclude tasks; share efforts and effects.
> Identify and facilitate group agreements.
> Identify and interpret group disagreements.
> Use persuasion to influence group members and to facilitate
>   intergroup cooperation.
> Coalesce with other groups.
> Negotiate membership group plans; facilitate intergroup
>   cooperation or coalescence.
> Bargain to influence consequential actions.

Cooperative Learning

Cooperative learning is rarely discussed in a classroom management textbook. The more typical text urges that teachers keep students on task through appropriate assignments that are within the student's "success level" and that teachers monitor and provide feedback. This is good advice, but it means that the emphasis is on learning alone, which promotes a competitive classroom environment. In the competitive classroom environment students usually try to be "first": the first to be finished; the first to be correct; the first to sit up tall and fold hands! In this environment students are urged not to talk and not to disturb classmates, but to ask for help from the teacher, if it is needed. Again, this is not necessarily Bad (with a capital "B"), but it is the opposite of a cooperatively structured classroom that favors interaction. Let us consider what happens in a cooperative environment.

◆ In Julie Kramer's classroom the students were working in five groups. The groups' assignment was to develop a set of principles for designing a house that would follow from the logical use of the elements: heat from the sun, insulation of the earth, cooling resulting from shade and breezes. The groups could use their science, social science, health texts or any resource material in the classroom. The students, accustomed to working in groups, immediately organized themselves so that each person had a task; when someone had a problem, he or she asked a team member for an idea. The teacher monitored progress and offered resource suggestions and asked pointed questions to promote students' understanding.

In a seventh-grade mathematics class the students were given story problems dealing with distance, rate, and time. Their tasks were to solve the problems, come up with a formula for solving similar problems, and to make sure that everyone in their group understood how to solve the problems.

In both of these examples the students were grouped heterogeneously. The students are dependent on each other for listening, for encouragement, for assistance, and for task completion. Group and individual success are contingent upon social participation skills of the entire group. The teacher is still monitoring and providing feedback, but the atmosphere of the classroom is different because students are actively promoting each other's learning. The emphasis is on student-student interaction, constructive peer relationships rather than teacher-student interaction.

The importance of peer relationships continues through the high school years. This does not mean that nonguided group work will provide the quality of interactive relationships that is desired. The teacher's classroom management tasks are specific if group work is to happen advantageously. *Teachers who learn the management tasks related to group work strategies never have classroom management problems.* This cannot be overemphasized. Let us now look at the purposes for large- or small-group organization in the classroom and then at the management tasks associated with each organizational strategy.

PURPOSES OF ORGANIZATIONAL STRATEGY

The organization of students into either small groups or treating them as a whole group is a strategy to further learning outcomes (Table 3.1). The teacher's decision needs to be based on the intent of the lesson. If the whole class needs to be introduced to a specific skill, such as adding a one-place number to a two-place number, it is probably more efficient to introduce the skill to the whole class at one time. Similarly, if a biology teacher needs to motivate small-group laboratory inquiry related to a

Table 3.1. Purposes of Large- and Small-Group Instruction

Large-Group Instruction
1. Communication of information/knowledge from single signal source (teacher/guest lecturer) to whole class
2. Demonstration (skills, experiments) from single signal source to whole class

Small-Group Instruction
1. Communication among students
2. Interaction among students
3. Student involvement and valuing
4. Student responsibility for self-learning
5. Cooperative learning (responsibility for others' learning)
6. Development of social participation skills including decision making
7. Differentiation of instruction based on individual differences

specific problem or demonstrate safety techiques, it is more efficient to demonstrate to the whole group before sending students off to their labs to engage in problem solving. But if the intent is to teach democratic behaviors, then students need the opportunity to work in small groups and learn group process skills. Instruction that fosters communication, decision making, and peer relationships cannot occur through large-group organization.

Effect of Group Organization on Multicultured Students

When students are required to participate at school in ways that are different from the students' participation style at home, students will be affected by the clash between the two participation structures (Erickson & Mohatt, 1982). For example, if students are accustomed to talking in an "add-on" style, the rule to raise your hand and wait to be called upon will inhibit participation. (Adding on means that child A makes a statement and child B adds a comment or completes the thought.) In large-group organization the rule of hand raising typically needs to be enforced; therefore, some students from multicultured backgrounds may be negatively affected.

When discussion is orchestrated by the teacher in a teacher-student interaction configuration, real conversation does not occur. The management devices used by teachers to control (socialize) a large group inhibit face-to-face communication. Teachers communicate certain expectations for whole-group participation. These expectations may include ways to take turns in speaking, posture, and eye contact. Since students perceive these communicated "messages" differently, they will also react in different ways.

Wilcox (1982) studied the different ways that teachers socialize students in the classroom and noted differences between teachers who emphasize external controls and rules and those who attempt to inculcate the internalization of norms. Teachers who want students to take responsibility for their own actions require that students share in selecting and shaping participation in activities. This requires a different type of interaction than in the classroom where the teacher is committed to setting the rules and procedures and directing students' actions by virtue of authority. Once again students of different cultural background and socioeconomic level may react differentially to these treatments. Wilcox, however, notes that teachers may treat students differentially based on sociocultural information that influences teacher expectations for students' future occupations. So, although it is important to base grouping decisions on the purpose of instruction and to consider the population to be taught, it is also important to verify that decisions are not based on faulty expectations related to sociocultural information.

MANAGEMENT OF LARGE- AND SMALL-GROUP INSTRUCTION

Maintaining Control during Large-Group Instruction

What management tasks do teachers need to know for effective large-group instruction? Table 3.2 provides an overview of the management tasks experienced teachers perform for effective teaching using large-group instruction. There are always advantages and possible disadvantages in every instructional approach and organizational strategy. For this reason it is important to recognize the options, or trade-offs, and be prepared to counter the potential problems. Let us first look at some of the advantages of using large-group instruction.

As noted earlier, large-group instruction is an efficient means for whole-class input utilizing lecture technique, films, guest speakers, or demonstrations. Often students will gain a sense of belonging by being a member of the whole group and treated the same as everyone else. Large-group instruction facilitates the teaching of new skills. The teacher does not have to repeat information that everyone will need, and so classroom time is utilized productively. Large-group instruction also promotes teacher-centered authority. At the beginning of the semester when it is important to set standards and critical that students recognize the teacher's leadership, this strategy is very effective.

Table 3.2. Management of Large-Group Instruction

Teacher Management Tasks	Problems to Avoid
1. Select lesson (information, skills) needed by most students.	1. Lesson geared to few students deficient in some area.
2. Elicit attention of all students.	2. Inattention due to students' continuing own work tasks.
3. Verify that all students can see and hear (accommodate handicapped students).	3. Students too spread out in classroom or too crowded to see and hear; deviant behavior results.
4. Motivate interest.	4. Students fail to generate interest.
5. Constantly scan entire class; encourage eye contact.	5. Deviant behavior is contagious.
6. Provide basic information; reassure students who do not understand that additional assistance will be forthcoming, if needed.	6. Special information needed for high and low achievers; failure to assess individual needs accurately.
7. Verify understanding through short and frequent questions; wait and encourage student responses.	7. Students lose interest because they do not comprehend.

Finally, it is significant to recognize that the use of large-group instruction provides a single continuous signal source to focus students' attention. Research by Kounin and Sherman (1979) provides evidence that certain environmental settings have more holding power than others. If the teacher has truly interested the students, the teacher will be the sole "signal" source. If the lesson does not lag, it is likely that the teacher will hold students' attention and as a consequence the large-group setting has the potential to decrease students' social ineffective behavior.

Are there disadvantages related to the use of large-group instruction? Yes indeed! Quite frequently individual needs are subordinated to group needs in order to demonstrate a skill or make a presentation to the whole class at the same time. When teaching to a large group, it is necessary to keep everyone on task (the same task); as a result the strategy impedes differentiation of instruction.

Large-group instruction typically discourages social participation because interaction is controlled by the teacher, and the typical pattern moves from teacher to student and back to the teacher. As a consequence instruction tends to be impersonal, and some students begin to feel alienated. Another consequence is that task involvement is often reduced.

Students with handicapping conditions may have problems during large-group instruction if teachers do not remember to provide for their needs. In particular one needs to be concerned with students' vision and hearing. Sometimes the physical size of some students may be a factor in affecting other students' vision and hearing, and so seat assignments or the spatial arrangement of students sitting on a rug should be monitored during large-group instruction. Sitting too close together is also a problem since it tempts misbehavior.

Another problem to be aware of is that teachers are sometimes tempted to make an "example" of disruptive students during large-group instruction. It is very annoying to be on the verge of presenting a marvelous idea when one student begins to whisper to a classmate. (Review the ripple effect presented in Chapter 1.)

Maintaining Control During Small-Group Instruction

What management tasks do teachers need to know for effective small-group instruction? Table 3.3 provides information about the management tasks involved in small-group instruction and the potential problems to avoid for effective use of the strategy. Once again, it is useful to be familiar with the advantages and disadvantages of the organizational use of small-group instruction.

If teachers were in the business of passing out awards or medals, during large-group instruction teachers would hand out awards to students for being quiet and attending to the demonstration or lecture; but in small-group instruction, awards are given for interaction and communication. Small-group instruction motivates student involvement, promotes interaction, and facilitates communication. A natural consequence of this is that students are encouraged to assist others and to accept responsibility.

Small-group instruction necessitates listening to others' viewpoints and sharing values; as a result students move from egocentric points of view to more sociocentric perspectives. Group decision making is promoted as students develop group productions and engage in group planning sessions. Group work involves negotiation and bargaining with classmates, and it is in this way that democratic group processes are taught.

Other obvious advantages are that the teacher is free to observe, listen, and diagnose students' needs and abilities during group work while monitoring group involvement and on-task behaviors. Differentiation of instruction occurs in two ways: The teacher can assign work based on the needs and abilities of the members of the group; groups will always approach an assignment differentially based on their own interests and abilities.

What are the potential disadvantages? Group process skills are developmental; this means that students need practice to be "skillful."

Table 3.3. Management of Small-Group Instruction

Teacher Management Tasks	Problems to Avoid
1. Motivate class interest.	1. Situation, problem, or task not of interest to majority of students.
2. Identify and verify understanding of group work rules.	2. System of rules and procedures for group work not clear.
3. Group students and appoint group leaders and recorders.	3. Students do not understand roles and responsibilities during group work.
4. Provide clear task assignment(s).	4. Students cannot identify task to be performed.
5. Verify group understanding of task.	5. Students do not understand how to get started.
6. Assign physical space for group work.	6. Students do not know where to work.
7. Identify means for you to signal attention.	7. Students do not recognize signal for attention. Emergency conditions or too much noise necessitate that you get attention immediately.
8. Identify means for groups to signal your attention, if assistance is needed.	8. Students need help and *all* come to find you.
9. Provide material resources for group work.	9. Too few appropriate materials to accomplish task assignment.
10. Provide information about time utilization for group work.	10. Students waste time and are not cued to complete work.
11. Monitor group work: a. on task b. group processes c. material resource needs.	11. Groups fail to get started; groups do not really understand task; one student monopolizes conversation; others fail to cooperate and participate; inappropriate materials.
12. Signal whole-class attention for evaluation (have students turn chairs or return to original places).	12. Students fail to listen to and assist *other* groups during evaluation; students fail to identify with *own* group.
13. Evaluate: a. substantive accomplishment b. group needs c. group processes.	13. Groups tend to evaluate behavior rather than content accomplishments and group processes.

Teachers tend to be fearful of the organizational strategy because the strategy encourages talk and excitement, and the sound level increases. (Experienced teachers can differentiate between the good hum of work noise and play noise!) If process skills are poor, students will waste time.

Another disadvantage cited by some teachers is the subordination of academic content for group process skills.

Cooperative group work necessitates the accommodation of both high and low achievers in possibly the same group to accomplish group goals; although this may be a disadvantage, the same is really true when teachers use large-group instruction. Another possible problem that teachers need to be aware of is the potential conflict of extroverted, aggressive students and subordinate, introverted students.

The tasks identified in Table 3.3 provide a sequential list of suggestions to control small-group work. Perhaps most important is the realization that students will get better at group work if (1) they practice, and (2) it is evaluated *each* time they participate. Another point that needs to be considered in the placement of groups in the classroom is that if students sit at desks in small groupings, the desks tend to inhibit good communication. It is far better for students to just sit on chairs in a small circle, facing each other. (If the desk and chair are attached, then they should still be placed in a circle.) In Chapter 5 instructional suggestions will be given for beginning and improving small-group work.

Tables 3.4 and 3.5 provide checklists for large- and small-group instruction to help you anticipate the potential management problems. Use them as you plan instruction.

COMMON QUESTIONS ABOUT GROUP WORK

"What is the ideal size of a small group?" Five to seven students in a group has been found to be a desirable size. The odd number of students facilitates decision making. A larger group makes it difficult for everyone to share ideas and to make plans. A smaller group is often nonfunctional because there is not enough stimulation.

"Should there be group work rules?" Yes indeed! Students need to be aware of class procedures and what they are expected to accomplish. Group work rules are reinforced through a formative or end-of-period

---

Table 3.4. Checklist for Anticipating Problems Using Large-Group Instruction

1. Did you select an appropriate lesson for all students?
2. Did you elicit everyone's attention?
3. Did you verify seating arrangements so all can see and hear?
4. Did you motivate interest?
5. Did you scan class; monitor attention?
6. Did you verify understanding?

Table 3.5. Checklist for Anticipating Problems in Small Heterogeneous Groups

1. Did you assign each group a place to work?
2. Did you choose or suggest that the group choose a leader?
3. If needed, did you choose or suggest that the group choose a recorder?
4. Did you verify that each group understands its task or purpose?
5. Do the students need materials?
6. Have you provided a means whereby the students can find materials or resources?
7. If reading is required, are there at least two members of the group who can read the needed resource material?
8. If graphs, charts, or maps are to be used, do the students have the necessary skills to perform their task?
9. If intergroup interaction is necessary, are the students aware of the process they are to use?
10. Is there a time limit for the group work? If so, do the students know what it is?
11. How will you get the students' attention if you need to? Have you communicated the means to the students?
12. What should the students do if they need help? Have you communicated the system to them?
13. What should some groups do if they finish before other groups have concluded their tasks? Have you communicated your plan to them?

evaluation. Group work rules may include allowing every member of the group to talk out and share ideas; focusing on their task without wasting time; obtaining and returning materials expeditiously; and accepting responsibility, acting rationally and respectfully. Group work should become more purposeful each day if students are aware of time constraints, planning expectations, and the formative evaluation each day in which they are asked to share plans and accomplishments.

"If all students are working in small groups at the same time, what is the role of the teacher?" The teacher should be circulating, listening, observing, and taking notes about student participation and problems. The teacher should provide materials when needed or suggest resources to students. If a group seems to be off the track, then it is the teacher's responsibility to refocus their actions or thinking, to provide guidance and motivation. The teacher acts as a facilitator. It is the teacher's task to guide the daily formative evaluation by asking probing questions and by focusing the whole class's participation on the evaluation so that each group benefits from all the others.

"How can you meet the needs of exceptional students?" Heterogeneous grouping in small groups means that the exceptional learner will be a

group member. If the exceptional learner is below grade level, he or she should receive peer assistance in the small group. If reading is necessary for group activities, the teacher should arrange groups so that there are at least two good readers in each group.

Open-ended group activities will meet the needs of the gifted exceptional learner. There are a variety of ways that group work can be used for the extension of thinking; for example, the use of task cards or learning packets can have additional reports or experiments performed by more capable students.

If the exceptional learner is a hyperactive student, then manipulative group activities should be planned. The teacher can have the hyperactive student assist by handing out materials and by helping during a demonstration so that the youngster has the opportunity to touch things immediately.

"If the teacher has purposefully grouped students homogeneously or heterogeneously, does the teacher ever teach all of the students the same concept?" Yes, sometimes during group work activities you discover that many of the students need similar information or that a skill deficiency must be overcome. When this occurs, you should terminate activities temporarily, call the students together (be sure to elicit everyone's attention; switch to large-group instructional strategy) and teach them what they need to know.

However, in most cases the teacher groups the students in order to meet needs more efficiently. Therefore, whole-class teaching would be wasteful. It is important to remember that grouping offers the teacher the opportunity to differentiate assignments by extending and enriching instead of just assigning additional work.

EVALUATING GROUP ACTIVITIES

Both the process and the substance of group activities should be evaluated. In the beginning, students are tempted to dwell on group behavior, so they need to learn the difference between evaluating group successes and failures and evaluating substantive goals. If students have never worked in small groups before, it is possible that they will be unable to separate group behavior from the task orientation. If this occurs, reassure the students that group work is difficult (it is!) and evaluate what it should be.

The teacher may begin questions concerning the task assignment by asking one member of each group to share the group's problem, plans, actions, resources used, and accomplishments. This summation should occur daily whenever group work occurs and may be the job for the group recorder, leader, or any group member. If group work continues for several days, the children should take turns preparing the summarizing statements for the class. Group evaluations are more effective when the groups are still gathered together in their working positions because this facilitates the feeling of groupness and responsibility.

During this formative evaluation, the groups should be asked about any problems pertaining to their task. Students should be encouraged to evaluate whether or not they defined their problem clearly. Have they identified the issues involved? Did they decide how to find out? What resources will they use? Do they need some suggestions? ("Boys and girls, do you have any ideas to help them?") By bringing in the other groups and asking them to focus on the problem of the evaluating group, class attention and involvement are enhanced. The teacher should also question whether or not the students need some outside resource assistance. Finally, each group should be asked to project, "What will you do next (tomorrow)?"

Group behavioral evaluation is directed at improving social participation skills. For instance, the following kinds of questions might be asked to facilitate group introspection:

1. Did everyone share one viewpoint?
2. Did you always agree?
3. How did you decide what to do when different viewpoints were expressed?
4. In what ways is it valuable when individuals in a group do not agree?
5. How did it help the group when (Sheila) expressed (her) point of view (or disagreed)?
6. Sheila, how did you feel when you were in the minority?
7. Why is it important that we listen to a minority viewpoint?
8. Give us an example of how your group made a compromise.
9. Explain how you persuaded...
10. What was your hardest task today?
11. What was your easiest task today?
12. In what ways was your group work successful today?
13. In what ways will you need to improve your group work?

The evaluation portion of group work should be planned as carefully as the initial assignment. A common error lies in not providing sufficient time for the evaluation. It is wise to remember when planning your group work that students will enjoy it more if motivation is sustained by a short work period rather than being diminished by too long a work period. The evaluation part of the lesson facilitates critical understanding for students and teacher concerning "what is," "what we need to do," and "where we are going."

The whole class needs to be prepared for the evaluation. Each group should turn their chairs around so that they can see and hear all the other groups. Sometimes it is wise to have the students put their resource materials in the equipment centers before the evaluation begins. However, sometimes a group needs to share its product with the other groups. In that case it may be wise to put off the cleanup period until after the evaluation.

Listening skills should be developed during the evaluation period. "Students (boys and girls), it is Bob's group's turn. Listen and see if you can offer them some suggestions." "Did your group have a similar problem?" "How many groups agree with the way they solved their problem?" "Bert, tell us why you disagree." "What do you recommend to the other group?"

We always need to keep an eye on ideal situations for student participation. Sometimes when students have behavioral problems during group work, it is helpful to choose several students to be observers. If desired, the observer may be one member of each group. The observer's role is to listen and to interpret group problems. The observer should provide feedback to the group observed rather than to the class as a whole. This feedback report should occur at the end of the group work time and focus on participation of group members and the observer's suggestions for improving group interaction. The observer should be prepared for the role by the teacher before the work time.

Thus far in this chapter the discussion about grouping students has focused on the purpose of grouping, the efficient management of group work, the potential problems to anticipate, and how to evaluate group activities. A current controversy in society and in the profession concerns the grouping of students sometimes labeled "exceptional." The exceptional learner has frequently been separated from the regular classroom of so-called average, or normal, students and taught by a specialist. But many educators and laypersons believe that the classroom should be so normalized that it reflects a heterogeneous community similar to the community outside the school. The next section deals with the controversial issue of mainstreaming the exceptional learner in order to normalize the classroom.

NORMALIZING THE CLASSROOM

Homogeneity does not exist except in the mind's eye. In every classroom there are students with learning problems; yet these students are not necessarily described as "handicapped." Instead, the classroom teacher may describe these students as "challenging." Rubin and Balow (1971) discovered that teachers of students in grades K–3 identified 40 percent of their students as having some sort of learning problem that required special teaching. Outside the classroom we are a nation of disparate cultures. Our population represents an abundance of interests and abilities and reflects human variability. Perhaps instigated by a nationwide humanistic movement or perhaps by the age-old tradition in teacher education to "begin where the child is," normalizing the classroom is significant only in the sense that it represents an honest appraisal of human life. A true learning community should be heterogeneous in order to provide all students with equal educational opportunities and mutual respect.

RESEARCH AND READINGS

Dunn, Lloyd M. (1967). Special education for the mildly retarded: Is much of it justifiable? *Exceptional Children, 34,* 5–22.

Dunn observed that the majority of students in retarded classrooms came from low socioeconomic status homes.

Zito, R. J., & Bardon, J. I. (1969). Achievement motivation among Negro adolescents in regular and special education programs. *American Journal of Mental Deficiency, 74,* 20–26.

Zito and Bardon questioned the effectiveness of special classroom placement.

Mercer, Jane R. (1971). Sociocultural factors in labeling mental retardates. *Peabody Journal of Education, 48,* 191.

Mercer investigated the disproportionate number of minority and low economic background children in special education classrooms.

Favorable judicial decisions in Pennsylvania (1971), the District of Columbia (1972), and California (1972) instigated legislative actions in behalf of handicapped children. In 1974 Congress passed amendments (PL 93–380) to the Education of the Handicapped Act. This act established full educational opportunities for all handicapped children and provided procedures to assure that these children would be educated with nonhandicapped children when the degree of disability was not so severe as to limit satisfactory education in a regular classroom.

Almost 16 percent of the school-age population has some type of handicapping condition (visual and hearing impairment, speech impairment, crippled and health impairment, emotionally and mentally retarded, learning disabilities). Many students in the public schools receive inappropriate services because their educational handicaps go undetected. Handicapped children or children with special needs are not unique in the schools; nor do students with special needs represent an unsubstantial proportion of the total school population.

Individualized Educational Program

Public Law 94–142 has been cited as a bill of rights for handicapped children. The law states that the educational program should specify the student's present educational achievement level. The next step is to decide upon appropriate educational goals, both annual and short range. Special services to achieve or to implement the goals must be designated, along with the extent to which the student can be placed in a regular classroom. For instance, some students who have been in special classrooms may be able to work only part-time in a regular classroom. Evaluation is to occur annually and progress toward goals assessed.

The purpose of PL 94–142 is to guarantee that all handicapped students will receive special education and related services as required by the nature of their handicap and that such education will be free and appropriate.

By normalizing the public schools so that teachers are not concentrating solely on so-called normal students, the education of all students will be significantly improved. But the integration of handicapped students (or students labeled handicapped) into regular classrooms poses management problems for classroom teachers.

RESEARCH AND READINGS

Dewey, John. (1897). *My Pedagogic Creed*. Republished in 1929 by the Progressive Educational Association: Washington, D.C., p. 6.

"Education . . . is a process of living and not a preparation for future living. The school must represent present life—life as real and vital to the child as that which he carries on in the home, in the neighborhood, or on the playground."

The first major need of any student new to the classroom is peer group acceptance. The child who has been ostracized, branded, or stereotyped has an even greater need for status, respect, and security. The first place to start in order to help the physically or learning handicapped student is with the students who are already in the classroom. The receiving class needs to be prepared for what to expect, and this can be done in a variety of ways. Initial discussions can focus on the ways in which all individuals differ: abilities, skills, looks, culture, likes, problems, health. Then discussions can progress to consider ways in which all individuals are similar: feelings, emotions, needs, growth, change.

Resource people or students with similar handicaps may be another way to build understanding of how it feels to be handicapped. Students may contribute their own experiences about temporary problems, such as "When I broke my leg," or "got hit in the eye," and listening to or reading stories about handicapped youth can also provide insight for the students. In this sensitizing stage it is important to develop understanding about the nature of individual differences and handicaps. The purpose is not to pity the different child but to develop empathy for and acceptance of individual differences.

Another aspect of the preparation is to deal with students' fears. Both the handicapped student and the normal peers will face a period of uncertainty about and fear of one another. All are worried about others' reactions. Normal age mates should be reassured from the initial discussions and activities that consider likenesses and differences that disabled students share the same interests and the same capacity for fun. If the physically handicapped student uses mechanical devices such as a wheelchair, crutches, or braces, then other types of preparation are needed. Students should be prepared to anticipate seating arrangements to accommodate the handicapped youth. Aisles may need to be widened or perhaps the handicapped student should leave class earlier than others if it takes longer to arrive at lunch or learning facilities or if more space is required to accomplish a task.

The teacher's own fears must also be faced. It is not possible to alleviate students' fears or foster peer group acceptance if the teacher does not have a positive attitude about mainstreaming. A successful classroom program will be dependent on the teacher's optimism, understanding, and encouragement as well as on his or her technical skills for the development of a viable program. (Is it possible to provide too much assistance to handicapped students?)

RESEARCH AND READINGS

Stipek, D., & Sanborn, M. (1983). Preschool teachers' task-related interactions with handicapped and nonhandicapped boys and girls. Paper presented at the American Educational Research Association, Montreal, Canada.

Preschool teachers tend to offer more unrequested assistance and praise to handicapped children and "high-risk" academic problem children than to their more normal age mates. It is possible that this may result in the promotion of more passive role behavior by these target children.

PEER TUTORING

Peer tutoring extends the teacher's ability to provide individualized instruction and can occur within the classroom. By using students as resources for other students, responsibility and mutual respect are learned along with needed skills. With learning teams flexibly determined for learning or for practicing specific skills, tutoring can be an intergrade, multiaged process. Tutoring that takes place within the classroom is more likely to be a reciprocal relationship in which tutor and tutee understand the helping relationship. The pairing of students friendly to each other facilitates the process of asking for and accepting assistance.

Advantages of Peer Tutoring

Since the primary purpose of peer tutoring is the accomplishment of individualized instruction, this strategy should relieve the classroom teacher of some instructional tasks so that the necessary planning, diagnostic, and assessment tasks can be carried out. Probably no other strategy says as explicitly to students that individual rates for learning are natural and accepted.

If tutoring is used as a recurring process during the school week, students will find that for some tasks they will be teachers and for other tasks they will be receiving assistance. Self-evaluation by students will be more precise and effective as they determine their own capacity to accept or to provide help.

Another advantage of peer tutoring is self-learning. When students make plans for and work at teaching others, they become more effective learners and more proficient at the task they are teaching. Students begin to assume responsibility for personal planning as well as for planning tasks for the step-by-step learning of a peer tutee.

Mutual respect, socialization, and understanding increase as students plan and work together. Students take pride in teaching others and assume pride in learning. Students learn to care about one another. The peer tutor becomes a model who enhances and reinforces the skill or behavior that is to be taught. (Rarely is a peer perceived as an authority figure.) Since students "speak the same language," the communication process is more open, and they are more likely to understand each other.

RESEARCH AND READINGS

Newmark, G. (1976). *This school belongs to you and me.* New York: Hart Publishing, pp. 40–41.

"As children become involved in teaching other children they begin to feel good about asking for and offering each other help. Competitiveness is replaced by cooperation as students work together on learning teams."

Johnson, D. W., & Johnson, R. T. (1982). Healthy peer relationships: A necessity not a luxury. In P. Roy (Ed.). *Structuring cooperative learning experiences in the classroom: The 1982 handbook*. Minneapolis: Interaction Books, pp. 45–82.

"When children have poor study skills or are unmotivated, cooperative interaction with peers who support academic achievement has powerful effects on learning and educational aspirations. Supportive relations with peers are also related to using abilities in achievement situations."

Disadvantages of Peer Tutoring

The tutoring process needs to be taught. One cannot assume that a student has the necessary skill to teach another just because the student can perform the needed behavior. Some skills are learned serendipitously, and the performer may not be able to break them down into the essential instructional sequence in order to teach a peer learner. Therefore the teacher must take the time to develop a step-by-step process for the tutor to implement. Another aspect of the problem is that the desired behavior may not be performed precisely as the teacher wants it modeled. If such is the case, the teacher will first have to model the behavior to the tutor, which brings us to the second problem.

Valuable time can be lost in preparing students to tutor and to receive assistance from other students. The time invested in planning instructional sequences for tutors to use and in modeling desired behavior may well be more than if the teacher provided the necessary instruction in small homogeneous groups.

Students being tutored may feel that they are not getting the full benefit of a teacher-student relationship. Parents may also feel this way. The teacher will have to exercise special care in praising and encouraging students' learning behavior, and care will also have to be exercised to be sure that every student experiences both the tutor and tutee roles.

Although the tutor and tutee need to be friendly in order to establish an effective helping relationship, if the students are too close or too friendly, their attention may wander to pursuits of greater interest or fun.

Class organization may suffer during the initial stages of tutoring until students learn how to talk quietly together, how to help, when to get supplies, when to ask for teacher assistance, how to keep track of progress, and so forth.

Classroom Management Guidelines for Peer Tutoring

1. Preplan classroom organization and procedures.
   a. Decide how often tutoring is to occur and the time of the day that is to be used for tutoring.
   b. Are all the children to be involved? If not, what other things will they be doing?
   c. How will you ensure that all students will perform both tutor and tutee roles? Will there be a tutoring partnership of two students or a learning team of three or more?
   d. How will the room be arranged for tutoring? Where will the children sit?
   e. When will you diagnose needs and assess achievement?
   f. Who will perform record-keeping chores—teacher, aide, or students? Have you developed the appropriate record-keeping devices to facilitate peer tutoring?
   g. Have you communicated to parents and principal your plan for peer tutoring?
2. Preplan with students for tutoring.
   a. Do the students understand the concept of individual differences?
   b. Do the students understand that we learn from one another?
   c. Do the students understand the modeling process? This needs to be demonstrated to them.
   d. How will you communicate with tutors and tutees about what is to be learned?
   e. How will you develop tutor responsibility for planning? Will tutor and tutee plan jointly?
   f. How will you verify that the students are good at whatever it is they are going to tutor?
   g. How will you ensure proper teaching procedures?
   h. Will you advise the tutor about potential learning problems? Will you suggest techniques for overcoming them? Are the students advised to seek your assistance if learning problems develop? How are they to obtain teacher assistance?
   i. How will the students self-evaluate?
   j. How will you verify achievement?
3. Preplan teacher behavior and tasks during tutoring.
   a. How will you keep track of learning needs and achievement?
   b. How will you provide assistance to tutors?
   c. How will you monitor teaching procedures?
   d. What skills will be taught by tutors?
   e. How will you vary tutoring experiences so that every student has an opportunity to model what he or she is good at?
   f. How will you vary assignments to include tasks other than drill

work so that boredom does not set in? (For instance: library or map skills, pottery making, music notation, science experiments).

MANAGING GROUP
DISCIPLINARY PROBLEMS

Individuals influence groups and groups influence individuals. If students lack a sense of purpose and of caring about one another, there is bound to be conflict and friction. Effective group discipline is dependent on the leadership capabilities of the teacher in stressing positive and desirable behavior. The teacher's first task is to establish rapport with the class and to facilitate the development of a classroom community. As a community of individuals who will work together over a relatively long period of time, certain relationships need to be established. These relationships involve work and play roles for class members, values and rules, and procedures to govern progress inside and outside the classroom. The greater the group participation in deciding on classroom organization and structure, the greater will be the involvement and solidarity of the total group.

Teachers have more interactions with individuals and with small groups than with the entire classroom of students. The teacher's control is dependent on personal leadership in using group process strategies for the development of groupness and for preplanning appropriate learning experiences in which students work as members of learning teams. With the teacher's guidance students will grow in their ability to assume responsibility and to analyze and evaluate their own group process behavior and skills, and the life of the classroom community will improve correspondingly.

Small-Group Misbehavior

When misbehavior occurs, it should be handled on a one-time basis similar to the suggestions for handling individual misbehavior. Admonishing or punishing an entire class or group is impractical and can injure the teacher's classroom rapport as well as escalate the negative behavior. In most situations a private talk with the misbehaving students will suffice. Small-group disruptiveness should be handled in terms of the effect on the entire class. Students should learn to view their own behavior as affecting their classmates. The classroom is a learning community, and its members are responsible to one another. Teachers are sometimes inclined to lose their temper and to pronounce a classroom sentence that rarely fits the crime. For instance, if students are disruptive, nasty, or disinterested, it would not make sense to shout,

"Just for that there will be a double homework assignment tonight." Or, "Just for that, there will be no PE today!" In the case of the "no PE," physical education is a subject to be taught, and achievement standards apply to physical education as well as to any other subject. Second, it is not a privilege to be withdrawn if students misbehave, and physical activity is probably just what the group needs at this particular moment. The real point is that before one reacts, one must think: Why are the students behaving in this manner? In what ways have I personally contributed to their negative behavior? How can I help them?

Punishing many for the actions of a few has often resulted in teachers assigning homework or a drill procedure as a deterrent to future misbehavior. The consequence of using a work assignment for punishment is distrust by both students and parents of homework assignments as mere busywork. In addition, students are robbed of learning motivation; the teacher has implied to the students that academic work is punishment.

There are no magic solutions or techniques for handling small-group misbehavior; however, successful teachers deal with disciplinary problems in the following ways:

1. *Take immediate action.* Walk over to the misbehaving group and use your physical presence to inhibit more mischief. If what is happening is clear, give the group your best "I mean it" expression.

2. If what is happening is not clear, *talk quietly to the group.* Determine what is wrong, why it is happening, what needs exist.

3. If members of the group need to be separated from one another, do it quickly and efficiently. *Do not alert the entire class,* unless it is a situation in which you can say, "(Boys and girls, Students), we have some (friends, classmates) who are having a problem. They need our help. Who can tell them what we are supposed to be doing?" Continuing in this vein, primary school children will learn appropriate classroom behavior. With slight language variations, older students will realize that you are not going to allow off-task behavior. It takes patience and really being on top of the situation to use misbehavior to teach appropriate social behavior. This leads to the next point.

4. The very best technique for handling misbehavior is to *monitor the classroom and inhibit misbehavior before it occurs.* Teachers who pace their classroom—using eye contact, gesturing (finger at lips), listening, suggesting—know what is going on and have convinced their students that they know what is happening. In these classrooms minor infractions do not have a chance!

5. *Some misbehavior ought to be ignored.* The loud yawn that encourages another student to laugh should probably be handled by a raised eyebrow aimed at the yawner and the laugher. Then forget it; one

shouldn't make a big deal about nothing. Interrupting the classroom lesson will cause more of a disruption than the yawn did.

6. *Evaluate group work.* Praise the way in which different groups handled their problems and worked together. As stated earlier, both the substance of group work and the ways in which the group participated together are fair play for an evaluation.

Investigate Major Problems

Classroom group problems that occur on the playground, when the teacher is absent, or are of a serious nature should be investigated carefully. Such investigations should occur after school, before school with the offending students, or if all the students are involved and have information, then class time should be used to hold a class meeting in order to gather facts. Because students must learn that everyone is accountable for personal actions, the teacher must help the students resolve the situation if it is at all possible.

Disinterest and Inattentiveness

Individual students or groups of students who are uninvolved during class activities, lectures, or individual work tasks are more likely to cause classroom problems. These students will soon lag behind their classmates in achieving learning outcomes. They are also likely to engage in behaviors that cause other students to be distracted. It is important to find out why these students are not attending to the appropriate activity. If necessary, clarify the work task and remind the student(s) to "get going." Then monitor the student's work to verify that your directions have been followed. Remember to talk quietly to the student or group of students so that you do not interrupt the concentration of the rest of the class.

Punishment: What Kind?

Penalties need to be appropriate to the seriousness of the misbehavior. The penalty should be used to deter recurrence of the violation of classroom rules or procedures. This means that students need to be aware of what they have done wrong.

Penalties should be pretty standard so that all students are treated equally. Students should recognize that certain behaviors, such as failure to complete assignments, aggressiveness, destruction of property, abusive language, and so on, will be punished.

A very effective technique used by teachers of students in grades 3 through 8 is to assign a composition of 50–150 words in length, depending on the seriousness of the misbehavior. The composition should focus on what happened, why it happened, its effect on others, and how it can be prevented in the future. The composition must be written in the student's or group's spare time and must be taken home for parental signature.

But compositions are not effective with very young students or older high school students. For young students sometimes it is important to separate the members of a misbehaving group and to disallow their association together either in the classroom or on the playground. School citizenship chores can also be assigned to misbehaving groups of students to keep them out of the area where they are having problems. Chores can be cleaning up the lunch pavilion, weeding, planting, collecting milk cartons for kindergarten paint containers, and so on. These kinds of jobs allow a cooling off period for the misbehaving group of individuals and suggest ways of helping others instead of causing school problems.

It is also necessary to consider serious offenders. These students or groups of students should be dealt with by other personnel such as the grade-level counselor, the assistant principal, or the principal. Serious offenses should also require parental advisement. Teachers should not try to solve all behavioral problems; school resource people as well as community resources should be called upon for assistance.

SUMMARY

In this chapter there has been an emphasis on managing group behavior. Two purposes for grouping were identified: individualization of instruction and socialization. The use of flexible grouping procedures was discussed to provide for individual needs and to avoid dull and repetitive teaching. The purposes of large- and small-group organizational strategies were identified and the teacher's management tasks for each were discussed from the perspective of the advantages and disadvantages of each grouping strategy. Checklists for anticipating problems in large and small groups were provided. Normalizing the regular classroom by integrating exceptional children was discussed and anticipatory preplanning suggestions to implement mainstreaming were given. Peer tutoring was considered as a teaching strategy to extend individualization. The management of group disciplinary problems was discussed, with similar emphases on the management of individual disciplinary problems.

CASE STUDY PROBLEMS

1. Cooperative Learning. You just observed your students' agonized expressions when you announced that there will be a science test of the unit they have just completed. Develop a cooperative review activity in which students are dependent on each other for assistance to prepare for the examination.

2. Small-Group Work.   Mr. Kelly was disgusted with small-group work. He found that the students were highly motivated but didn't seem to accomplish very much. He would tell the students what they were to work on and then send them off to their groups. The students would talk a bit and then seem confused and finally quit. What was wrong with Mr. Kelly's procedures? What are some things Mr. Kelly could do to improve the students' group work?

3. Large-Group Work.   Ms. Barry was suddenly aware that in the last several minutes her voice had been rising. She was demonstrating a problem at the chalkboard, but now it was apparent to her that the students were not all attending to the demonstration. What do you think went wrong? What should she say to the students?

4. Handicapped.   A handicapped youth in Mr. Frances' classroom would repeatedly burp loudly during class, usually during a teacher-directed lesson. Most of the other students were successfully ignoring this behavior, but Mr. Frances noted that several students were beginning to smirk when this occurred. Suggest some things that Mr. Frances could do to correct this behavior. How could a peer model assist the handicapped youth? What directions should the peer model be given?

QUESTIONS

1. What are the pedagogic implications of flexible grouping?
2. Discuss cultural conflicts between home and school affecting multicultured students.
3. Do you think small- or large-group organization is more difficult for a beginning teacher? Why? How can a teacher become more proficient in using both strategies?
4. Using the text definition of classroom management, discuss the rationale for putting information about mainstreaming in a classroom management text.
5. You have decided that some of your students would profit from individualization of learning activities. Develop some appropriate activities at the level you are teaching or observing.
6. "Time" is often cited as the reason for utilizing the lecture approach in classrooms versus other approaches. How valid is this reason? (What do students gain? What do they lose?)

CHAPTER 4

Evaluating Progress

CHAPTER HIGHLIGHTS

Gathering data about student progress

Checklists for evaluating progress

Anecdotal records

Conferences

Diaries and logs

Teacher-made tests

Sociometric tests

Grading

PURPOSES OF EVALUATION

Midge Brady was one of our fictitious teachers in Chapter 1. Her prime concern as she prepared for the new school year was her ability to report student progress to parents in an accurate and specific manner. Student progress should be routinely and cooperatively evaluated in terms of cognitive understanding, skills, attitudes, and values. Through the evaluation process teachers learn how to improve learning and how to improve teaching; students learn what it is that is important to learn and how successful they are at it. Many teachers share their teaching objectives with students in order to clarify the relationship between what is taught and what is evaluated. The evaluation process should be a communication system that keeps everyone who is involved (students, parents, community members, educators) informed about the effectiveness of the educational program.

Evaluation occurs continuously in the classroom in both formal and informal ways. Parents are well aware of the formal measures that are used. The results of state and nationally designed tests are often reported in local newspapers and magazines. But the judgments that are made daily as teachers diagnose situations, redesign objectives, reteach and reinforce learning, are seldom reported to parents in ways that communicate the teacher's leadership and professional expertise in the instructional process.

RESEARCH AND READINGS

Ragan, William B. (1966). *Modern elementary curriculum* (3rd ed.). New York: Holt, Rinehart & Winston, p. 452.

Purposes of Evaluation

1. To reveal to teachers what is happening to each child.
2. To motivate learning through furnishing pupils with information concerning success in various areas of the curriculum.
3. To furnish teachers with a means of appraising teaching methods, textbooks, and other instrumentalities of the educative process.
4. To provide a basis for continuous improvement of the curriculum.
5. To give pupils experience in evaluating their own progress.
6. To reveal the progress the school program is making toward the achievement of the accepted objectives.

Retrieval System

Midge Brady was interested in ways to record progress so that she would not be forced to overburden her memory about the students in her classroom. Teaching is exceedingly complex, and teachers need a written record of the students' learning performance, including their changes in attitudes and values. Midge Brady taught about 32 students throughout the school day in 19 different subjects; Stewart Jackson would be teaching about 125 students each day with slight variations in the subject field.

Students' work is an output of learning and provides an excellent sample of how students are progressing. Other exhibits are teacher-made tests, anecdotal records, sociometric devices, student diaries, checklists, and conference records. Each of these items provides a unique measure of student behavior and has value because such records allow the teacher, the student, and the parents to evaluate learning over a period of time in order to determine progress and to set future goals.

Evaluative means are limited only by the teacher's imagination and record-keeping skills. There should be a place in elementary classrooms where each student has a file of work samples, test papers, diaries, or

records, observations, and sociometric responses. To a lesser extent secondary teachers can also keep selected samples of student productions. All of these records should be shared with parents so that teacher and parents can assess the student's growth together.

The exhibits in this chapter can be used as points of departure for obtaining feedback. The skills, behavior, and attitudes chosen for these instruments are not more appropriate for evaluation than others; they are merely illustrative.

Gathering Data

To facilitate the data-gathering process, Midge Brady thought over what she wanted to know about her students and how she would go about getting the information. She asked herself the following questions:

1. Who is to be evaluated? (She decided she wanted to evaluate the students individually, in small groups, and as participating members of the class as a whole.)
2. What is to be evaluated? (She decided to spell out specific skills, concepts, attitudes, and values.)
3. Who will evaluate? (She hoped that besides being her own responsibility, much of the process would be done by the students themselves.)
4. How will it be done? (She decided on the techniques, the procedures, and devices to be used.)
5. What will be learned? (The outcomes would relate to changes in cognition, attitudes, and skills.)

Using her questions as guides, Midge developed a chart (Table 4.1) that corresponded to the five questions so that she would know precisely what needed to be developed or designed and what her responsibilities would be in terms of student and parent conferences, observing, and testing. Of course, both what is evaluated and the means for evaluation change depending on the age of the students involved. The greater the specificity in the preplanning outline for evaluation and feedback, the easier will be the actual developmental stage of feedback instruments.

TECHNIQUES FOR EVALUATING PROGRESS

Some of the most important techniques for evaluating progress are checklists and teacher-made tests.

Table 4.1. Program for Evaluation and Feedback

1. Who?	2. What?	3. By Whom?	4. How?	5. Outcome?
Individuals	Skills: group process, oral, communication (identify specific skill)	Self-evaluate	Checklist	Distinguish *specific skill use*, such as speaking, leadership, participation, use of contextual clues, etc.
	Reading, mathematics	Teacher	Checklist	Note skill discrepancies, problems, competence
		Teacher and student	Conference	
	Discussion, participation, physical education, music, art	Teacher	Observation	Observe skill application in group situations
	Reading, mathematics, social studies, science	Teacher and student	Tests	Record diagnosis and evaluation of progress in specific skill usage
	Projects, tasks, follow-up work	Teacher and student, peer tutor	Products (student work)	Diagnose need for reteaching, reinforcement, continuing use and progress
Individuals	Cognitive growth: all subject fields	Teacher and student	Checklists	Evaluate specific objective: Note use of factual details, conceptual understanding
	(Identify specific concepts)	Teacher and student	Tests	Record concept understanding and application and interpretive growth
		Teacher and student	Conference	Discover need for assistance, remediation
		Teacher and student	Product	Application of concepts—work samples indicate continuing growth
		Student	Diaries	Indicative of continuing growth
		Teacher	Anecdotal record	Open-ended means to report on specific items of behavior as related to specific understandings and needs

Target	Focus	Evaluator	Method	Notes
Individuals	Attitudes, values	Student (self-evaluation)	Checklist	Students may record changes in personal interests, feelings about self and others
		Teacher	Observation; Anecdotal record	Observe interaction with other class members; task orientation, responsibility, sensitivity
		Teacher	Sociometric measures	Will indicate leadership role, acceptance by others
		Teacher and student	Tests	Open-ended questions will reveal feelings, emotional impact, interests
		Teacher and student	Product	Will reveal choices and priorities
		Teacher and student	Conference	Interests, choices, preferences
Small groups of students	Skills: discussion, group process, physical education, music, art (identify specific tasks involving skill use)	Self-evaluation	Checklist	(Note individual skill outcomes)
		Group evaluation; Self, group, teacher	Observation	Modeling experiences should reveal skill discrepancies and problems
		Group evaluation and teacher	Product	Continuing progress evaluated; new needs, reteaching tasks can be noted (Note individual skill outcomes)
Small groups of students	Cognitive growth	Teacher/group	Conference	Conceptual misunderstandings and deficiencies will be apparent
		Teacher/group	Product; Observation	
		(Application of conceptual understanding through participation in simulations, role playing or projects)	Conference	(Note individual cognitive growth outcomes)
	Values, attitudes	Self-evaluation; Group evaluation	Checklists; Logs; Discussion; Product	Acceptance of responsibility, leadership, participation, likes and dislikes, initiative, creativity, respectfulness, cooperativeness
		Teacher	Conference; Observation	

CHECKLISTS

Skills sequences, specific behavior, interests, and concepts can be evaluated using a checklist. The checklist can be developed for self-evaluative use, group use, peer tutor, or teacher evaluation. It is often valuable to allow students to develop their own checklists to self-evaluate their accomplishments. Tables 4.2–4.6 are examples of devices that can be used in various subject fields and in the evaluation of social behavior:

The discussion checklist (4.2) for the class as a whole can be used to determine student participation and discussion competencies. The teacher can share the evaluation with the class, and after some practice the students can help the teacher evaluate how well they did. Another type of teacher evaluation, using a checklist, can categorize the items to be evaluated and place the students' names on the chart so that repeated evaluations can occur over a period of time (Table 4.3). By duplicating the checklist, the teacher has it ready for use during the entire semester.

Using ratings, the checklist can also be used for grading. The checklist in Table 4.4 evaluates comprehension skills and was used by a teacher to evaluate individual growth while working in a small reading group. Some of the behavior (9–13) represents group activities after the initial story was presented.

Table 4.2. Discussion Checklist
Objective: To increase student participation; to improve discussion skills for the class as a whole

	(Teacher Evaluation)		
	Few	Many	All
1. How many students participated?			
2. How many speakers used important ideas?			
3. How many speakers used factual details?			
4. How many speakers kept to the point?			
5. How many speakers used ideas of others to develop their own thoughts?			
6. How many speakers supported their ideas with evidence or examples?			
7. How many speakers challenged the ideas of others?			
8. How many speakers refuted ideas using evidence?			
9. How many speakers stated the main point in summation?			

Table 4.3. Communication Skill Growth
Objective: To determine student participation; communication skills

			(Teacher Evaluation) Children's Names		
Behaviors	*Abel*	*Boren*	*Brown*	*Cherney*	*Cox*
1. Listens, observes attentively					
2. Expresses thoughts with clarity					
3. Describes verbally observation of pictures, films, audio presentation					
4. Describes observations in writing					
5. Identifies source of data					
6. Sequences ideas logically					
7. Uses appropriate language					
8. Organizes own and others' viewpoints					
9. Evaluates own and others' efforts					

Table 4.4. Creative Reading Skills Comprehension
Objective: To extend interpretive and creative reading skills

			(Teacher evaluation) Children's Names		
Behaviors	*Abel*	*Boren*	*Brown*	*Cherney*	*Cox*
1. Listens attentively to story/ event	3	5			
2. Retells story in own words	2	4			
3. Sequences ideas in story	2	4			
4. Describes characters in story	1	4			
5. Expresses opinion about story	0	5			
6. Interprets meaning of story	0	5			
7. Projects different ending for story	0	5			

Table 4.4. *(Continued)*

			(Teacher evaluation) Children's Names		
Behaviors	Abel	Boren	Brown	Cherney	Cox
8. Creates a similar story	2	5			
9.* Enacts story, sequentially	2	5			
10. Elaborates story theme	0	4			
11. Selects similar story to act out	0	3			
12. Creates similar story to act out	0	4			
13. Characterizes appropriately	3	5			

0 = No response 3 =
1 = Poor 4 =
2 = 5 = Superior
* Items 9–13 represented small-group work after the initial story was presented.

Table 4.5. Decision-Making Skills
Objective: To extend decision-making skills

			(Teacher Evaluation) Children's Names		
Behaviors	Abel	Boren	Brown	Cherney	Cox
1. States main point; defines problem					
2. Identifies relevant information					
3. Seeks information from others; utilizes resources					
4. Identifies bias and values					
5. Accepts others' values nonjudgmentally					
6. Willingly examines own values					
7. Debates values, issues					
8. Orders and classifies information					
9. Uses information to predict, project					
10. Considers alternatives					
11. Decides on a preference					

Table 4.6. Vocabulary Checklist
Objective: To extend vocabulary skills

Recognizes and uses:	(Teacher Evaluation) Children's Names				
	Abel	Boren	Brown	Cherney	Cox
1. Synonyms					
2. Antonyms					
3. Homonyms					
4. Homographs					
5. Idiomatic language					
6. Figurative language					
7. Colloquial language					
8. Abbreviations					

Code: + √ −

Table 4.7. Ego-Satisfying Behaviors

(Teacher Evaluation)

Children's Names

1. Expresses personal viewpoint
2. Shares concerns, feelings
3. Responds to ideas, feelings, behaviors of others
4. Accepts ideas of others
5. Accepts criticism and praise
6. Constructively criticizes others
7. Debates an issue or viewpoint
8. Does not require praise or encouragement to proceed
9. Does not dominate others
10. Shares successes and failures
11. Chooses own task, activity, goal
12. Assumes responsibility
13. Demonstrates interest in others
14. Cooperatively assists others
15. Voluntarily identifies, demonstrates information and skills
16. Accepts leadership activities
17. Accepts membership activities
18. Chooses activities commensurate to ability
19. Self-evaluates
20. Infrequent need for discipline

Code: + √ −

Both school and general academic success may be dependent on a variety of factors that include how a student feels about him or herself; ability to work independently, be assertive, and to participate with others in a variety of group situations. Tables 4.7–4.10 provide ideas for evaluating these behaviors.

Table 4.8. Learner Assertiveness

	(Teacher Evaluation)
	Children's Names

1. Seeks independent tasks
2. Defines problem accurately
3. Locates appropriate resource materials
4. Gathers data
5. Analyzes information for relevance
6. Prepares report, project, plan
7. Evaluates output

Table 4.9. Independent-Oriented Behaviors

	(Teacher Evaluation)
	Children's Names

1. Defines a personal goal
2. Plans and organizes means to accomplish
3. Chooses resource materials
4. Develops project or task
5. Maintains interest
6. Changes goal
7. Concludes project, task
8. Seeks appropriate assistance, guidance

Code: frequently, sometimes, rarely

Table 4.10. Social Participation Skills

	(Teacher Evaluation)
	Children's Names

1. Participates and cooperates with others
2. Observes and shares observation
3. Listens to others
4. Expresses own viewpoint
5. Plans with others

Table 4.10. *(Continued)*

	(Teacher Evaluation)
	Children's Names
6. Assists others	
7. Accepts personal responsibility	
8. Carries out group tasks, plans, actions	
9. Shares efforts	
10. Concludes tasks	
11. Identifies agreements, disagreements	
12. Interprets agreements, disagreements	
13. Facilitates cooperation	
14. Bargains, negotiates	

Code: Yes, No

SELF-EVALUATION

The use of self-evaluation instruments prior to a teacher-student conference can help teacher and student focus on essential aspects of student behavior. Many teachers (particularly at the secondary level) like students to rate themselves on report card items. At the secondary level this is often done during each class period and related to each subject. As the elementary level the students can be given a list of the different subject fields and the typical citizenship or work habits categories (Tables 4.11–4.13).

After students have graded themselves, there should be a teacher-student conference to discuss the ratings and the possible discrepancy between teacher and student. Realistic self-appraisal is difficult, and teachers need to handle the situation sensitively. Students need practice; thus it is a good idea to have students self-evaluate in different ways

Table 4.11. Self-Evaluation of Group Work

Do I . . .	Yes	No
1. Suggest ideas?		
2. State an opinion?		
3. Supply information?		
4. Find resources?		
5. Contribute work effort?		
6. Listen to others?		
7. Help others?		
8. Clean up?		

Table 4.12. Self-Evaluation of Work Habits

Do I...	Always	Sometimes	Rarely
1. Listen to directions?			
2. Begin work promptly?			
3. Take care of my own work materials?			
4. Work quietly?			
5. Finish my task?			
6. Return materials and papers?			
7. Clean up?			

Table 4.13. Self-Evaluation of Work Habits

Do I...	Yes	No
1. Enjoy working with others?		
2. Prefer to work alone?		
3. Like to ask other students for help?		
4. Like to ask the teacher for help?		
5. Like to be the boss?		
6. Like to help others?		
7. Get along with others?		
8. Like to impress others?		
9. Like to listen to others?		
10. Express my own ideas?		
11. Prefer quiet work?		
12. Like to be told what to do?		

prior to the report card grading period. The student-teacher conference should occur prior to any conference between teacher and parent so that students will not be surprised by any information that is transmitted from teacher to parent, and so that the student does not feel resentful about the conference. (Parent conferences are discussed in Chapter 9.)

SUGGESTIONS FOR THE DEVELOPMENT OF CHECKLISTS

The checklists included as exhibits in this chapter are but a few of the many types that can be made to monitor student progress in skills, behavior, and attitudes. A checklist can have as few as four items or as many as twenty. The following points summarize preplanning ideas for the development of checklists.

1. Decide what needs to be evaluated by using a chart similar to the one Ms. Brady developed for her class.

2. Do you need a checklist to evaluate a skill, a behavior, or attitudes? Be precise; emphasize what you need to learn about student performance in order to accomplish instructional objectives. For example, if you need to know whether students have mastered location skills, be sure that you have defined those skills exactly. To illustrate, students are able to:

Use the table of contents to locate the title of a story. Use volume
   letters and key words to locate information in an encyclopedia.
Alphabetize a list of words using second and third letters.
Use guide words in a dictionary.
Use a reference library to find a textbook on drugs.
Use the card catalog in the library three ways: to locate author, title,
   and subject.
Identify and use sections of a newspaper to locate key articles.

3. Decide on a coding system. The following list of words indicates those which are commonly used on checklists:

Frequently, sometimes, rarely
Many, few, none
High, average, low
Always, usually, seldom, never
Superior, satisfactory, inferior
Often, seldom
Excellent, good, satisfactory, poor
Too much, all right, too little
Understand, understand slightly, do not understand
Like, dislike
Agree, disagree
Yes, no

Some imaginative teachers draw happy faces, passive faces, or sad faces for their students to check. Musical sharps and flats can also record positive and negative feelings. Number ratings (1–5) provide an easy system to record data.

4. When you are the evaluator, do you prefer to use children's names in columns at the top of the checklist and symbols or numbers as an indication of growth (Table 4.14)? If so, give yourself enough room on the evaluation sheet to record data over a fairly long period of time.

Or do you prefer to use a separate checklist for each child, with the student's name at the top of the checklist (Table 4.15)?

Table 4.14. Checklist for Several Children

Behavior	Abel	Brown	Cox	Duffey

Table 4.15. Checklist for One Child

Ron Abel	(1)	(2)	(3)	(4)	(5)
Behavior					

5. You need to be realistic about your own time and energies. Every student cannot be evaluated on the same day. Plan evaluating time over a number of days.

6. Use the data obtained to develop new instructional objectives. As you evaluate, assess whether students have developed the selected competencies or whether perhaps they needed prerequisite skill development. Do the students need material to be retaught? Do they need reinforcement?

Rating scales or reaction instruments that require the respondent to check a box or point on a scale are considered to be closed-end evaluation instruments. A closed-end instrument is simple to respond to and easy for the teacher to record; however, it does not provide any special insight into students' feelings, ideas, or problems because of a lack of specificity. For this reason it is valuable to develop open-ended instruments for special uses.

Open-ended instruments require the respondent to write in suggestions or perceptions. This type of instrument can be considered an opinionnaire, reactionnaire, or questionnaire rather than a checklist. The open-ended instrument requires more time to interpret. The instrument shown in Table 4.16 was used by a fifth-grade teacher for students to evaluate their small-group work. The students used the evaluation after each session and then reported to the class using the form as a guide for their evaluative presentation.

The open-ended instrument provides a keen way to discover the affective dimension and to learn about critical thinking skills. The instrument shown in Table 4.17 was distributed after a classroom discussion. Each student completed the opinionnaire.

Sometimes it is appropriate to have students rate others whom they work with in order to teach accountability. The positive aspects of evaluation can be stressed with the form shown in Table 4.18.

Table 4.16. Small-Group Discussion/Learning Activity

(Student Evaluation of Group Work)

1. How many took part in planning/discussing?
2. How many different suggestions were made?
3. What helped the discussion/planning?
4. What spoiled the discussion/planning?
5. What agreements/plans were made?
6. What did you accomplish?
7. What will you do the next time you meet?
8. What materials will you need?
9. What help do you need?

Table 4.17. Discussion Evaluation

1. Which argument was most convincing? Why?
2. Which argument was least convincing? Why?
3. The following emotional words were used during the discussion:
4. In what ways were ideas exaggerated?
5. I changed my mind about. . .
6. I still believe that. . .

Table 4.18. Rating Others

1. Who had the best ideas?
2. Who was most willing to listen to the ideas of others?
3. Who helped the group the most?
4. Who always gets the job done?
5. Who suggests getting started?
6. Who organizes the group for work?
7. Who helps others?

The list in Table 4.19 can be used as an informal type of review after a learning activity has been completed. Students write their responses and, if desired, may share some of their reactions with the class as a whole. Before beginning the evaluation, students should be assured that there are no right or wrong answers.

Planning forms for group work often help students focus on what they ought to be doing. The form in Table 4.20 was used in a third-grade classroom. The students fill out the form; then teacher and students evaluate using the form at the end of each work period.

TEACHER OBSERVATION

Many evaluation techniques are dependent on teacher observation of students. To use an observer's report compiled by another adult or to record data from your own observation, it is important to know the purpose of the observation. What was the observer looking for? How did the observer (how will you) recognize the behavior? A review of the various checklist categories will reveal that each is designed to gather data about specific behaviors, skills, or attitudes. An observer's report

Table 4.19. Learning Activity

	(Student Self-Evaluation)

1. I learned that—
2. I am interested in finding out about—
3. I was unaware that—
4. I changed my mind about—
5. I was sorry that—
6. I felt good about—

Table 4.20. Team Planning Form

Task	Goal	Steps (Methods)	Who	Material	When (Due)
Task:					
Goal:					
Steps to perform:					
Who will do what?					
Materials needed:					
When to be completed?					

should indicate observed behavior apart from interpreted behavior as well as the purpose for the observation. To verify the interpretation of an observation record, one should see that the interpretation is based upon observed facts.

Anecdotal Records

The anecdotal record is used to write down the teacher's observation of specific behaviors that appear discrepant, problem causing, or of interest because of their evidence of predispositions requiring analysis. The basic format for the preparation of the record is the transcription of behavior as observed by the teacher (Table 4.21). This column could be entitled "What Happened." Some anecdotal records do not go any further than this observed behavior column. After a record has been kept for a week, several weeks, or even a semester, the record can be analyzed. However, in the case of Bill Martin, the teacher wrote down his interpretation of why the behavior happened and then the teacher prescribed remedial action. After a period of time, if the planned actions are ineffective, then the teacher may want another professional to read the record and suggest other actions.

Table 4.21. Anecdotal Record: Bill Martin (Third Grade)

Date	Observation (What happened?)	Interpretation (Why did it happen?)	Planned Action (Prescription)
Oct. 1, Mon.	Kicked Barry during reading follow-up time. Did not finish work.	Disinterested in work; may not understand follow-up directions; appears to want attention.	Will verify that Bill understands what he is supposed to be doing.
Oct. 2, Tues.	Began follow-up immediately, but lost interest after a few minutes. Wandered around the room; disturbed others.	Verifying directions seemed to help, but Bill still lost interest and does not seem to understand about not disturbing others.	Perhaps if Bill worked alongside a friend it would make him more conscious of appropriate work habits.
Oct. 3, Wed.	Bill and Marv sat together at back of room. Some silliness and loud voices, but Bill finished his work today.	Greater interest in work. Needs a peer model.	I will talk to Marv about the importance of being a "serious" model and real friend to Bill.

Conferences

An individual conference with a student can be handled in a similar manner as the anecdotal record. After the conference the teacher should make notes identifying the questions asked, the responses, the interpretation, and the planned actions. The advantage of the conference is that the student can also be asked to interpret and plan appropriately. The conference provides the opportunity to evoke commitment from the student and develop personally satisfying behaviors. The conference may begin with teacher and student reviewing the student's self-evaluation of work habits.

Diaries or Logs

Diaries or logs can be used as an accountability measure to help students examine and compare their own behavior in terms of accomplishments and goals. Diaries can be accounts of individual behavior or even small-group behavior. When groups work on projects or tasks over an extended period of time, it is sometimes valuable to have the group record tasks, responsibilities, cooperation, accomplishments, and needs. The diaries or logs can be shared if desired with the class or just with the teacher. In lower elementary classrooms, students can dictate their logs or illustrate their activities.

Evaluating Peer Tutoring

The teacher's observation of tutor and tutee as they work together is probably the most accurate evaluation of the effectiveness of the relationship and value of the time expended. Also, if the tutee's performance improves in the desired skill, then the teacher has a positive indication of growth. An open-ended instrument (Table 4.22) can also reveal some insight into how the students are doing in terms of attitudes about self and each other. Both tutor and tutee can use the evaluation instrument, Table 4.22.

Table 4.22. Tutor/Tutee Evaluation
Objective: To improve interaction and skill performance

1. What do you think you did best today?
2. What do you not like about your own performance today?
3. What did your (tutor, tutee) do best today?
4. What did you not like about the performance of your (tutor, tutee) today?
5. How would you change your own performance?
6. What would you like your tutor/tutee to change?

Table 4.23. Concept Learning Evaluation
Write the concept. For instance, "addition of whole numbers," or in social studies the concept might be "conflict."

1. State the big idea of the concept.
2. State as many little facts about the concept as you are able.
3. Write at least three examples of the concept.
4. Write at least two examples that do *not* demonstrate the concept.

The instrument shown in Table 4.23 can be used after a tutoring session that focused on practicing a concept or after a teacher-directed lesson in which the class as a whole participated. The concept to be tested should be identified by the teacher. The questions can be written on the chalkboard.

TEACHER-MADE TESTS

To evaluate subject matter knowledge and diagnose learning problems, teachers generally design informal objective-type tests. Usually these tests have been simple recall devices to test factual memory. In recent years teachers have been urged to balance their tests between knowledge objectives and application-level objectives. True-false, multiple-choice, simple completion, and matching tests are normally used to test recall. Higher level objectives can be tested by utilizing a variety of other strategies such as supporting with evidence a chosen true-false response or changing statements in order to make them valid, distinguishing between relevant and irrelevant information. The concept learning evaluation can also be used to test students' ability to apply learning.

GUIDELINES FOR TESTING

1. Introduce and motivate test taking to students. Treat the test in the same way you do other learning experiences.
2. Explain the purpose of the test.
3. Provide clear instructions to the students. Allow the students to ask questions; verify that the directions are understood.
4. After the test, review questions with the students to provide immediate feedback to them.
5. After the test has been scored, confer individually with students who have not done well.

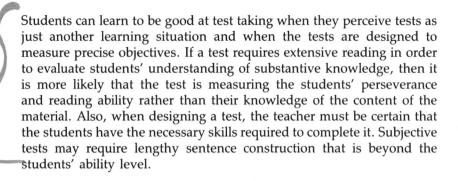

Students can learn to be good at test taking when they perceive tests as just another learning situation and when the tests are designed to measure precise objectives. If a test requires extensive reading in order to evaluate students' understanding of substantive knowledge, then it is more likely that the test is measuring the students' perseverance and reading ability rather than their knowledge of the content of the material. Also, when designing a test, the teacher must be certain that the students have the necessary skills required to complete it. Subjective tests may require lengthy sentence construction that is beyond the students' ability level.

Sociometric Testing

Sociometric devices are used to evaluate changes in the students' attitudes and values. Although most teachers feel that they know their students, sociometric testing often reveals social patterns in the classroom, leadership roles, and student preferences that may come as a surprise to the classroom teacher. Acceptance and rejection patterns influence the ways in which students relate to one another in the classroom and in school activities; these in turn affect classroom management in the classroom. Data are gathered by asking students for first, second, and third choices about whom they would prefer to work with, get together with (for young children, play with), be tutored by, like to assist, and so on. To obtain the information from kindergartners through second-grade students, the pupils may come and whisper their choices to the teacher. Older students can list their preferences on a slip of paper. To tabulate the data, a very simple matrix can be made to list the choosers and the chosen. Graph paper is ideal for tabulating the choices. Students' names could be numbered or their initials used in order to fit on the graph paper.

Using the sociomatrix in Table 4.24 for reference, cursory interpretation yields information that suggests that Davis may be a loner except for his or her friendship with Abel. Abel on the other hand appears to be a school/classroom leader. To increase the acceptance and participation of Davis in the classroom, the teacher could arrange to team Davis with Abel for some activities. This decision would of course depend on the reasons the teacher believes Davis is rejected by classmates.

Another technique is the sociogram (Figure 4.1), which represents students as geometric shapes with connecting lines and arrows to indicate choices. "Which two people in the room would you choose to sit next to you?" This was the question asked by these students' teacher. Figure 4.1 illustrates the students' choices.

Although the sociogram can be used to illustrate several choices by using different colored ink or different types of lines, it is usually used to designate one or two choices. In contrast, the matrix table can be tabu-

Table 4.24. Whom Do You Prefer to Play with/Get Together with?

Choosers (1st, 2nd, 3rd choices)	Chosen				
	Abel	Brown	Cox	Davis	Eberly
Abel		1		2	3
Brown	1		2		3
Cox	2	3			1
Davis	1	2	3		
Eberly	1	2	3		
Total, 1st choice	3	1	0	0	1
Total, 2nd choice	1	2	1	1	0
Total, 3rd choice	0	1	2	0	2

lated to represent many choices and a number of different questions. This sociogram indicates that Bill and Vicky are extremely popular and are chosen to sit next to, whereas Jane and Mike are isolates. It is also interesting to note that Bill and Vicky are chosen by both boys and girls; in all other cases girls chose other females and boys chose other males. Larry, Dick, and Roger represent a clique in the classroom.

Figure 4.1

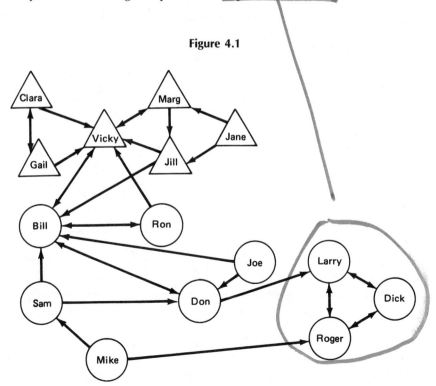

The sociogram and the matrix table yield specific information depending on the question(s) students are asked. It may be very important to know whether students will choose the same person to sit next to as they would to invite to a party. Do they want to be tutored by their best friend? If you needed to choose a peer model for Davis, whom would you choose from the matrix table? Since Abel is a choice of someone to get together with, perhaps the matrix table will not provide the information sought.

Histogram and Frequency Polygon

Two graphic techniques for picturing data are the bar graph (histogram) and the broken-line graph (frequency polygon). Both of these representations can be kept by teachers to depict total class scores for a specific test or scores on a continuing basis (Figures 4.2 and 4.3). They can also be maintained by students to monitor their own growth over a period of

Figure 4.2

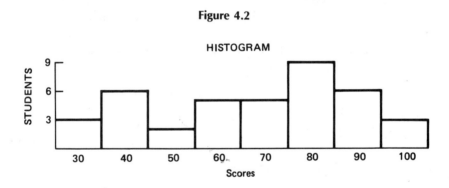

Figure 4.3

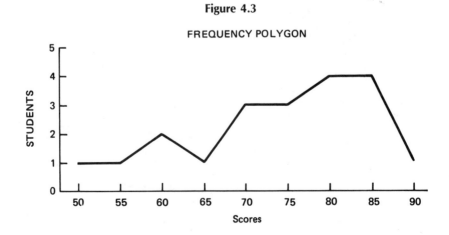

time. Graphic representations are extremely valuable to use during a conference with students and parents.

Students can be asked to keep records about their own progress in completing assignments, in spelling test achievement, in the decreasing frequency of teacher reminders, or in the number of books read. In the bar graph maintained by Mary Kelly (Figure 4.4), it is apparent that something seems to happen on Tuesdays and Thursdays or perhaps on Monday and Wednesday nights that affects her schoolwork. A conference with Mary would probably reveal the problem.

GRADING

Grading students is an important teacher task. Almost all school systems expect teachers to report student progress to parents, as well as to students, using a report card. Evaluation methods suggested in this chapter can be used to help determine grades.

Typically your school or district will have a grading policy. The policy indicates how often students and parents/guardians are to receive progress reports. The policy may also provide specific grading standards. The grading standard gives the numerical range for grades (70–79 = C; 60–69 = D) and whether or not a D grade allows the student to pass. Grades are more important to secondary students and their parents because grades affect academic eligibility to attend postsecondary institutions and sometimes to engage in athletics and other extracurricular activities during high school.

If your school does not have a policy to guide your grading system,

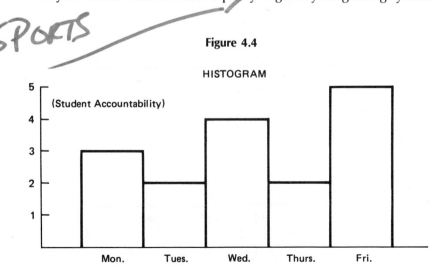

SPORTS

Figure 4.4

HISTOGRAM

(Student Accountability)

Mon. Tues. Wed. Thurs. Fri.

Assignments Completed: Mary Kelly

you will need to make decisions concerning the range for each grade. You also need to decide the worth of your assignments and the value of individual projects. Some of your decisions include the following:

How many tests will you give?
How important will the tests be?
Will you give quizzes?
What is the value of individual projects?
Will you give letter grades or scores on tests and projects?
Will you grade daily assignments?
Will you grade homework?
Will assignments that extend over a long period of time be valued accordingly? (For example, term papers?)
How will you convey the value of class participation?

These decisions need to be communicated to students, and for junior- and senior-high-school students you may want to prepare a hand-out to guide students about grading in your classroom. Criteria for grades should be included. (Will you base grades on neatness? Punctuality? Clarity? Use of resources? Depth and understanding?) It is a good idea to have parents sign this so that you know that students have shared the information with their parents.

You will also need to develop a record book for grades. In elementary classrooms you will need a different record for each subject and in secondary classrooms you will need a separate record for each period. Grade books can usually be purchased with an indentation system already established to allow you to use different parts of the book for different subjects or different class periods. Some teachers like to keep attendance and tardiness in the same record book. If you are going to have students take attendance you will want to anticipate where your grades are to be placed so that students do not have access to others' grades. You want an efficient bookkeeping system so that when it is time for report cards or for a parent conference you can retrieve the needed information conveniently and quickly. It is professionally embarrassing to have insufficient information upon which to base grades or to be unable to retrieve information when needed.

SUMMARY

This chapter has presented a number of techniques for gathering data about student progress. The purpose of these techniques has been to tell teachers, students, and parents what is happening in terms of the students' success in the classroom. Through the evaluation of student progress, teachers learn about their own teaching effectiveness and about the students' learning problems. The evaluation process facilitates the development of teaching objectives and reveals needs for remediation. Improvement of the total school curriculum can occur through a cooperative and continuous evaluation program.

CASE STUDY PROBLEMS

1. **Homework.**   Maureen rarely completes her homework assignments. When she does finish and turn in the assignment, it is extremely messy. Her work in class is reasonably neat. She seems to be an average student, but lately her test scores have been dropping. Ms. Gladstone has the impression that something is not right. What should Ms. Gladstone do to determine what is affecting Maureen's behavior?

2. **Teacher Evaluation.**   The last time your principal observed in your classroom several students did not seem to know what was expected of them and several others were not doing their best work. The principal was not pleased, and the evaluation noted that students' work habits needed to be improved. How can you help students to take responsibility for their work habits so that you do not have to resort to penalties and more rules?

3. **Parent Conference.**   One of your students seems to be failing, and you have sent a failure slip home to the student's parent. The parent has called and requested a conference. Identify the evidence you will assemble to prove to the parent that the student needs assistance.

4. **Tutoring.**   A student has come to you and said that he wants to be tutored in mathematics. The student is correct; he needs additional help, but you do not have time during class and cannot do it after school. You have never tried peer tutoring, but you don't know what else to do. Suppose that you find a tutor for the student, how will you monitor success?

QUESTIONS AND PROBLEMS

1. Why is it important to tell students the purpose of a test?
2. Checklists provide an objective and reliable means to verify teacher observations. Develop several checklists to evaluate students' understanding of social science concepts, knowledge and understanding of art history, and attitudes about music.
3. Why is it important for students to evaluate their own performance? Develop several means for your students to self-evaluate.
4. You have one student in your class who really troubles you. Keep an anecdotal record of that student's behavior for a one-week period. At the end of the week try to interpret the behavior and develop a plan of action.
5. You are teaching a new unit and you want information about both how you are doing as a teacher and how your students are doing in learning. You have decided to ask your students to write a log about what they are thinking during and immediately after the lessons. What do you think you will learn from the students' logs?

CHAPTER 5

Instructional Skills
Managerial Success I

CHAPTER HIGHLIGHTS

Transitions
Pacing
Purposeful activities
Student involvement
Overlapping
Improving students' attention
Differentiating instruction
Cueing
Cognitive and affective taxonomies
Encouraging responses
Encouraging responsibility
Initiating small-group work

Our definition of classroom management contained some key words: planning, organizing, arranging, monitoring, and anticipating. All of these words relate to two conscious acts: contemplation and prediction. The old adage about the teacher with eyes in the back of the head obviously described a teacher with highly developed classroom management skills. This storybook teacher was able to predict what the students would be doing even though he or she was not looking. Classroom management does not really pertain to handling misbehavior, but rather to having a sense of how classroom energies ebb and flow.

Doyle (1986, p. 424) writes that "a program of action, and thus classroom order, is jointly enacted by teachers and students in settings of enormous complexity. Teachers obviously play a key role in initiating and sustaining classroom activities." The initiation and nurturing of classroom activities requires both the prethinking (planning, contemplation) and the ability to predict students' responses to the activity. (Are students capable of the tasks defined by the activity? Will students be motivated by the activity? Will students lose interest quickly? Will some students finish long before others?)

Misbehavior or nonengagement in work activities is typically the consequence of lack of planning of appropriate activities and/or inability to meld the program of activities with social participation within the context of academic work and the classroom system.

Doyle (1986, p. 423) summarizes the multitude of classroom management studies and comments about the common themes underlying research conclusions:

◆ Classroom management is fundamentally a process of solving the problem of order in classrooms rather than the problems of misbehavior or student engagement. These latter issues are not insignificant, but they are not primary targets of a teacher's management energies. Indeed, high engagement and low levels of inappropriate and disruptive behavior are by-products of an effective program of classroom organization and management. At its foundation, then, the teacher's management task is primarily one of establishing and maintaining work systems for classroom groups rather than spotting and punishing misbehavior, remediating behavioral disorders, or maximizing the engagement of individual students.

Some of the managerial techniques that influence success include changing activities, keeping students' attention, and varying the learning activities. Classroom episodes of teachers with varying degrees of success will be used to illustrate the key concepts.

MANAGERIAL TASKS

Transitions

Ms. Jones called on her colleague across the hall and complained, "Every time I change activities I lose at least 10 minutes of time. Why does that happen; what can I do?"

Ms. Jones's problem is shared by many beginning teachers. Kounin (1970) described the problem as abruptness versus smoothness. Both Arlin (1979) and Doyle (1984) noted that successful teachers minimized the natural loss of energy that occurs during a change of activities, whereas teachers with management problems tended to blend activities together, failed to monitor what students were doing during the change period, and took an excessively long time to complete the transition. Ms. Jones was probably typical of those teachers with management problems. We are observing her as she dismisses her second graders to go out to physical education on a cold, windy day.

TEACHER: It's time for P. E. now; everybody get ready. Table 1, line up at the door. Don't forget to pass your papers in. OK, Table 2, go ahead. Put your counting sticks away, everyone. Billy, be quiet. Why aren't you cleaning up?

STUDENTS: Ms. Jones, we need our coats; it's cold out.

TEACHER: For goodness' sake, everybody sit down. You are much too noisy.

The exchange between Ms. Jones and her class will probably continue for at least 7 minutes of precious classroom time before Ms. Jones calms her students and provides clear and concise directions. Ms. Jones has not anticipated organizational problems such as the students' personal needs and environmental needs when she moves from one activity to another.

Ms. Jones's colleague explains to her that she should have cued the children about her plans and programmed them to (a) pass in papers, (b) put learning materials away, (c) demonstrate their readiness for physical education, and (d) obtain jackets and line up at the door.

Smooth transitions are extremely important as the teacher melds the components of a lesson (motivation, concept teaching, reinforcement assignment, evaluation), and they are important in moving from one subject field to another. Smoothness versus abruptness means that disruptions and delays are minimized.

RESEARCH AND READINGS

Good, Thomas L., & Brophy, Jere E. (1972). *Looking in classrooms.* New York: Harper & Row, pp. 174–175.

"Bear in mind that when students are asked to wait with nothing to do, four things can happen and three of them are bad: the student may remain interested and attentive; he may become bored or fatigued, losing his interest and ability to concentrate; he may become distracted or start daydreaming; or he may actively misbehave."

The trick is to anticipate the students' personal needs, instructional needs (paper, pencils, books), and environmental needs (traffic patterns, storage of equipment).

Smooth transitions between subjects can be facilitated if students are aware of the daily program. Students should be able to anticipate program needs as well as the teacher. They should know when math or reading or physical education is to be taught. If there is to be a special program on Wednesday, then the teacher can write a reminder on the chalkboard at the beginning of the day or the period so that students can expect a program change, and they can be told how the program change will affect them.

In a well-organized classroom everyone knows what is expected during and in between activities. Students accept responsibility for the preparation of materials and for cleanup; businesslike behavior helps eliminate teacher time expended on admonishment and punishment.

Instructional Pacing

When to teach more and when to teach less is another important decision that teachers need to make, sometimes many times a day. Somehow the teacher must find out whether all students understand. Do some students need more practice? Are there such things as "over-teaching" and "overlearning?"

Overlearning can be defined as the point in time just beyond mastery when additional practice provides retention gain. Overlearning contributes to retention, but the teacher must be highly skilled in perceiving the point of diminishing returns.

How much to teach is determined by how successful students are in learning. How long to teach is determined both by student success and by student interest. Students who continually fail at learning tasks will not be motivated to continue trying. However, it has been found that making mistakes can be motivating if the mistakes contribute to learning, which means that the student receives feedback about progress. It is often beneficial to low-achieving students to teach step by step in short segments or activities and assess student understanding frequently.

Teachers, too, seem to be affected by the Aha! principle. Some teachers know instinctively when students have "got it" or when they still need more in order to clinch the point. But sometimes it is practice that the student needs and not teaching, and so appropriate instructional pacing also means the consideration of practice time. Evidence supports the effectiveness of distributed practice periods that entail short periods of practicing a skill followed by a different activity or a rest period.

Teachers also need to recognize that different activities and tasks influence student involvement. Kounin and Gump (1974) use the term *signal systems* to indicate that some activities are affected by the teacher, equipment, the environmental setting, or the expected behavior pattern of the activity. When teachers present a lesson to the whole class, less deviance on the part of student behavior is expected, and the pacing is totally controlled by the teacher. This type of lesson has *continuity* because there is a steady flow of information from teacher to student. When students are dependent on themselves or other students for the flow of information, there is less continuity and lags in communication. (The signal source is shifting from individual to individual.) During such times, monitoring pacing is more difficult for the teacher.

When students are highly stimulated in physical activities, such as music activities, drama, and dance, even though there may be a single signal source, students may not recognize what it is they are supposed to be doing. Other stimuli intrude and motivate off-task behaviors. During these stimulating activities teachers are challenged to maintain the appropriate flow of activity and involvement.

Activities: How Much Is Too Much?

The successful teacher instinctively plans just enough activities (assignments) to keep students working purposefully. "Working purposefully" should be contrasted with the idea of "busyness" because the length of assignments is not the crucial factor. The level of difficulty of an assignment should be matched with the ability level of the student. Frequently it is impossible to plan the same assignment to fit the needs of an entire class. In social studies or science where activities can be open ended, high-ability students can automatically seek their own level of accomplishment. In teaching skills such as reading, spelling, and math, the teacher must plan ways to extend thinking. The learning centers approach in elementary schools and learning packets in secondary schools are extremely helpful for enrichment and extending thinking for students who are high achievers or extremely speedy in their accomplishments.

Planning the optimal level of difficulty for each student means that the teacher has accurately assessed the ability level of each student and has considered interests and other affective factors. Another concept that the teacher must consider in planning activities is challenge. As already noted under instructional pacing, if students cannot answer any of the questions, they will not be motivated to continue; however, if students are able to answer all questions correctly, they still will not be motivated. Consequently, the teacher must provide a learning challenge if students are to progress. The key to this situation appears to be the students' achievement motivation; tasks too simple or too difficult do not motivate students to achieve.

RESEARCH AND READINGS

Good, T. L., & Brophy, J. E. (1986). *Educational psychology* (3rd ed.). New York: Longman, p. 436.

   Some students resort to failure avoidance strategies. These strategies include (1) avoiding participation, (2) blaming failure on others, and (3) setting low goals to ensure success. Each of these strategies assures failure because the individual has been unrealistic in self-evaluation.

Students' Involvement: "What Do I Do When I'm Done?"

The successful classroom manager always has one or more alternative plans. If the lesson that was planned doesn't fly or you thought you could teach without a plan, or you failed to assess accurately the Herculean nature of the task(s), then you had better have a contingency plan.

   Students always need to know (a) where to put their finished work, (b) what to do if they need help, and (c) what to do next. Classroom standards should be established to provide students with the answers to these questions. If students have completed their tasks, then there ought to be a location to place their work (on their own desk, in a folder, in their textbook at the appropriate page). If students need help, should they raise hands, ask a buddy, or go sit in a special place? If students are satified with their accomplishment, should they work in a learning center, perform spare-time activities, or assist another student?

   There are dozens of reasons why students may have time on their hands, but most of these reasons have to do with planning. Before students are put to work, the effective teacher verifies that they know what they are to do and how to do it. Chapter 4 presented ideas for student accountability, and students should be made aware that they are accountable. This can be achieved by providing students with immediate feedback about their assignment. Optimal learning occurs in classrooms where students know what is expected of them. Active participation in planning room standards, communicating ideas, and sharing in classroom decision making increases both student involvement and enjoyment.

Peripheral Vision: Overlapping

Good teachers seem to have outstanding peripheral vision and be able to attend to more than one issue at the same time. Kounin (1970, p. 88) described this attribute as *overlapping*. He defined it as simultaneous attendance to two issues and related it to the teacher's managerial success. The following classroom incident should illustrate the concept (Lemlech, 1977, p. 35).

◆   Ted Dixon was late to class. As he entered the classroom, he could see that one group of students was reading with the teacher at the front of the classroom, the rest of the students were working either at desks or at different "centers." He proceeded to scuff his shoes as he walked, slammed his books down on his desk, and then he sat looking expectantly at the teacher.

His teacher nodded at him, raised her voice slightly, as she continued her reading lesson with the children in front of her. As the other students in the classroom looked at the teacher and then at Ted, they realized that their teacher did not feel badgered, nor was she lured to interrupt the classroom routine.

When it was time for the groups to "change places," the teacher walked over to where Ted was sitting. She pulled out the chair next to Ted and sat down. Very quietly, so that other students could not hear, she talked to Ted.

"Did you have breakfast this morning, Ted?"

"No. Nobody got up."

"Is that why you were late?"

"Yes."

"What about your sister, did she go to school?"

"I woke her. She came."

"Do you have any money for a snack today?"

"I got a dime."

"It will be recess soon. Buy yourself a hot drink or a roll."

The teacher then went on with her teaching, and after a bit Ted began to work.

Analysis of this incident reveals that the boy was probably embarrassed because of his tardiness and interrupted the class purposefully in order to get the teacher's attention. If the teacher had ceased teaching in order to warn or punish Ted, the students' level of concentration would have been spoiled and, as noted in Chapter 1, depending on what the teacher said, the students witnessing the admonishment would have been affected (see discussion on ripple effect).

Instead of breaking the classroom mood and concentration, *the teacher nodded at Ted to verify to Ted and the rest of the class that she had heard him.* This is the precise act that demonstrates the concept of overlapping. The consequence of this action was that the class did not cease its work; Ted was neither a villain nor a hero.

Also, it should be noted that this teaching incident provides an example of a neat transition. As the groups changed places, the teacher used those precious minutes to talk to Ted privately in order to clarify the situation and to demonstrate personal concern.

Improving Students' Attention

Hardly a teacher alive can honestly say that there have not been countless times when he or she has perceived that students have not been paying attention. (It even happens in the college classroom!) Why does this happen? How can attention be improved? The first thing to think about is that attending is a factor of the input process. We take in information using our senses, but hearing is not "auding," so the fact that the students are capable of hearing you does not mean that they are listening to you. Similarly, the lights are out and the students are supposedly watching a film, but that does not assure the teacher that the students are "seeing." The problem may be that the students were not motivated in the beginning to attend to the task or that the task itself lacks clarity or impact.

To improve attention and listening, the first step is: Do not begin a new task, assignment, or subject without *getting the attention* of all students. "OK, boys and girls, let's look up here." "Time to begin." "I really appreciate the way everyone is paying attention." "I've got something special to share, but I can't tell you about it until everyone's eyes are looking this way." Or, "Joe, will you let your friends next to you know that it is time to look this way?" "Suzy, we need your attention too." "Johnny, I really like the way you are paying attention. I know that you will do excellent work today." Some teachers drop their voice when beginning a new task so that students will pay stricter attention. (Teachers who talk louder on such occasions only increase the level of noise in the classroom.) Sometimes teachers use special signals to begin new tasks, for instance, flicking the light switch or ringing a bell.

The second step is: *Motivate*. If the students are all paying attention and then your presentation is a bore, or it lacks impact, or you say, "Turn to page 99," then some of the students will continue to pay attention but some, having lost interest, will not. The important aspect of step 2 is to interest them in the task to be performed. This may be accomplished through normal lesson motivation or perhaps by doing something different. Sometimes the motivation should be some unpredictable questions asked of the students. Whatever it is, the purpose is to pick up the *pace* of the lesson, get attention, and obtain interest.

Step 3 is to focus attention on the concept that is to be taught or on the task assignment and to *teach* it (demonstrate or model). Lesson content should be challenging.

Step 4 is *verify* that you have taught it. Ask students to demonstrate what you have taught. *Ask questions about it.* Have students provide examples of the application of the lesson. Call on students randomly; use choral responses on occasion; scan the class. Tell students you are challenging them with a difficult question.

Step 5 is *give the task assignment* and be sure that every student knows what is expected.

Step 6 is *monitor attention (on-task behavior)*. If it is a skill assignment, walk around and verify that students are performing the task(s) successfully. If it is a group assignment, observe and take notes, ask questions of the students, refocus them if they are off base. If you are teaching a group of students and the rest of the class is involved in related tasks, scan the room frequently to let the students know that you are observing.

Step 7 is *evaluate and provide feedback* but do not do it in the same way every time. If students are to recite, be sure that you again focus attention and help students listen to one another. This can be encouraged if the teacher does not repeat what a student has said but instead says, "Janie, I'm not sure I understood what you said. Can you explain it again?" Or, "Boris, are you shaking your head because you disagreed with Matilda? Tell us your opinion."

TEACHING HINT

Improving Students' Attention

1. Gain attention of all students.
2. Motivate interest.
3. Teach (model, demonstrate) concept.
4. Verify understanding (ask questions about concept).
5. Provide follow-up task assignment.
6. Monitor on-task behavior.
7. Evaluate and provide feedback.

DIFFERENTIATING INSTRUCTION

This concept has been discussed repeatedly throughout the text. What does it really mean? In order to provide for individual differences, teachers need to consider learning styles, students' interests, the rate or speed of learning, conceptual level or style, and ability levels. Suppose you are teaching science or social studies (social sciences), the following are planning suggestions for meeting individual needs:

1. Use a typical textbook.
2. In addition to the text that is at grade level, use multitexts at varied levels.
3. Rewrite and duplicate the text information using words that are within the reading vocabulary of specific students in your classroom.
4. Rewrite text information and put it on a chart.
5. Develop a picture file. Index the file. Have students use the picture file instead of print material.

6. Use a filmstrip or slides that you have made yourself to convey similar information.
7. Tape-record the information you want to convey.
8. Allow students to interview knowledgeable people in order to learn about the desired information or concepts.

Differentiating skill needs using small-group instruction and learning centers (and learning packets) is quite simple once the teacher has assessed the students' learning progress. If one group of students needs extra help in language and vocabulary development, they can be given some directed instruction and reinforcement in identifying and using synonyms, homonyms, and antonyms. Another group perhaps needs assistance with structural analysis, so they use materials to aid them in discriminating between words with similar configurations, different endings, prefixes, suffixes, root words. A third group may need to focus on contextual clues by using pictures and applying contextual clues when reading.

After assessing skill needs, the teacher then groups the students in order to differentiate instruction. Grouping is flexible because students do not necessarily learn specific skills in a sequence. The aforementioned groups that need instruction in language and vocabulary development, structural analysis, and contextual clues may all need practice in location and study skills. If this were to occur, then the teacher might want to bring the students together for directed instruction. The point is that students should progress at their own rate and not be constrained by the learning sequence of others or by a learning sequence conceived in a textbook.

CUEING STUDENTS

Teachers need to provide students with both verbal and nonverbal cues relating to academic tasks and to behavior. During reading instruction the teacher models how to hold the book correctly. When the teacher observes that a child is not holding the book appropriately, he or she gains eye contact and gestures with the book to demonstrate the correct posture and way to hold the text. This cues the student about expected posture, way to hold book, and expected behavior during reading instruction.

When we suddenly look at our watch in front of another person, we are conveying the context of time and our concern for timeliness. When students are wasting time, many a teacher has pantomimed tapping the watch and shaking the head at the same time.

Cueing occurs when a teacher picks up the tempo of an activity; even when the teacher begins to talk faster. Sometimes teachers write messages on the chalkboard to cue students about events, time, or behavior. Turning out the lights may cue students to be quiet, come to attention, or cool it.

PARAPHRASING

This is a useful skill for teachers to use to let students know that you are listening to them. By paraphrasing the student's ideas, feelings, or content communication, you are integrating what the student has said and putting it into another form for more discussion. Paraphrasing is *not* just empathetic, nonevaluative listening characterized by the "Uh-huh" or "Hmm" kind of statements. Paraphrasing is used when the student has not expressed ideas clearly and when it is important to pull together statements into a content summary. Paraphrasing should not be used to manipulate students' thoughts but rather to help them extend thinking; therefore it is important to be faithful to the original meaning of the statements.

QUESTIONING STRATEGIES

Class participation and effective thinking are affected by the questions teachers ask. In Chapter 1 research was cited that indicated that participation by classroom members could be increased if teachers would increase the wait time between asking questions and expecting responses. An increase in the wait time also affects the quality of the students' responses because with more time to answer, students tend to reflect on their responses.

Questions are used for a variety of purposes in the classroom:

To motivate interest and "thinking about"
To encourage participation and attention
To sequence problem solving
To evaluate and to assess needs

Although the types of questions one asks cannot necessarily be categorized as good or bad, teachers soon learn that the yes/no variety of questions often closes out further thinking or motivates simultaneous responses that are undesirable. Sometimes, however, there is a purpose for a mass response, such as when the teacher wants to verify student attention and understanding. Since questions are used for a variety of purposes, the teacher must be sure that the question asked reflects the instructional purpose. Bigge (1976) warned that the teacher should beware of the "lullaby effect" that occurs when a student answers a question with a response that sounds reasonable yet is the result of a hasty generalization or conclusion. When this occurs, the teacher should refocus the student's thinking about the original question and if necessary should provide content clues so that other students do not jump to a conclusion and stop thinking.

In asking a question, the teacher needs to anticipate the possible response as well as the next step in thinking about whatever was originally asked. If the teacher intends to be a participant in the classroom discussion, the following points must be considered:

How will student responses be encouraged?
How will increasing levels of thought be motivated?
How will listening behavior be encouraged?

Because the teacher is "onstage" during a classroom discussion, the teacher's impact as a model is greater than at other times during the day. So if the teacher responds negatively to some students, or does not provide content clues when needed to all students, or does not ask students to clarify their thoughts, then the teacher is modeling negative discussion standards, closing off classroom communication, and exhibiting disrespect.

Encouraging Students' Responses

Provide enough time for a classroom discussion so that there is no need to hurry along. Avoid accepting the first answer or the first response to a question. Give accepting but noncommittal responses when a student has answered, such as "Ah-huh," "Good," "Yeeesss," or asking another student, "What do you think?" Smile and raise your eyebrows encouragingly, then turn to another student. But if you say, "OK, I'll buy that!" then you have successfully closed off further discussion on the point.

Remember that the process of hand raising will inhibit natural discussion because it makes the discussion process dependent on the teacher's calling on each speaker. For this reason many teachers prefer to sit down during a discussion so that they do not tower over the students, and if teachers intend to be a part of the discussion group, they try not to contribute to a student-to-teacher-to-student interaction cycle.

Sometimes where a student sits determines participation. The zone farthest away from the teacher tends to be the least active during a classroom discussion, so the teacher can actively encourage all students to speak by arranging a discussion circle or square, by changing his or her position during a discussion, or by changing the students' discussion seats frequently.

As a general rule, it is wise to ask questions and then wait for students to think about the question before randomly calling on a student to answer. Good and Brophy (1986) comment that patterned turns for answering questions in whole-class settings usually slow the pacing of the lesson and may create a mismatch between students' ability to answer a specific question and the question that is programmed for them.

The shy student may need special encouragement, particularly in lower elementary grades. Because the shy child is afraid to answer, it is a good idea to provide a little bit of extra warning time. Therefore, call the child's name and then ask the question. The student who is not listening may need to be jolted a bit; so again, call the student's name to awaken thought, then ask the question.

Since good questions help students produce, the sequencing of questions is especially important. Careful sequencing lifts the level of thought and encourages greater participation during a discussion.

The *Taxonomy of Educational Objectives Handbook I: Cognitive Domain* (Bloom, 1956) provides a system for the classification of educational goals. Curriculum developers have used this taxonomy to plan and to evaluate the relationship between learning experiences and learning programs. Teachers have found that the taxonomy provides a system for the evaluation of their classroom questions, skills, and activities. Using the taxonomy it is possible to plan questions in a sequence so that problem solving moves from the obtainment of facts about a given hypothesis to the testing and evaluation of the hypothesis. A brief version of the cognitive domain with illustrative questions using the classification system as a guide is shown in Table 5.1. (The reader is urged to read the original text.)

Table 5.1. Cognitive Domain with Illustrative Questions*

	1.00 Knowledge
1.0	The learner recalls specifics (facts, terminology), a pattern, structure, or a setting. The emphasis is on remembering. Recall involves the process of "data retrieval."
1.10	Knowledge of specifics
1.11	Knowledge of terminology
1.12	Knowledge of specific facts: (Name seven large cities in the world.)
1.20	Knowledge of ways and means of dealing with specifics
1.21	Knowledge of conventions
1.22	Knowledge of trends and sequences: (What are some causes of poverty?)
1.23	Knowledge of classifications and categories

1.24 Knowledge of criteria: (Which of the following cities are considered large?)
1.25 Knowledge of methodology
1.30 Knowledge of the universals and abstractions in a field
1.31 Knowledge of principles and generalizations: (What do we need to know about poverty?)
1.32 Knowledge of theories and structures

2.00   Comprehension

2.0   The learner "hears" and understands what is being communicated. This is a relatively low level of understanding.
2.10 Translation: (In what ways does poverty affect the rich?)
2.20 Interpretation: (What causes some cities to become dense population centers?)
2.30 Extrapolation

3.00   Application

3.0   The learner remembers, understands, and applies ideas, rules, methods, or theories. The learner uses the known and may apply to an unknown situation: (How would you explain the growth of a city? In what ways are the causes of poverty similar worldwide?)

4.00   Analysis

4.0   The learner will take apart the various components or elements of an idea in order to clarify or organize the elements for communication.
4.10 Analysis of elements: (Why might a population center expand and then at a later date, decrease?)
4.20 Analyses of relationships: (What is the relationship between a cycle of poverty and change?)
4.30 Analysis of organizational principles

5.00   Synthesis

5.0   The learner "puts together" the components or elements into a whole and perhaps original way for communication or produces a new plan.
5.10 Production of a unique communication: (What steps could be taken to break the cycle of poverty?)
5.20 Production of a plan or proposed set of operations: (If you were a demographer, what signs of change would you look for?)
5.30 Derivation of a set of abstract relations

6.00   Evaluation

6.0   The learner judges quantitatively and qualitatively using personal criteria or criteria given to the learner.
6.10 Judgments in terms of internal evidence: (How will changes in population affect public services, major industry, agriculture?)
6.20 Judgments in terms of external criteria: (How would the elimination of poverty in other nations affect us?)

* From Bloom (1956), pp. 201–207.

The Taxonomy of Educational Objectives Handbook II, Affective Domain (Krathwohl et al., 1964) provides a system for the evaluation of effective goals and objectives (Table 5.2). Again the reader is urged to read the original document.

Table 5.2. System for the Evaluation of Effective Goals and Objectives*

1.0   Receiving (Attending)

1.0	The learner is passive. The learner may be aware and attending, but is neutral.
1.1	Awareness: (Name seven large cities in the world.)
1.2	Willingness to receive
1.3	Controlled or selected attention

2.0   Responding

2.0	The learner demonstrates willingness by responding to a suggestion, complying with a rule or raising hand to communicate. For instance, the leader might say, "How many agree?" The learner in this situation would hold up a hand to agree or disagree.
2.1	Acquiescence in responding: (Describe how living in a farm community would affect you and your family.)
2.2	Willingness to respond
2.3	Satisfaction in response

3.0   Valuing

3.0	The learner commits by assuming responsibility, debating a point of view, expressing own feelings or convictions.
3.1	Acceptance of a value: (Debate the advantages (disadvantages) of large city life versus small town life.)
3.2	Preference for a value
3.3	Commitment

4.0   Organization

4.0	The learner organizes own and others' ideas or values into a system for analysis.
4.1	Conceptualization of a value: (In what ways would population expansion or decline cause changes in the way of life of your family?)
4.2	Organization of a value system

5.0   Characterization by a Value or Value Complex

5.0	The learner internalizes personal values and adapts own behavior so that actions are consistent with beliefs.
5.1	Generalized set: (Explain why you would prefer to live in a (large city, small city, rural community).)
5.2	Characterization

* From Krathwohl et al. (1964), pp. 176–185.

In the use of the affective domain it is important to remember that there is literally no way to find out if students are receiving as they observe a film, listen to directions, and so on, unless they willingly perform a task such as responding. When a student volunteers to respond, then the teacher knows that the student derives satisfaction from participation. The student who willingly debates an issue is expressing a preference and commitment to a value or group of values. If students are able to say, "Billy believes that—and Mable believes such and such, these ideas tell us that..." then we are able to conclude that students have perceived others' values and organized them into systems for understanding. The expression of a personal preference using an organization of values to explain personal judgment is described as characterization. Each domain is dependent on the other. The individual does not make a decision without considering the personal effect of the decision. Rational decisions are based on knowledge of relevant facts, issues (values) involved, understanding of possible alternatives (organization), and an evaluation of choice.

The use of affective questions facilitates the accomplishment of cognitive objectives. One of the main functions of questions in the classroom is to motivate or develop interest. By personalizing questions teachers encourage student involvement. Affective components emphasize participation in an appropriate manner; the focus is on choosing to do versus "can do" if requested.

The sequencing of questions to lift the level of thought is particularly important to the process of problem solving. If teachers ask only factual questions (knowledge level), then students scan books and ask themselves questions to improve memory, but the capacity to explain events, anticipate alternatives, or judge the importance or impact of a course of action is not cultivated nor attempted. However, when teachers focus on skill teaching, there is considerable evidence that questions should be direct and narrow and focus student attention on what is to be learned.

ENCOURAGING RESPONSIBILITY

Successful students can usually work both independently and with others. As an independent learner, the successful individual often is self-initiating, expresses individuality, and accepts responsibility to accomplish prescribed tasks. In other words the individual is accountable for personal performance. As a group member, the successful student is socially disciplined and able to work cooperatively and respectfully with others, differentiates between rational and irrational ideas, and accepts responsibility willingly.

Teachers encourage these behaviors in several ways. First, by emphasizing that students are responsible for their own learning and that their success hinges on their efforts. To emphasize personal responsibility for learning, students need to be given clear task assignments—what they are responsible for and when it is due. Students may need help learning to organize work materials and time to accomplish tasks.

Second, teachers need to share responsibility for the classroom environment. This is accomplished by giving students work tasks to perform to support classmates and the room environment. In early elementary grades these tasks may include handing out supplies, opening windows, feeding fish, sharpening pencils, and so on. In secondary schools these tasks may relate to school and homeroom leadership responsibilities.

The third way in which teachers can encourage responsibility is to have students work with classmates in small groups. Cooperative group work promotes responsibility as students accept social roles within the group and work together to solve problems or perform research. Working with peers, students gain an understanding of what others expect, as well as what the teacher expects, and group pressure affects the acceptance of responsibility.

In Chapter 3 there was a discussion of the purposes of large- and small-group instruction and the advantages and disadvantages of each approach; now it is time to examine the ways in which experienced teachers initiate small-group instruction.

INITIATING SMALL-GROUP INSTRUCTION

Effective teachers accept that there are a number of advantages to having students work cooperatively with peers. These advantages include the development of responsible attitudes toward learning and school and positive peer relationships. A review of Chapter 3 will provide additional purposes for grouping students for instruction. It may be helpful at this time to review Table 3.3 so that you are familiar with the management tasks for small-group instruction and the problems you will try to avoid.

Although some inexperienced teachers may dread beginning group instruction, students become efficient group members and learn to analyze group processes quite easily. To illustrate the techniques involved, we shall spy on our fictitious teachers. First, let's peek into Midge Brady's lower grade classroom.

◆   As we enter the room, we see the students sitting on the rug in the front of the classroom with Midge Brady sitting on a chair in front of them. Midge is integrating several subject fields. Her students are learning about similarities in families. Midge began the lesson using a large picture of a family playing softball together. She asked the students, "What is happening in this picture?" After several responses, she asked: "Can you tell a story about this picture?"

Next she introduced a picture of a father and daughter leaving home in the morning with the mother and a younger child waving goodbye. She asked: "What do you think these people are saying to each other?" Her questions continued directing students' attention to interaction processes, roles of the persons, and questions about economics. Next Midge asked the students, "Do you live in a group at home? What kind?" After some discussion she told the students that they were members of a group here at school. ("What do we call it?" "A classroom group.") Then she told the students that they would be working with some of their classmates in a small group. The purpose of the group is to do some thinking together, to share, and to listen to each other.

"I'm going to give each group some pictures to look at. The pictures will be about families. Your job will be to decide how are these families alike and how are they different?" Each group will have different pictures.

"So that you can work together, we will take chairs to different places in the room, and I will ask you to place your chairs in a circle so that you can see each other. Each group will have a leader. What do you think the leader of each group should do?"

Midge elicited from the students that the leader of the group was to see that everyone got a chance to talk and to help keep the group working and not let people do things that would spoil the group work. Midge asked the students, "What would happen if we used our playground voice in the classroom?" The students giggled and finally said that they would have to speak quietly in their groups.

"When you are working in your groups, I may need to talk to you. How can I get your attention?" With her help, the students decided that flipping the light switch would probably be the best idea. Midge also told the students that they would only have about 10 minutes to do their group work.

Next Midge got up and walked to a spot in the classroom and told the students that one group would work in this spot; then she proceeded to identify several other places in the room that would accommodate group work. Moving back to the front of the classroom, she told the students that she was going to call their names if they were in the first group, and they were to go quietly and get their chairs and place them in spot 1 by the bookcase. She immediately handed one student in the group a packet of pictures for the group to use. The students were rather noisy, and so Midge called them back. The students did it again; this time much better. Slowly she helped all of the students find their places. She quickly moved to each group and tapped a student on the shoulder and asked that person to act as the group leader.

As the groups began to talk she walked around to each group and listened and helped the students get started. When their voices began to rise, she flipped the light switch and asked them, "Why do you think I stopped you?" The students were quick to acknowledge that the room had become noisy. They settled down again and Midge again monitored their work.

On this first day of group work, Midge did not want the session to be too long. After about 6 minutes she once again flipped the lights: "Boys and girls, will you turn your chairs so that you can see me? Good. Now, I want all of you to think about what your group decided. Who can tell me what our question for discussion was?"

(Child repeats question, which is written on chalkboard.)

"Good. Group 1, who can tell us how families are like? What did your group decide?"

Each group gets a chance to report. Then Midge asks: "Did your group decide how families are different?"

Further discussion from each group is elicited. Midge asks: "Did the spokesperson from your group forget anything? Who would like to add to the group report?" After substantive discussion is exhausted, Midge states:

"Let's talk about what it's like to work in a small group." Midge asked the following questions to help the students discuss their behavior while working together in a small group:

Did everyone get a chance to talk?
In what ways did everyone help?
What problems did you have?
How can we improve our group work?

How Julie Kramer Initiated Group Work

◆   On the second day of Julie Kramer's science unit, she had the students turn their chairs to face the front of the room. She said to them, "I want to show you something." Then she suspended a lodestone on a string and the students watched as the stone moved around and around and then stopped. Kramer said, "What do you think is happening?"

Motivation

"Anything suspended will do that," said one student.

"Naw, only magnets—in that way."

"I don't understand it. Why isn't it moving now?"

"Turn it around again, Ms. Kramer." [Kramer complied.]

"Hey, I think it's in the same position."

After many ideas had been exchanged and the students seemed to be thinking about the problem, Julie Kramer asked, "What do we really need to know? I will write your questions on the board."

Assignment

STUDENT: Do only lodestones do that, or will any magnet when suspended seek a particular position?

KRAMER: Well stated, Pete.

STUDENT: Ms. Kramer, does it make any difference which is the north or south side of the magnet?

KRAMER: You will need to find out. [Kramer restated it as a question and wrote it on the board.] Also, make sure that you know what substances are attracted to magnets. In addition, after your experiments, you should be able to make a general rule about the poles of all magnets.

Organization

"Since we are going to work in groups, I want to give you some special instructions. First of all, here is a guide to help you get started. [The students read it silently.] If you have any difficulties in your group, raise your hand and I will come over and help. When we have our discussion, we will talk about what you have learned and group problems."

Guide to Science Group Work

1. Choose a group leader.
2. Choose a group recorder.
3. Plan your experiments.
4. Perform your experiments.
5. Talk about your experiments and record what you have learned.
6. Plan what you will tell the other groups.
7. Clean up and turn your chairs for a class discussion.

KRAMER: I have six boxes of science materials, and each box has enough equipment for five to seven people to work together. It is important to choose your group carefully so that you are able to work cooperatively. You will only have 20 minutes to work. When I finish speaking, I want Table 3 people to select whom they want to work with. When you have all selected your groups, please look up so that I will know you are ready to begin. Then I will bring you your box of materials. OK, Table 3.
Good. Now Table 2 and Table 1.

When the lesson was concluded, Julie Kramer had each group tell how they had proceeded and what they had learned. The evaluative discussion focused both on group processes and on the content of the lesson. She helped the students generalize about and state the law of poles and articulate why the lodestone sought a particular position.

Analysis of the Two Group Work Lessons

Both teachers began with whole-class motivation. This was followed with an assignment communicated to the whole class. The organization of the groups followed with specific information about where each group would work. Midge Brady elicited group work rules from the students; Julie Kramer provided the students with written instructions to guide their group work. (Many teachers like to chart their group work rules.) Both teachers made sure that students understood how to get assistance, and Midge Brady verified that students would come to attention if it were necessary by having the students identify a means for the teacher to alert them. We can only assume that Julie Kramer had a system already developed with her students for obtaining their attention. Both teachers let the students in on the time constraints so they would not be surprised when asked to stop work. Both teachers let students know how the lesson would be evaluated. Both teachers evaluated both group processes and subject matter content.

◆   In Stewart Jackson's classroom the students were studying the causes of revolution in a society. To help the students recognize the similarity of social problems that lead up to societal disintegration, Jackson decided to have his students study revolution in different countries. He wrote the assignment on the board: What causes people to want and to bring about radical and complete change?

"OK, let's have Bill and the people at his table work as a group. Bill, you chair the group and select a recorder. Your group should research the French revolution."

"Mary, you and the folks at your table work as a group and study the Cuban revolution."

"Sidney, your group is to study civil war in El Salvador."

"Shawn, your group should focus on Cambodia."

"For Shawn and Sidney's groups I have handouts for you to use. Bill and Mary's groups will need to select texts from the back of the room to find information. I want to caution you folks, you have only 30 minutes today for work so decide as a group

Table 5.3. Checklist for Small-Group Instruction

Management Tasks	Plans
1. Motivate class interest	
2. Identify and verify understanding of group work rules	
3. Group students; appoint group leaders and recorders	
4. Provide clear task assignment(s)	
5. Verify understanding of task	
6. Assign physical space for group work	
7. Identify means for you to signal attention	
8. Provide material resources for group work	
9. Provide information about time utilization for group work	
10. Monitor group work: on task, group processes, resource needs	
11. Where will students sit for evaluation?	
12. Evaluate substantive accomplishment, group needs, group processes	

what you are looking for and how each group member will help. You are to prepare a group oral report; however, the group report will not be due until Thursday. Before we quit today, I shall ask each group for a report on progress. I shall want to know what organizing questions your group used for its investigation. If you need assistance, raise your hand and I shall come over to assist you. Remember, don't waste time with idle chitchat. You may get your materials and texts now."

In Stewart Jackson's classroom the students will be working at their own table. He did not have to select a special place for the students to work and he was not concerned about who would work together. Note that he preplanned his research question and had thought out his material resources before class began. He let students know how long they were to work and what would be expected of them.

Group work must be preplanned. One cannot expect students to work well together if the task to be accomplished is uninteresting, if material resources are inadequate, if group members cannot communicate within normal talking distance with each other. Because all groups need rules, small-group work in the classroom must have clearly identified procedures. Because working in groups necessitates some form of consensus, group work is more difficult than independent on-task behavior; therefore, we need to remember that group work needs to be practiced. These considerations are thoughtfully orchestrated prior to coming into the classroom and telling students, "Today we will work in groups!"

Small-group organization is effective and efficient when the purpose is for one or more of the following:

1. To provide opportunity for practicing discussion skills
2. To provide opportunity for decision making
3. To motivate affective involvement and interaction
4. To facilitate team learning, cooperation, and production
5. To practice leadership and modeling behavior
6. To differentiate instruction

Table 5.3 provides a checklist for small-group work. The items are the same as those identified in Table 3.3. Be sure to review the specific problems to be avoided also listed in Table 3.3.

SUMMARY

The emphasis in this chapter was on conscious planning *before* instruction is initiated. In the first half of the chapter a number of managerial tasks were identified with teaching episodes to demonstrate them.

Experienced teachers perform these techniques automatically; for example, an experienced teacher who detects classroom boredom will automatically pick up the pace of instruction or change gears in some way. Inexperienced teachers need to overplan specific operations in order to be ready for emergencies.

The second half of the chapter discussed how to initiate small-group instruction. Once again planning was the key to good management. Our fictitious teachers anticipated the need for group placement, group leadership, resources, assistance, knowledge of time constraints, and information about evaluation. Students need practice in group work, just as they need practice in working independently.

CASE STUDY PROBLEMS

1. Grouping for Instruction. *Incident 1.* Julie Kramer intended to introduce the multiplication of unit fractions to her class. None of the students had had prior experience multiplying fractional numbers. She began by supplying each class member with a piece of paper. She asked the students to fold the paper four times. Using the sheet of paper, the children discovered that ½ of ½ = ¼. Kramer demonstrated on the chalkboard by drawing a rectangle. The initial discussion and investigation by the children lasted 6 minutes.

Kramer then began the second part of her lesson: "Boys and girls, please turn to page 27 while I give you another sheet of paper." She assigned one problem out of the textbook and asked the students to do it. She chose three students to demonstrate the problem on the chalkboard. All of the students seemed to understand the concept, but she verified by asking, "Are there any questions?" No one responded. At that point Kramer wrote an assignment on the board and told the students to "get started." Kramer reminded the students to raise their hands if they needed help, and she began to circulate and give assistance where needed. The lesson had proceeded smoothly.

Incident 2. In another sixth-grade classroom the students had prior experience with the multiplication of fractions and the teacher's objective was to have the children find the products of mixed numerals.

TEACHER: Boys and girls, take out your books and turn to page 44. OK, now everyone look this way. [The teacher begins to write on the chalkboard.] Billy, can you come up and explain this?

BILLY: Sure. You change the mixed numbers to improper fractions and then you multiply them.

TEACHER: No, Billy. I want you to explain the distributive principle and how you multiply whole numbers first.

BILLY: But, Ms. Marston, we already know how to do that.

TEACHER: Billy, some of the children had trouble with it yesterday. Brad, you're not paying attention. Everybody close your books and look up here right now.

Some of the children closed their books, other did not. One child asked to leave the room; another proceeded to sharpen a pencil. In desperation, the teacher wrote an assignment on the board.

TEACHER: All right. I'm tired of this nonsense during math. Your assignment is on the board. Everybody get busy. I don't want to hear a sound out of you.

EMILY: Ms. Marston! You forgot to pass out any paper.

DAVID: But, Ms. Marston, I don't understand.

Both teachers used large-class instruction, but only the first teacher was successful. A closer look at the two teachers' procedures should reveal the differences. See if you can explain why the large-class grouping was appropriate in one case yet inappropriate in the other. Your author's analysis of the two incidents is shown in Table 5.4.

Table 5.4. Case Study Problem Grouping for Instruction

What happened	Consequence
Ms. Kramer's: Incident 1	
Children are given sheet of paper for folding to learn about fractions.	A concrete activity motivates all of the children to participate.
Teacher demonstrated at chalkboard.	Children are interested, and there are not distracting materials available.
Children told to take out books and turn to specific page.	Time is not wasted.
New sheet of paper is distributed.	The paper was ready for distribution. Children had no time to fuss.
Students do a practice problem. Problem discussed and demonstrated.	Teacher verified children's understanding of the concept.
Assignment given.	Teacher reinforced understanding through practice assignment.
System for receiving help explained to children.	Teacher provided for slow learners or misunderstandings.
Ms. Marston's: Incident 2	
Children instructed to take out books and turn to specific page.	Children comply and expect an assignment.
Children instructed to look at chalkboard.	Children distracted by two competing directions.
Child asked to explain problem.	Child responds.
Teacher disagrees with explanation and refocuses on her instructional purpose.	Student participation closed off.
Child defends prior understanding.	Child defensive and withdraws.

Table 5.4. *(Continued)*

Ms. Marston's: Incident 2	
Teacher reiterates purpose of lesson.	Teacher is forced to state her rationale.
Teacher demands individual and class behavioral compliance.	Misbehavior in classroom compels teacher to exercise control.
Class rules and class behavior at variance.	Behavior management of entire class perceived necessary by teacher.
Assignment is given. Children admonished.	Assignment used to control behavior.
Children request supplies.	Need for paper causes additional misbehavior.
Children request assistance.	Children confused and do not know an accepted system to obtain teacher assistance.

In Incident 1 children's conceptual needs were apparently assessed accurately, and the teacher managed procedural items, such as the passing out of paper and opening of textbooks smoothly, without any problems. In Incident 2 the teacher's directions lacked clarity, were abrupt, and caused misbehavior that in turn affected teacher behavior. This incident provides insight related to typical classroom management problems. Ms. Marston's children appeared to be at varied conceptual levels in the multiplication of fractions. Some had no need for her lesson, while others needed assistance. Her instructions were imprecise, and the children's work patterns were interrupted; materials were not provided when needed, transitions were abrupt, and no provision was made to assist slow learners.

The two classroom episodes reveal that large-group organization is an efficient means to introduce a *new concept* or a *new skill* to the entire class when all of the class members need and are ready for the same concept or skill. Ms. Marston had failed to assess students' instructional needs.

2. Time Management. Mr. Smith was lecturing to his class when he realized that he was running out of time. He proceeded to give a homework assignment, tell the students there was to be an assembly in the auditorium, and then he said, "OK, back to the lecture." The students were scrambling for paper to take down the homework assignment, clean up for the assembly, and then they were stunned when he proceeded to continue his lecture. You are observing in this classroom, and it is your job to help Mr. Smith waste less time; what will you tell him?

QUESTIONS

1. At the grade level you are teaching, identify ways that you might diagnose whether students need more practice on a given task.
2. Make a list of learning activities and identify the signal source during these activities. Think about how continuity will be maintained and how you will monitor the pacing during the activity.
3. At the grade level you are teaching, suggest ways to improve students' attention during a variety of activities.

4. At the grade level you are teaching, identify ways to differentiate instruction.
5. Identify ways that teachers cue students using nonverbal communication.
6. At the grade level you are teaching, plan small-group work and identify several ways to motivate the lessons.
7. If you were Stewart Jackson, what evaluation questions would you ask your students? (Refer back to the small-group research on revolutions.)

CHAPTER 6

Beyond Skills
Managerial Success II,
Teaching Models

CHAPTER HIGHLIGHTS

Direct instruction
Group investigation
Concept attainment
Advance organizer
Expository teaching
Guided discussion
Interaction mode

PIZZA, EVERY DAY?

In this chapter instructional tactics will be expanded to include several models of teaching. Experienced teachers recognize that there are a variety of ways to accomplish instructional goals. For example, if a teacher wants to teach a math concept such as addition of fractions, the teacher might bring concrete objects and have students manipulate the pieces to gain the concept of addition of fractions. Or, the teacher might draw a circle on the board and demonstrate using the chalk and chalkboard. Another teacher may use the abstract fraction and demonstrate how denominators are changed to perform addition. This third teacher may be assuming that students understand fractions already and only need instruction in the process of addition. Still another teacher may begin with the concept of "fraction" and help students comprehend the idea of what a fraction is before attempting to teach addition using fractions.

There are several good reasons for using a variety of teaching strategies. Sitting in the same classroom every day and experiencing the same methods of teaching is like eating pizza every day of the week. After a while it becomes pretty boring for both student and teacher. Another really important reason for using a variety of teaching strategies is the need to match instructional strategy with instructional goal. Still another reason for using different modes of instruction is that students are diverse in their learning styles so if one methodology doesn't work well, another mode may be more appropriate. Let us spend a little more time exploring these ideas.

1. It is generally recognized that there are a variety of approaches to instruction. Both teacher and learner become satiated by a steady diet of sameness. Although students may become aware of boredom long before the teacher recognizes the dullness of teaching in the same way, many teachers who complain of burnout have failed to vary the instructional process and become a slave to tedious lectures and drills.

2. Teaching method affects what students learn. Thornton (1984) describes a history teacher who wanted students to be critical thinkers, but his teaching methodology was restricted to a lecture and question methodology followed by testing. The tests were objective and tested lectures and readings. The students learned that to do well in this classroom necessitated memorizing the lecture material for the unit test. Thornton concluded that, "what you do is what you get." Teaching methodology determines educational outcomes. If students are to become critical thinkers, they need to practice this behavior through interaction with teaching materials that require them to use their critical faculties. Both the teaching methodology and the test must require the students to process data and think critically.

3. Student characteristics affect the learning process. A student who is visually oriented learns more easily when what is to be learned can be seen via a live model or by film or chalkboard. Some students are really good listeners. These students like to listen to tape recordings, the radio, a lecture. Still other students prefer to interact with what is to be learned using their sense of touch. Even though students may have a preferred means of learning, they may be able to learn in a variety of ways, but when students have difficulty with a concept or if they become bored with a steady diet of experiences in a less desirable mode, then learning problems develop. For this reason teachers should try to present key concepts in several different ways so that all students have the opportunity to learn in an advantageous mode.

MATCHING INSTRUCTIONAL STRATEGIES AND LEARNING OUTCOMES

In this chapter we shall explore several models of teaching. The idea of precise teaching models with specific terminology for defining the actual syntax of teacher and learner behavior comes from a marvelous textbook, *Models of Teaching* by Joyce and Weil (1986). (The first edition of this text was written in 1972.) Joyce and Weil synthesized the work of (1) experienced teachers in elementary and secondary schools and (2) social scientists. Experienced teachers have long recognized the value of utilizing different techniques for accomplishing the range of instructional objectives. But classroom teachers lacked a common vocabulary for describing their teaching methods. In addition to the classroom teachers' approaches in classrooms, a number of social scientists and education professors began to experiment with and write about instructional approaches to accomplish specific goals. Joyce and Weil utilized these sources and developed precise teaching models. Several of these models will be described in this chapter.

DIRECT INSTRUCTION MODEL

The direct instruction model is a training model. The roots of the model come from behavioral psychology. In this model the teacher breaks tasks down into small components and teaches systematically until mastery is achieved. Learning is sequentially arranged with prerequisite learning coming before more complex learning (Joyce and Weil, 1986). The model has four basic characteristics:

1. It is controlled by the teacher.
2. It is oriented to large-group instruction.
3. It is focused on the individuals in the group.
4. It has a clear academic focus.

Teacher Controlled

The teacher imposes high structure on students when using this instructional model although it is possible to modify the degree of structure in the approach. Structure refers to the degree the teacher controls the activity in terms of organization, pacing, and as the source of information. Instruction is not begun until students are quiet and attending to business. The teacher controls instruction, feedback, practice, and evaluation. A major purpose of direct instruction is to increase the student's involvement in the learning task. This is sometimes called active learning time. The teacher maintains a supportive climate in the classroom to encourage student performance.

Large-Group Instruction

The direct instruction approach may be used with the class organized in a large group or the teacher may work with a small group of students while most of the class is involved in practice activities. In either case the method of teaching involves six components: diagnosis, prescription, modeling, practice, monitoring, and feedback. These components will be discussed further.

Focus on the Individual

During direct instruction the teacher pays particular attention to the achievement of each student. The teacher has confidence that each student can learn if instruction is based on the prerequisite knowledge and skills of each student, the student is interested in learning, and the student is given the appropriate amount of time to complete the task.

Focus on the Academic Goal

The instructional purpose is communicated to the students, the presentation is clearly demonstrated, and instruction is relevant to the goal. The teacher conscientiously includes all appropriate content. Now we shall observe Julie Kramer as she teaches using direct instruction. After the observation we shall analyze the instructional processes.

RESEARCH AND READINGS

Stallings, Jane A., & Stipek, Deborah (1976). *Handbook of research on teaching.* New York: Macmillan Publishing, pp. 738–739.

   Stallings and Stipek describe the Bereiter and Engelmann Oregon Direct Instruction program for K–3 children. "The Direct Instruction program is based upon the premise that positive reinforcement is essential to modifying student behavior and maximizing children's academic success. To implement the belief that children can be trained to succeed, a carefully sequenced curriculum and a rigidly controlled instructional process are required."

   To demonstrate teaching models, student talk will not be verbatim, but teacher talk to pace and organize the model through the various stages will be precise.

◆ Julie Kramer is teaching math to her sixth graders. Students are seated at tables and chairs are turned to face the chalkboard. She is teaching the students as a whole group. She has taped two "pie" pictures of fractions on the board.

TEACHER: Yesterday we practiced reducing fractions to lowest terms. Today we are going to study equivalent fractions. Fractions are equivalent when they have equal portions of the wholes used. Look at these two pies, in what way are these two pictures of fractions alike?

STUDENT: One-half of each pie is shaded.

TEACHER: Good. What is unlike about these two pictures?

STUDENT: One picture shows a pie divided in halves; the other shows a pie cut in fourths.

TEACHER: Can you give me the fractional name for the shaded part in each circle?

STUDENT: One-half and two-fourths.

TEACHER: Good. We call these fractions "equivalent" because they show the same amounts. [Kramer wrote the word "equivalent" on the chalkboard.] Let's look at some more equivalent fractions. [She taped several sets of pictures to the board.] Look at set 1. Are they equivalent? If two people were given pies as in the first two pictures, would they have the same amount?

Kramer went through four sets of pictures; two sets were equivalent, two were not. She had the students identify the fraction in each picture.

TEACHER: All right, everybody really pay attention. Come on Billy, look this way. Sue, what happens if we multiple a fraction by 1?

STUDENT: It remains the same.

TEACHER: All right, how can we change the 1 into an equivalent fraction? This is more difficult, but you know the answer. Think. Jerry, can you come to the board and write a fraction equal to 1?

STUDENT: Yeah, I guess so. Would $\frac{2}{2}$ be right?

TEACHER: Good. What are some others?
[Many students talk out, and Kramer accepts the responses.]
OK. You have the idea. Now let's make a rule about multiplying a fraction by a fraction that equals 1. [Kramer wrote several problems on the board: $\frac{1}{2} \times \frac{2}{2}$; $\frac{3}{4} \times \frac{4}{4}$; $\frac{5}{6} \times \frac{6}{6}$; she called three students to the board to work the problems.]
Who can state a rule?

STUDENT: Would the rule be, when you multiply a fraction by 1, the answer equals the same number you started with?

TEACHER: Excellent. Why don't you all write these problems on your paper and see if the rule works. [Kramer wrote three problems on the board for the students to copy. Then she walked around the room and observed the students' work. She stopped at one desk where a student appeared confused and she provided assistance.]

TEACHER: I want to make sure that no one is confused. What happens when we multiply $\frac{3}{9}$ by $\frac{9}{9}$?

STUDENT: We get $\frac{27}{81}$.

TEACHER: Is $\frac{27}{81}$ the same as $\frac{3}{9}$? Who can prove it to us? [Students respond, and

Kramer calls on two students to come to the board and demonstrate.] All right, well done. Now we have one more thing to learn today. Let's all really look up here. I'll fool you if you are not paying attention. [Kramer wrote on the board the following problem: $3/4 = ?/12$.] We need to end up with a fraction whose denominator is 12. What do we need to multiply the 4 by in order to equal 12?

STUDENT: Three.

TEACHER: Good. Let's multiply by $3/3$, which is a fraction of 1. Sam, please come to the board and do it for us.

STUDENT: $3/4 \times 3/3 = 9/12$.

TEACHER: Good, Sam. Is $9/12$ the same as $3/4$? Everyone? [Students all respond, "Yes."] OK, folks I'm going to give you a sheet with just a few problems on it. We will work them together.

Julie Kramer walks around the room and continues to teach, helping the students with one problem at a time, calling often for group responses and observing students who do not seem to be responding or paying attention to their work. When she is satisfied with the work she asks: Is there anyone who does not understand? May I help someone? [The students do not respond.] All right, now we're going to each do our own work, but if you have a problem with it, raise your hand, and I shall come over to help. We'll work in our texts and correct our work in 20 minutes. Sharon, you pass out paper at Table 1, Bill and Sue, you pass out the paper at your tables. Turn to page 112 and work the problems in section B.

Now we are going to go through the instructional model called direct instruction using Julie Kramer's lesson to help understand what Julie was attempting to accomplish. First, Julie reminded the students about the previous day's lesson (reducing fractions). We can assume that the students did well on that lesson because Julie did not review it or have students demonstrate it.

Next Julie told the students what they would be studying today. She was precise and in fact defined the concept to be learned (equivalent fractions). In this way she shared the objective of the math lesson for the day.

Julie provided a visual representation of what they were to learn using two pie pictures. She called students' attention to the pictures and had them verbalize about them. She again reiterated the concept and used it as she talked about the two pie pictures.

Next Julie provided additional pictures; two demonstrated the concept to be learned and two did not. The purpose was to have the students identify the critical attributes of the concept and discriminate positive and negative examples.

Julie moved from the positive and negative examples using the chalkboard and demonstrating abstractly how to change a whole into an equivalent fraction. To verify that the students were following and understanding, she encouraged them to talk out.

To verify understanding, Julie had the students make a rule about multiplying a fraction by a fraction that equals 1.

Now Julie had the students use paper and pencil and practice several problems. She walked around monitoring their work and provided feedback. She continued to teach by having the students respond to the problems as they did them.

She selected two students to demonstrate at the board so that once again the students could see how to do the work and correct their own work.

She provided additional insight using the chalkboard. This time there was no visual representation. Once again she chose students to work at the board.

She passed out a sheet with several problems and had the students participate in structured practice while she verified their understanding by monitoring their work. She asked if everyone understood.

When she was satisfied that everyone had gained the concept, she assigned independent practice work. She continued to monitor their performance.

TEACHING HINT

Direct Instruction

1. Review prior learning.
2. Share lesson objective/purpose.
3. Explain or demonstrate concept/skill to be learned using visual or concrete objects when possible.
4. Check students' understanding.
5. Lead group practice.
6. Ask short-answer questions to verify understanding.
7. Provide corrective feedback as needed.
8. Provide additional structured practice.
9. Monitor students' work; provide assistance as needed.
10. Provide independent practice.
11. Evaluate students' work.

Classroom Management during Direct Instruction

As noted earlier, during this instructional model the teacher provides direction in a very traditional way. The teacher's priority is the academic task to be learned. Interaction between teacher and class is oriented to the task. Direct instruction means there is a patterned way of teaching using controlled practice, recitation, and seatwork. The teacher must keep students' attention on the task to be learned. The teacher does this through frequent questioning about the task, through the practice with feedback, and through the structured demonstrations.

A major goal of direct instruction is to maximize academic learning time (ALT). This means that the teacher attempts to keep all students engaged in the task to be learned. Julie Kramer did this by encouraging the students to "think," to respond, to practice, to "pay attention." Another way that Julie managed the class and maintained engagement was by walking around while the students practiced. She literally controlled the class through her constant monitoring (vigilance) of their work.

It is also important to note that Kramer avoided negative criticism. (This does not mean that she would not tell students when they were doing something incorrectly.) There is some evidence that indicates that criticism inhibits students during direct instruction.

When Should Direct Instruction Be Used?

Direct instruction is appropriate for teaching basic skills in reading and mathematics. Direct instruction is often used in physical education to teach a skill. This model helps students master academic content and skills. For some students it is motivating, for others it is not. Some researchers have found that direct instruction is especially successful with lower socioeconomic students (Joyce & Weil, 1986). When working with higher socioeconomic students, teachers often need to modify the amount of structure and adapt the approach to encourage greater discussion. The model is not suited to goals such as abstract thinking, creativity, inquiry, or problem solving.

GROUP INVESTIGATION MODEL

This instructional model has its roots in the work of John Dewey, William Heard Kilpatrick, Gordon H. Hullfish, and Phillip G. Smith. The work of Herbert Thelen also contributed to the formulation of this model. Dewey believed that the classroom should be a miniature democracy so that students obtain practice dealing with real-life problems. Kilpatrick suggested that students have purposeful projects to work on; these projects should cultivate and build on students' interests. Hullfish and Smith stressed that education should encourage reflective thinking, and so they felt that social processes in the classroom should be related to intellectual skills that would require analysis and synthesis. Herbert Thelen founded the National Training Laboratory; Thelen utilized democratic processes and believed in group inquiry.

Thelen's "inquiry" was similar to what Hullfish and Smith meant by reflective thinking. The group investigation model melds the ideas of Dewey, Thelen, Kilpatrick, and Hullfish and Smith. It is characterized by democratic processes and the scientific method. We shall observe Stewart Jackson as he uses the group investigation model.

◆   Jackson began talking to his students about the problems at Cayuga Lake, a recreation area in New York State. During the late 1960s residents in the northeastern United States were having power crises that resulted in blackouts. The power company, which is a public utility, proposed to build a nuclear station. According to the utility company, the new station would put an end to the blackouts, and it would increase the utility's profits.

Scientists at Cornell University were concerned that the plant was not designed well and would release radioactive particles and endanger the community. They also were concerned that nuclear waste from the plant would be dumped into the lake and pollute the water, affecting plants, fish, and other animals. The lake would then not be usable for fishing, swimming, and boating.

At this point Jackson showed the students a picture of Lake Cayuga and asked them: "What are the issues here?"

Jackson began to write on the board as the students identified the issues:

- Possible health danger to the community
- Loss of the lake for recreation
- Possible poor design of the plant
- Increased possibility of new jobs
- New tax revenue from plant would help community
- Businesses in community would thrive
- Environmental effect on animal and plant life
- Power needs of residents in northeastern United States

JACKSON: You've done a good job.
  SALLY: Mr. Jackson, I'd like to know who makes the decisions to build a nuclear plant. What if most of the people don't want one?
WILLIAM: Well, people who will get new jobs or people who live far away will want it built.
JACKSON: Are we agreed that the question depends on what is important to the individual? [The students nod and agree.] OK, then let's investigate this. I'm going to give you a case study to read about Cayuga Lake and the power plant problem. Each group is to decide what is valued in each of the issues and what is the ultimate goal involved in each of the issues. How can the goal be reached? Try to consider how a solution to the many issues can be attained. I'll write these questions on the board for you. Now let's divide into groups and get our materials. Bruce, Jay, Jennie, and Sally, you get the materials for the people around you and lead the groups. You will have about 22 minutes before we evaluate.

There was a good deal of buzzing in the room as students grumbled, moved, and settled in to their task. Jackson observed the beginning stage of work as students talked and decided they had better begin to read the case study before they made any plans. The case study was fairly short and after about 6 minutes most of the students had finished reading. Jackson observed the students as they began their deliberations. He moved to one of the groups and listened in. The students at this group decided to take the issues one at a time and identify the obvious value implications and then "brainstorm" possible solutions. He moved to another group; they decided to identify values for all of the issues first, then each person in the group would take one issue and be responsible for developing a solution to present to the other group members. A third group was having trouble deciding how to move on the project. Jackson detected a lack of understanding about the value side of the assignment. Jackson asked the group: Who cares about new jobs, taxes, and the businesses? The group responded, "The local community residents would care." "Exactly," said Jackson, "but would *all* of the residents feel the same way?" Slowly Jackson helped the students focus on their task and understand how to proceed.

Stewart Jackson continued to monitor the group work, and at the appropriate moment he asked the students to stop working and turn their chairs so that they could all see him. He said, "I know you have not finished, but you will get some time tomorrow on this. In the meantime let's report progress and see if we can help each other with the task. Group 1, tell us how you decided to proceed and a little bit about your progress."

Each group reported how many issues they had worked on, whether they were working together on the issues or whether each person was responsible for a separate task. It was agreed that they needed additional references dealing with power pollution. Because each group would ultimately be making a separate report on its solutions, they reported on the values involved in each issue but refrained from divulging their interpretations.

The period ended with Jackson giving the students a homework assignment to read about public decision making in their government textbook.

TEACHING HINT

Group Investigation Teaching Model

1. Begin with a problem/puzzling situation to motivate students.
2. Provide time for students' reactions/comments.
3. Organize the work tasks by clarifying the problem and the assignment; arrange groups, group procedures, space to work, material resources; clarify time limits.
4. Group study.
5. Groups report substantive progress; group work processes, group needs; listen and help others.
6. Group work is recycled for successive days, if needed.

Now let's take a closer look at what Stewart Jackson, the teacher, was accomplishing as he used the group investigation teaching approach. Jackson was using the text *Environmental Concerns, The World* by Sweeney (1977), and he was talking to his students about a possible values conflict regarding the building of a nuclear power station. He could have had the students read about it out of the textbook, but that would not have been as motivating as it was by providing selected information. He then showed a picture of the lake to provide visual motivation. His opening was short, and he immediately asked the students what are the issues because he needed to find out if they recognized the problem and possible controversy.

Stage 2 of the strategy began when the students identified the issues. If the students could not identify the issues, Jackson would have had to further motivate or recognize that the problem he had selected was unsuitable for his students.

Stage 3 begins when the students structure the problem. ("Who makes the decisions?") Jackson rephrases the question and the students agree. Jackson then organizes them for group work and writes the assignment on the board. He suggests a group leader for each group. He reminds the students how much time they will have for work and that he will be evaluating their work with them.

During stage 4, Jackson observes how each group begins their work task. Note that there are different sounds when students begin a new task and are unsure how to proceed and when students are involved and on task. He monitors each group by sitting in on their planning session. One of the groups is having difficulty, so Jackson helps to refocus their thinking; he does not ignore substantive work problems; nor would he ignore group behavior problems.

Stage 5 begins when Jackson asks the students to turn their chairs so that they can see him. This is the evaluation phase, and it is extremely important. Group work is evaluated by discussing the content of the lesson and by discussing cooperative work patterns (the process of group work). It is during this phase that groups may make suggestions to other groups about ways to proceed. Groups can alert the teacher and others to the need for additional material resources.

We know that this activity is to continue the next day because Jackson told the students, "I know you have not finished but..." This means that the activity will be continued. Sometimes activities are continued with a new focus to the problem, which means "recycled." If the evaluation completes the task, then there would *not* be a stage 6, and the teaching model would end after stage 5.

Classroom Management during Group Investigation

The teacher's role is quite different during group investigation as compared to direct instruction. Jackson acts as a consultant and an interested observer during the work period. He facilitates the students' work tasks; he is understanding and accepting as a counselor. He tries to refrain from telling students how to proceed. It is their task to inquire and to problem solve, and they are to do this in a cooperative environment with their peers. His task is to motivate, provide a certain amount of resources to get the inquiry going, organize the groups, and provide a place to work.

During group work, although the teacher tries to refrain from providing too much substantive guidance, it is the teacher's job to help students learn group process skills. If a group cannot work well together, then Jackson needs to find out why and provide help. He must do this immediately and not let a group wreck the work of others. If necessary, he should stop the whole class and have the other groups offer suggestions. ("How can we help Jay's group?") He may need to change members of the group, have members observe other groups in action, or perhaps just talk to the group about group work rules. During Jackson's lesson he did not call attention to group work rules. Probably his students were experienced in group work. It is important to recognize that group work skills are learned, and so students need practice. Be sure to review Chapter 3 and Chapter 5, which provide information about initiating group work.

Another important management task is to plan ahead about where each group will work. The arrangement of the classroom is vital to group work. Students must be able to see and talk to each other comfortably. In Jackson's classroom the students were probably working at tables because he did not give directions about moving to different points in the room except in the case of Sally's group.

When Should Group Investigation Be Used?

This model of teaching can be used in any classroom at any grade level and in any subject field. It merely requires willingness to allow students to sit next to each other and eyeball each other. It should not be conceived as a method for an "open" classroom. One can use direct instruction for teaching math and reading skills and use group investigation when the purposes for instruction include teaching cooperative group process skills. The model teaches democratic decision making. It helps students recognize and respect diverse viewpoints. The substantive nature of the problems should provide opportunity for students to learn inquiry skills. Group investigation teaches:

1. Group process skills
2. Democratic governance
3. Inquiry skills
4. Constructionist view of knowledge

CONCEPT ATTAINMENT MODEL

This teaching model is used to help students gain specific concepts by comparing and contrasting examples that contain attributes of the concept with examples that do not contain the characteristic.

The model comes from the work of Jerome Bruner. Bruner studied the means people use to categorize, form, and gain concepts. Cognitive psychologists like Bruner have found that people categorize to simplify conceptual learning. Joyce and Weil (1986) describe Bruner's theory of concepts. Concepts have four elements. For example, an apple is the *name* of our concept. Positive *examples* of apples would be Pippin, Granny Smith, and Jonathan; negative *examples* would be plums and pears. *Attributes* of apples would be the skin, seeds, colors, and shape. The fourth element has to do with the range of appropriateness or acceptability of the attributes. For example, if we were to talk about the *attribute range* of apples in terms of color, we would call attention to yellow, red, green, and variegated apples, but purple would be beyond the range of its defining attribute.

Some concepts can only be defined by the presence of one or more characteristics. Our concept example, apple, could be confused with a pear if it were not for its shape because both apples and pears have similar colors, skin, and seeds.

Sometimes concepts need to be described by the presence of some characteristics and the absence of others. (Apple is a fruit and similar to plums and apricots, but it has seeds, not a pit.)

Still other concepts must be described by the relationship between them and other types of concepts. We could not understand apple as a fruit if we did not understand the concept "fruit."

Students learn concepts in a variety of ways. Some students are efficient and others are not. It is for this reason that students are encouraged to share their strategies for attaining concepts during this instructional approach. We shall visit Midge Brady's class to watch her teach concept attainment; then we shall discuss the strategy some more.

◆   Midge Brady's class enjoyed a field trip to the zoo. On the following day in class, Midge asked her students to recall what they had seen. Their list included the following animals:

Lizards	Elephants	Dolphins	Crocodiles
Lions	Ostrich	Cheetah	Herring gull
Polar bear	Mole	Camel	Beaver
Eel	Whale	Crow	Penguin
Chimpanzee	Eagle	Zebra	Snakes

The class identified more than forty different animals, and Midge was amazed how much they remembered. She said, "Now that you are thinking about our trip to the zoo, I wonder if you can guess what I'm thinking about." Midge then wrote a list on the board:

Lizards (yes)   Turtle (yes)
Ostrich (no)   Snake (yes)
Dolphin (no)

"The yesses give you a clue as to what I am thinking," said Midge.

The students began to guess. "Are you thinking about animals that crawl?" "I think you are thinking about animals that lay eggs." "No, she is thinking about animals that live in water." The students continued to make comments and finally Midge suggested that they look at her next list.

Camel   Alligator
Monkey   Elephant
Iguana

"Now," said Midge, "which animals should I write yes after, and which ones should be followed by a no?" The students quickly identified the camel, monkey, and elephant as "noes" and the iguana and alligator as "yesses." "Well boys and girls, you certainly do have the right idea, but I wonder if anyone here can tell me the name that describes all of our yes animals." After several tries the children remembered the word "reptile," and Midge congratulated them for guessing what she was thinking about. Midge now asked them if they could help her identify additional "yesses" and "noes." After a few minutes students contributed: "The chameleon is a yes." "A cobra is a yes." "An eagle is a no." "A mole is a no." "Is a frog a yes or no?"

"Tell me, boys and girls, what were you thinking about while you were guessing the meaning of my yesses and noes?"

"I tried to see what was alike when I looked at the yes words."

"I tried to see how the no words were different from the yes words."

"I figured it had something to do with the way the animals move."

"Well, you certainly are good thinkers. We need to continue to classify the rest of our animals and help Jimmy find out if a frog is a reptile, but first, let's..."

Midge Brady motivated her class by having them recall their visit on the preceding day to the zoo. After determining that the students could remember many of the animals they saw, Midge asked the students to guess what she was thinking about. She identified three animals as positive examples of her concept and two as negative examples. She allowed the students to discuss this aloud. Joyce and Weil (1986) refer to this stage as the hypothesizing stage.

Midge does not confirm their hypotheses. This encourages the students to continue thinking. Instead she writes a new list of animals on the board, and this time she asks the students to tell her whether each animal is a positive example or a negative example of her concept.

The students appear to have the concept because they respond correctly. Midge asks the students to think hard and see if they can name the concept, which they ultimately do. It is here that Midge could have defined the concept for the students. Next Midge asks the students if they can generate positive and negative examples of the concept. Once again they do this correctly. However, one alert youngster questions whether a frog is a positive or negative example.

It is apparent that Midge intends to come back to Jimmy and talk about whether the frog is a reptile, but she postpones that discussion because she will probably discuss the attributes of reptiles and other classes of animals.

TEACHING HINT

Concept Attainment Model

1. Present positive and negative labeled examples of the concept.
2. Students compare attributes of positive and negative examples.
3. Students discuss ideas (hypotheses are generated).
4. Teacher does not confirm students' hypotheses at this stage.
5. Teacher presents additional positive and negative examples but does not label them.
6. Students identify the examples as positive or negative based on their prior hypotheses.
7. Teacher confirms ideas, hypotheses, at this point and names the concept, stating a definition.
8. Students are asked to generate their own examples of the concept.
9. Students are asked to describe their thoughts while trying to identify the concept. Teacher helps students understand the role of hypothesizing as a thinking strategy.

Classroom Management during Concept Attainment

This model is most typically used with the whole class as a group; however, it certainly can also be used during small-group instruction. There is moderate structure during the model. The teacher controls the pace of instruction but allows a free discussion and encourages interaction and hypothesizing. Cooperative learning strategies may be used if desired. The teacher needs to encourage students to try out their ideas. During the discussion of thoughts, the teacher helps the students analyze their thinking strategies.

The model is dependent on the teacher's preplanning of appropriate concepts and positive and negative examples. Although no instructional materials are necessary for the strategy, texts and other materials often provide the information needed for concept attainment exercises. Joyce and Weil (1986, p. 36) comment that "the three major functions of the teacher during concept attainment activity are to record, prompt (cue), and present additional data."

When Should Concept Attainment Be Used?

This strategy may be used for a variety of purposes. For example, suppose you want to initiate a unit on how human alienation leads to revolution. You may want to verify that students understand the term "revolution." Concept attainment would be perfect for this situation. Or, suppose you are teaching students poetic devices. You could have students read several poems, some identified as positive examples of the concept and some marked as negative examples of the attribute. In this way students will be forced to compare and contrast the selections. Suppose your students had just finished reports on the largest cities of the world, but you felt unsure whether they really had synthesized the information or instead thought about these cities in terms of their own contribution to the class report. You could use concept attainment in a variety of ways to help students synthesize what they learned by selecting cities with a large multiethnic composition as positive examples versus other cities, or you could select large cities near waterways, or large cities not near waterways, or cities expanding dramatically.

Concept attainment may be used to teach selected concepts, initiate units of study, and help students assimilate information. Concept attainment may also be used to improve students' thinking strategies. Under this circumstance the teacher would want to give fewer cues but more reinforcement to encourage hypothesizing, and more time to the analysis of the thinking process when students describe their thoughts.

Concept attainment is appropriate for every grade level. In fact it can be used quite well with kindergartners using concrete materials to identify the positive and negative examples. A teacher wanting to teach the concept "rough" would provide positive examples of the word "rough" (rocks, sandpaper, cinders) and negative examples (paper, silk). However, don't expect very young children to do much with the describing thoughts stage!

Concept attainment teaches specific concepts, concept development strategies, and the nature of concepts. Joyce and Weil (1986) note that this approach also helps students develop tolerance of ambiguity and sensitivity to logical reasoning.

ADVANCE ORGANIZER MODEL

David Ausubel (1963) theorizes that if meaningful knowledge is organized and presented in an orderly manner, then students will learn more efficiently and effectively. Ausubel wants teachers to structure information that students will encounter during a lesson prior to beginning reading or listening. By doing this, teachers will be providing students with an "intellectual scaffold" to fit and organize the ideas and facts they come upon. The use of an advance organizer, Ausubel believes, will improve understanding and retention.

The organization (scaffold) that is provided allows the student to relate the information he or she encounters in a meaningful way.

> This theory applies to situations in which the teacher plays the role of lecturer or explainer. Its major purpose is to help students acquire subject matter. The teacher is responsible for presenting what is to be learned. The learner's primary role is to master ideas and information. Whereas inductive approaches lead the students to discover or rediscover concepts, the advance organizers provide concepts and principles to the students directly. (Joyce & Weil, 1986, p. 72)

◆ In Midge Brady's classroom the children are going to engage in dramatic play. Midge is testing the children's understanding of how food is transported from the farm to the consumer. She has drawn an illustration on the chalkboard that illustrates the process. Her drawing indicates that the process begins on the farm, that some form of transportation is then needed to transport produce to the wholesale market where it is then once again transported to the supermarket and finally to the consumer.

Midge calls attention to her diagram and has the children "read" it. Then she organizes them for their dramatic play and intends to see if the diagram has helped them. During the dramatic play Midge walks around observing and taking notes. When she stops the activity for discussion, she will ask questions related to each component of the diagram. In this way she will determine whether or not the students link the actual movement of farm goods with their dramatic activities.

Julie Kramer expected her students to read in their social studies textbook, *Our World: Lands and Cultures* pages 429–433. "We are going to continue reading about the Soviet Union today." She introduced the following vocabulary to the students: collectivize, heavy industry, and consumer goods. She explained "collectivize" and had students give examples of heavy industry and consumer goods. Then she provided the students with an outline:

Collectivizing the land
Effects of collectivization on the peasants

Government planning and production of consumer goods
Industrialization in Russia
Stalin's plan for heavy industry
Production of consumer goods

Space was provided between the topics, and Julie instructed the class that they were each responsible for writing at least one question about the information pertaining to each topic. At the end of the reading time, she would call on students to ask a question and have others respond to see if students understood what they had read.

TEACHING HINT

Advance Organizer Model

1. Tell students the purpose of the lesson.
2. Present the organizer; provide examples if needed; clarify information. Verify students' attention.
3. Present material to be read or listened to; clarify the organization.
4. Be sure that material is organized logically and students understand how various pieces of information are related.
5. Use organizational outline for evaluating what students have learned. Be sure that students see how material relates to each aspect of the organizer. Utilize vocabulary. Have students summarize what they have learned. Ask students for underlying assumptions and inferences and/or contradictions. Provide clarifications as needed.

Midge Brady used the advance organizer approach in an unusual way. Her students were not going to read or listen to expository material. Instead they were to act out what they had been learning. Midge was concerned that her students were not integrating ideas about the wholesale market, so she used the organizer to clarify to students the flow of goods from farm to table. She illustrated the process and made sure that students paid attention and understood her diagram.

Next the students assumed roles of farmer, transportation people, and buyers at the wholesale market, supermarket employees, and consumers. While the students acted out these roles and responsibilities, she took notes. At the end of the role play she questioned the students and had them tell about their "work." Once again she used the diagram to help the students integrate what they were learning.

Julie Kramer gave the students an assignment and reminded them that they were continuing to read about the Soviet Union. She then introduced key vocabulary words and verified that students understood by having them give examples. She introduced her outline for the reading assignment and planned its use by the students, assigning them to write questions for each topic in the outline. In this way she ensured that they would utilize the organizer for their reading.

She evaluated and verified that they integrated the information by having students ask the questions related to each topic and call on other members of the class to answer the questions. In this way students were responsible for reconciling the material into the structure of the lesson and actively responding to the material.

Classroom Management during the Advance Organizer Model

This is a very structured teaching model. The teacher controls the presentation of material and relates it to what is to be learned. The teacher presents the organization to students and makes certain that they understand the structure of the lesson. It is necessary to maintain student attention during the presentation of the organizer. The lesson is dependent on the logical organization of the material for the students; this requires preplanning on the part of the teacher.

The teacher needs to clarify the organization for students and verify that they understand its logic. On-task behavior is critical throughout the entire lesson. During the evaluation the teacher once again structures the discussion to verify integrative reconciliation of knowledge. However, during the discussion interaction among students should be encouraged. Students should initiate questions and clarify ideas.

Which model of teaching would you use to transmit important spelling rules?

When Should the Advance Organizer Approach Be Used?

This approach can be used in any subject field to systematically introduce a unit of study to students. Key ideas can be clarified to expedite the structuring and assimilation of information; this is true in mathematics, the arts, and the sciences. A music teacher may present information such as "folk music tells us about the cultural life and times of the composer and the period in which he or she lived." Information such as this may serve as a clue and information for students in order to appreciate the works the teacher will next present. Thus the model can help shape students' critical thinking abilities as well as improve their skills for reception learning.

Quite often textbooks for elementary students fail to present an organizing structure with appropriate subheads and questions to motivate students to read. The use of an advance organizer becomes critical to students' understanding and motivation. While teaching, reading teachers typically introduce vocabulary and motivate reading through appropriate questions. These teaching behaviors serve the advance organizer function. The same behaviors in social studies, science, and health education would increase student understanding and help students integrate the learning material.

When teachers develop their own learning materials for students to read, the format should follow the principles of this approach. Organizing questions followed by an explanation of what is to follow will facilitate student understanding, reinforce learning, and motivate progress.

A common mistake frequently made in using this approach is to begin a lesson by asking students to recall past learned information. This is a valuable way to begin a lesson, but the recall activity does not serve as an organizer. The organizer must be systematically presented information that provides an overall structure for what is to come.

TEACHING WITH STRATEGY

Teaching goals differ throughout the school day; goals depend on the content to be taught and the students who are to learn. The instructional process needs to be congruent with the purpose for instruction, otherwise teachers would be attempting to reach diverse goals with one tried-and-true teaching strategy. This would be similar to serving pizza for all meals, to all students, every day.

Instructional approaches can be categorized into three basic modes: expository, guided discussion, interaction. Direct instruction and the advance organizer are expository teaching approaches. Concept attainment is primarily a guided discussion approach although it has moments of interaction. The group investigation approach would be categorized as interaction. An effective teacher is skillful in utilizing all three modes of instruction and modulating between the approaches. To facilitate understanding, the three modes will be contrasted.

Expository Teaching

Expository teaching is teacher-focused instruction. Exposition means to present and to interpret. In the classroom this translates into the teacher as a "presenter" and "interpreter." The teacher's purpose is to transmit knowledge. The student is responsible for listening and seeing. Often with older students, they are required to take notes while they are listening. The teacher's role is to "input" ideas and information while the student's role is to consume ideas and information.

Expository teaching is an efficient teaching strategy primarily because the teacher can input to a whole group at the same time. It allows the teacher to communicate needed information once instead of several times, but the teacher must monitor that everyone is paying attention. The classroom environment must be controlled; there should be moderate to high structure, and the teacher should be initiating questions, if necessary, and eliciting short-answer responses.

The expository mode of instruction is appropriate when the student is expected to consume information and learn a skill; therefore, reading out of textbooks, observing a demonstration, watching films, and listening to lectures are expository approaches. This is not to belittle the expository approach because transmitting knowledge and skills are important teaching tasks.

The teacher's role during exposition is to direct learning. The teacher is responsible for preplanning what is to be communicated to students and for obtaining the necessary learning materials—texts, teacher-prepared information, or films. The learning materials communicate specified and defined information to students. This means that students are not *seeking* information because the teacher has done the seeking and the asking of the appropriate questions. In other words the teacher is *preprocessing* the information for student consumption.

The standardized test is frequently used to evaluate what students have learned via exposition. Teacher-made tests are also used to find out if students have learned what teachers have taught through lectures and textbooks. These tests most typically ask students to reproduce specific facts and ideas versus asking students to analyze, synthesize, or evaluate. It is assumed that the curriculum can be specified into precise content terms and that what students are to learn can be predetermined and ultimately tested.

Which model of teaching would you use to help students focus on what they are to read?

Guided Discussion

Discussion strategies may be used by themselves as a teaching approach (Socratic discussion) or in conjunction with other teaching approaches. For example, in the direct instruction strategy, the teacher asks short-answer-type questions to help students stay on task. Because these questions are patterned to lead the students through the lesson, the discussion, while limited, is certainly "guided." In the concept attainment strategy the discussion is more "free form," which means that it is inquiry and problem solving oriented. The teacher allows students to digress a bit in order to cultivate and stimulate ideas and encourage hypothesizing.

It is important to contrast true discussion and a teacher-controlled discussion. A real discussion should allow widespread sharing of ideas, thoughts, and feelings. Discussion participants utilize their personal experiences, information, and data and are intent upon sharing these with the other participants. A discussion progresses through several phases: (1) getting acquainted with the issue/topic, (2) problem definition in which participants focus on the major issue, (3) data gathering through listening to each other's ideas, and (4) conclusion/summing up. Often the prime purpose of small-group work is discussion to allow students to share viewpoints and come to consensus.

Discussion requires that the participants allow the flow of conversation to move through the group. Group members need to be able to see each other to detect when someone wants to share. *Attending* to what others are saying means that the discussion flows without undue repetitions; participants listen to each other. Students need to learn not to monopolize the conversation—to allow others to take turns. In short, discussion manners need to be modeled and practiced.

True discussions are best in small groups; in the large group the discussion needs to be guided, which means there needs to be a discussion leader. In small groups students easily learn the role of the discussion leader, but in the large group this role is best performed by the teacher. Good discussions do not just happen; they are preplanned. The problem to be discussed needs to be clearly defined, and students must be in possession of information from either background knowledge and experiences or data from recent input to contribute to the discussion. Both the teacher and the students need to be prepared for a discussion.

Once again it is important that students can see each other if they are to participate meaningfully in the discussion. Many teachers like to use either a discussion circle or square formation to facilitate students' seeing and listening. This requires careful planning to teach students to move their chairs into the desired formation. Often only a portion of the class will need to change their positions for the discussion, so that students do not have their backs to each other.

As the discussion leader, the teacher needs to carefully plan the questions to initiate the discussion and to keep students on task. (The reader is urged to review the questioning strategies in Chapter 5 and the several discussion checklists in Chapter 4.) Some questions need to be used to open the discussion and draw students' interest; other questions are plotted to be thought provoking and increasingly complex. Some questions should produce divergent responses, and others are designed to lead to deductive thinking.

It is usually considered best to allow students to self-select who will answer a question, but on occasion it may be wise to call on a student to answer the question. This should occur under the following circumstances:

> You need to involve a new speaker.
> You need to alert a student to pay attention.
> You need to challenge the students.
> A shy child has not participated.

If you are calling on a shy student, it is best to give that student plenty of response time, so call the student's name before you ask the question.

Skillful questioning also requires that the discussion leader look around the group to encourage wide response, be nonevaluative in listening to responses to encourage several responses, and utilize add-on questions, such as: "What do you think, (Charlie)?" "Do you agree with (Baxter)?" "What else should we think about?" "What would you do, if you were . . . ?"

Nonevaluative listening means that the teacher is often silent after a response to encourage more discussion. Or, the teacher may utilize some counseling techniques like saying, "Hmm," "Uh-huh," "Interesting," 'I see." Another technique is to paraphrase what a student has said to let the student and the class know you are listening. The idea of paraphrasing is to integrate the cognitive elements of what a student(s) has said. This is most successful if students' thoughts have not been too clear and you want to encourage students to continue on, but perhaps in a new direction.

One last point about the guiding of discussions: Teachers need to remember that the questions asked control the subject matter learned. The sequencing of questions controls not only the responses but in fact makes the students dependent on what the teacher considers important.

RESEARCH AND READINGS

Barnes, Douglas (1984). *From communication to curriculum*. Middlesex, England: Penguin Books, p. 127.

"When teachers complain about classes who will not talk they often present this as a moral failing in the pupils: it is more likely that the pupils have learned from their schooling that their knowledge is irrelevant in a context determined by teachers, examinations, school syllabuses, and so on."

Interaction Mode

Interactive teaching approaches involve students in learning activities that require consideration of others. Students become interdependent. They depend on each other in a variety of ways:

For stimulation and ideas as in a discussion
To pursue knowledge; to link thoughts as in hypothesizing
To reason, compare, and contrast ideas and experiences
To test ideas, thoughts, and theories
To cooperate and coordinate skills, abilities

Interactive approaches include strategies such as group investigation, role playing, problem solving, some aspects of concept attainment, and inquiry approaches. The role of the teacher is decidedly different during interactive approaches. During expository approaches the teacher directs; during guided discussion the teacher guides and controls the discussion; during interactive approaches the teacher acts as an orchestra leader—facilitating, counseling, gently guiding. Interactive approaches are learner centered. The teacher selects an appropriate problem for study, but then helps the students define the problem in their own terms.

Learning materials are extremely important in this mode. The data base must be relevant and adequate. In contrast to the expository approach in which the teacher predigests information and ideas and presents these to students already processed, in interactive approaches the students process the information. Therefore, they need contrasting content to practice and learn how to categorize facts, ideas, or events. Students need to learn to evaluate information for interpretive purposes, and they need to generalize about why something is true or usually happens.

Learning materials may include realia, laboratory materials, or art supplies. They are not limited necessarily to print materials. Even for role playing or gaming strategies students may need some type of data base for processing. In planning these approaches, the teacher needs to preplan the learning resources. These resources may require students to read, to talk, to listen, to construct, to raise questions, to interpret, and so on.

The classroom environment must encourage interaction. If students depend on each other, they must have a way to work together and engage in discovery learning. The environment should encourage and promote both independence and the ability to establish meaningful relationships with others. Students are not encouraged to wander either mentally or physically during interactive approaches; the teacher should provide enough guidance to help students "settle in" to inquiry. This may mean that the teacher asks the right questions or directs students to the appropriate materials or challenges and prods. We have now looked at three major modes of teaching; let us now contrast the classroom management strategies required for each approach.

Classroom Management: Three Modes of Instruction

Exposition	*Guided Discussion*	*Interaction*
Teacher directed	Teacher guided	Teacher facilitative role
Teacher controlled	Teacher controlled	
High structure	Moderate to high structure	Low to moderate structure
Academic focus/skills	Focus on cognitive functions	Group process oriented: inquiry/problem solving
	Teacher monitors student processing	

SUMMARY

Four teaching approaches have been highlighted in this chapter. The purpose has been to demonstrate the wide range of approaches appropriate for classroom instruction. All four strategies are suitable for all grade levels. Direct instruction is a structured way of teaching the basic skills. The advance organizer is also a structured approach for systemically introducing learning material to students. Concept attainment is moderately structured by the teacher and is appropriate for teaching all subject fields. Group investigation emphasizes cooperative learning and can be used in any classroom in all subject areas and with all age levels when the purpose is to emphasize *problem solving* rather than knowledge that is predetermined.

Teaching strategy affects classroom management. During direct instruction the classroom is quiet, all eyes should be on the teacher; the teacher controls and paces the lesson. The advance organizer strategy is much the same; the teacher presents the organizer, and students should be listening or visually taking in the structure of the presentation. Concept attainment is less structured. The teacher encourages some interaction so that students will be listening to others as they hypothesize and as they describe the thinking process. In group investigation there is low structure and the sound of groups at work. The teacher monitors group efforts but does not stifle group work by controlling interaction.

Match Instructional Purpose and Instructional Strategy

	Concept Attainment	Group Investigation	Direct Instruction	Advance Organizer
Explain why an event occurred				
Memorize a poem				
Seek information about pollution				
Introduce new information				
Compare meter in several poems				
Investigate urban problems				
Outline social studies chapter				
Learn economic concepts				
Read graphs				
Improve cooperative work skills				
Understand what adjectives are				
Introduce historical time period				
Teach what "many years" means				
Master factual material				
Learn to square dance				
Apply concepts, principles				

CASE STUDY PROBLEMS

1. Group Work. Mr. Merrill looked at his students and said, "We will continue our group work task today. Group leaders, get the materials, and everyone move to your group for work."

The students started to work, but it was apparent that there was a great deal of confusion in the room. Some students were milling around. Two of the group leaders were arguing over materials. Three students approached Mr. Merrill and said that they didn't know how to proceed, could he help them?

It is obvious that Mr. Merrill will need to stop the students and provide some guidance. You are an observer in this classroom; what did Mr. Merrill neglect to do before sending the students off to work?

Solution: This is a continuing assignment, and it probably does not need to be motivated; however, group work should never be started without helping the students recall what they did on the previous day—their accomplishments and their needs. Each group should be asked to respond as to what their task would be today and how they will go about it. Mr. Merrill should ask: "What do you need to do today? What materials will you need to accomplish the task?" Then if students are confused or need help, Mr. Merrill should ask: "Who can suggest how this group should proceed?"

Mr. Merrill needs to be concerned that he has provided the appropriate materials and the right conditions for each group to make headway and that students know what is expected of them each time they work together. Then Mr. Merrill must monitor and guide the groups, if needed. At the end of the work period Mr. Merrill needs to evaluate the work session in terms of what was discussed at the beginning of the work period. ("Did you accomplish the task?" "What new needs do you have?")

2. Direct Instruction. Ms. Crane spent over an hour per day teaching reading skills using the direct instruction approach. But when she taught social studies or science or health and used textbooks, she never thought about helping her students with reading skills. As a consequence her students were having many problems reading these textbooks, and they were not enjoying them. If you were Ms. Crane's colleague, how could you help her?

Solution: Ms. Crane's students were not learning to apply reading skills during content instruction because Ms. Crane did not provide systematic instruction in reading in content fields. She needs to demonstrate and have students practice applying those skills during social studies, science, and health instruction.

QUESTIONS

1. In what ways will the environment of the classroom, content of instruction, and the skills that are taught affect the outcomes of instruction?
2. How does classroom management differ for each of the three modes of instruction? Give specific examples using the four models of instruction described in this chapter.

3. Suppose you want students to analyze their thinking strategies, what model of instruction should you use?
4. Suppose you want students to generate and test hypotheses and work co-operatively, what model would you choose?
5. Suppose your students need systematic and sequential instruction in mathematics, what model would you select?

CHAPTER 7

Creating and Managing the Learning Environment

The physical environment of the classroom affects the dynamics of learning. The formally arranged classroom typical of high schools and colleges, with chairs and desks facing forward and students sitting neatly in rows staring at the head of the individual in front, is a familiar schoolroom arrangement. The arrangement of this type of classroom determines the role behavior of both teacher and students. For students in this environment motor activity and sensory perception are "other" controlled, as is the use of language. In elementary, middle schools, and junior high schools, the physical arrangement of the classroom is often quite different, and so the dynamics of classroom life will be different. The physical environment may be defined as the space, chairs, desks, tables, lighting, ventilation, acoustics, and instructional supplies, but the ways in which teachers use and arrange these aspects of the environment affect the intellectual, social, and emotional climates of the classroom.

A primary purpose of bringing children together in an institution called a "school" is to arrange and to control the learning environment.

RESEARCH AND READINGS

Dewey, John (1944). *Democracy and education.* New York: The Free Press, pp. 18–19.

"The only way in which adults consciously control the kind of education which the immature get is by controlling the environment in which they act, and hence think and feel. We never educate directly, but indirectly by means of the environment. Whether we permit chance environments to do the work, or whether we design environments for the purpose makes a great deal of difference. And any environment is a chance environment so far as its educative influence is concerned *unless it has been deliberately regulated with reference to its educative effect*" (emphasis added).

The teacher who gives no thought to the classroom environment is influencing learning just as much as the teacher who designs the surroundings to encourage and motivate a special effect. Because the environment can be used as an effective teaching tool, objectives can be formulated to foster desirable behavior, skills, attitudes, and understandings. The classroom environment can be used to develop problem-solving skills and creative thought.

Since children learn very efficiently from one another, the classroom can be arranged to encourage (or discourage) students' interrelationships. Physical arrangements and learning activities can be focused so that student discussions are deliberately planned. Teachers can influence friendships and modeling experiences through the classroom environment. By arranging interactions, structuring activities, and distributing responsibility, teachers can develop the leadership skills of students.

Dewey has said that "we learn what we do," and McLuhan has added to that dimension by stating that "the medium is the message." Therefore, even though a teacher says, "Boys and girls, let's debate our ideas about the importance of...," if the classroom does not promote individuality, the students will be unable to define, evaluate, choose relevant information, and, in fact, go through problem-solving steps in order to debate *any* question or issue. The structure of the classroom can stimulate and challenge students or it can motivate passivity.

RESEARCH AND READINGS

Schmuck, Patricia, & Schmuck, Richard (1977). Formal and informal aspects of classroom life: Can they be harmonized for academic learning? *The History and Social Science Teacher 12*, 75–80.

McLuhan, Marshall, & Fiore, Quentin (1967). *The medium is the massage.* New York: Bantam Books.

CLASSROOM ORGANIZATION

The classroom can be arranged so that it is appealing to students by having areas of activity interestingly equipped with materials and resources. These activity centers can be organized for directed teaching and for individual and group work. Actual centers for learning should be designed to appeal to the students' natural interests and should be relevant in terms of curricular content. Consideration should be given to both the storage of and the access to materials and resources as well as to the traffic patterns in the classroom.

Judgment is necessary in the selection of materials for the classroom. There should be a variety of materials to provide for a range of differing needs and ability levels. Provision should be made for structured uses (reading); tactile, auditory, visual-aesthetic, and manipulative needs; raw materials (sand); dramatic play; and so on. But most important is that the materials evidence use. If students are not allowed to touch, explore, and use the materials, then the materials are purposeless.

The classroom organization should also provide opportunities for teacher-student interaction and student-student interaction. Individual, group, and class meetings should be possible. In some lower grade classrooms, it is unnecessary for students to have a permanent personal desk as long as there are designated places for specific work activities. As children mature, they usually prefer to have their very own place in the classroom and so the interest/learning centers must be arranged peripherally.

Room Arrangement

Your room arrangement must fit the learning activities you intend to engage in with your students. It is extremely important, if you intend movement activities, center activities, group work, discussions, whatever, that you plan your physical space appropriately. First, eyeball your room and decide which chalkboard will be the "front" of the classroom. Where will you stand when you want to talk to all of the students in your class? Because you probably will not sit at your desk when students are in the room, where can you put it to keep it out of the way? If you intend to use an overhead projector much of the time, where will you position it and where is your screen, and how will all the students see the screen?

Your next task is to plan where students will sit. Once again you need to consider your activities, but more important, consider your traffic areas. Locate your exits and decide how students will walk to the doors to leave the room. Next decide where you will locate your resource materials (texts, dictionaries, encyclopedia, maps, etc.). Where are your storage shelves for paper and other supplies? Once you have located where you will keep your resource materials and you have considered your storage shelves, you must once again look at the traffic pattern in your classroom. Will students be able to get their supplies without bothering others? Will there be congestion? Consider the pencil sharpener, waste basket(s), and water fountain. These are typically high-traffic areas. Will students be able to reach them easily?

Do a mock-up plan of your tables and chairs (elementary, middle school) or desk/chairs (high school). Identify how you will have students move around the classroom; does your plan permit orderly movement to storage, exits, resources?

Now consider the position of students in their seats, will they be able to see the board? The screen? Will the students be able to see you if you are in the front of the room? If you are in the front of the room, will you be able to see everyone? If you are able to answer affirmatively to all of these questions, then you are ready to set your furniture in place. Remember not to neglect your own teaching comfort. There will be many occasions when you will want a work table in the front of the classroom to store lesson materials, to demonstrate to students, or to hold your own books. Place that table in position and verify that students will be able to see it if you perform demonstrations in that position.

Directed Teaching Center

In elementary classrooms and often in middle school classrooms, you need an area where you can teach basic skills to a small group of students. Generally this is best arranged in front of a chalkboard. Be sure in planning this area that you will be able to see the majority of the class at work when you are directing this small group of students. You do not want to position yourself so that you have your back to the rest of the classroom. Note the primary classroom in Figure 7.1. The teacher can work with students at the skills center or the teacher can have the students sit on the rug or on chairs in the meeting area. The teacher will

Figure 7.1. Classroom Floor Plan, Primary Elementary Grades

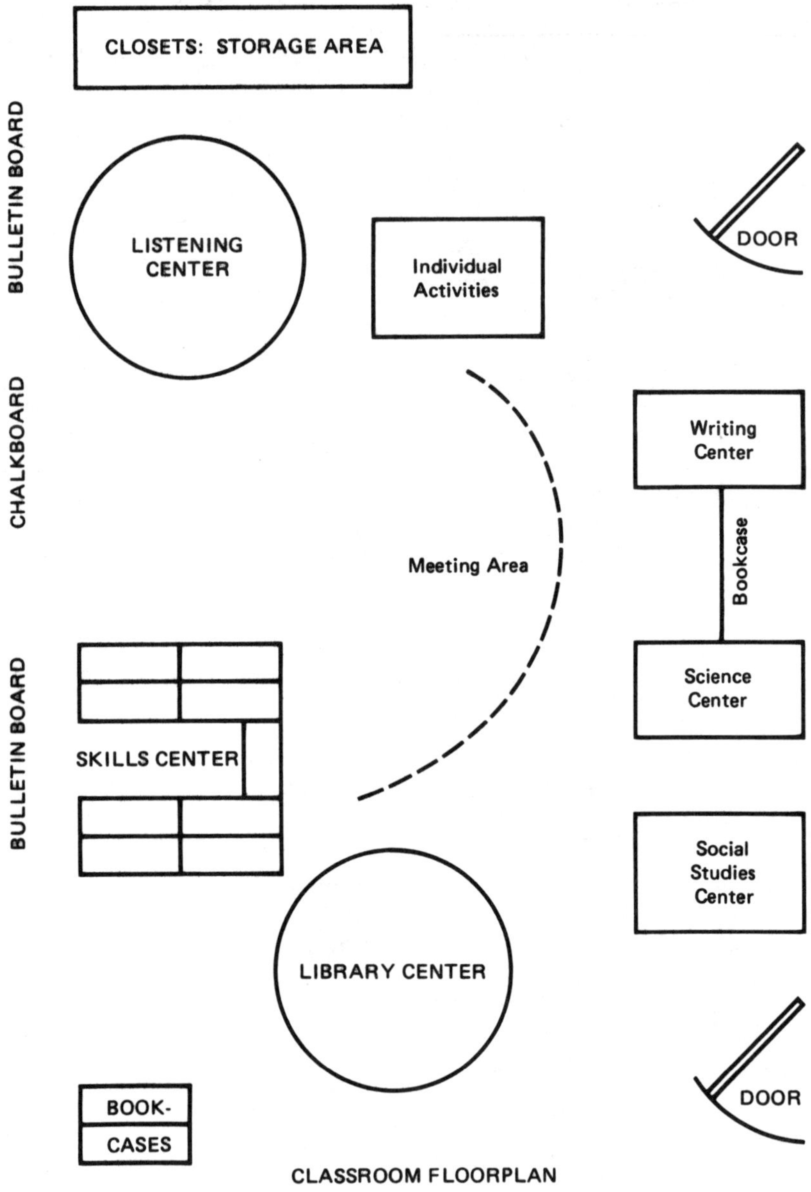

CLOSETS: STORAGE AREA

BULLETIN BOARD

CHALKBOARD

BULLETIN BOARD

LISTENING CENTER

Individual Activities

DOOR

Writing Center

Bookcase

Meeting Area

Science Center

SKILLS CENTER

Social Studies Center

LIBRARY CENTER

BOOK-CASES

DOOR

CLASSROOM FLOORPLAN

be able to see the rest of the class, who are presumably at the different centers. In Figure 7.2 the directed teaching center is in front of the tables and chairs and next to the chalkboard. In this plan the teacher will need to have students carry their chairs up to the front of the room and sit in a semicircle in front of the chalkboard.

Figure 7.2. Classroom Floor Plan, Upper Elementary Grades

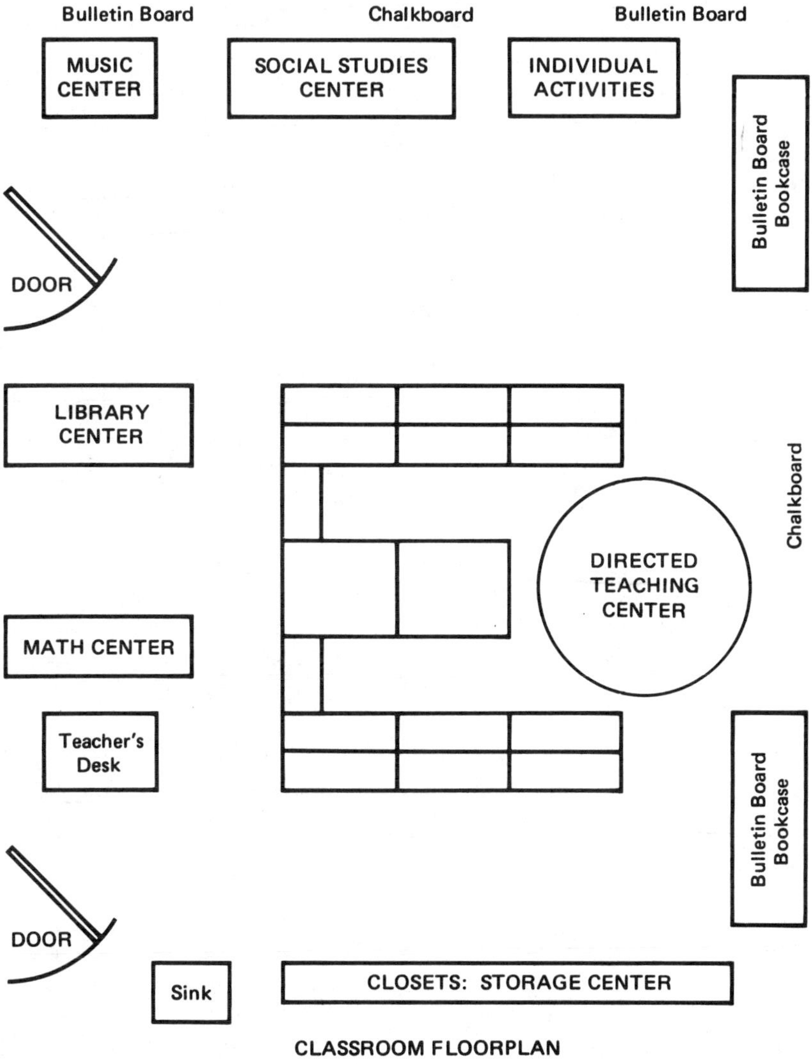

CLASSROOM FLOORPLAN

Bulletin Boards

Plan what is to go on your bulletin boards carefully. This will be one of the first things students and visitors in your classroom will observe. Consider what you are teaching and plan areas of emphasis to focus students' attention on the content of instruction. Make the bulletin boards interesting and motivating. Use color and border your pictures to make the boards attractive; be sure to carry out your color scheme throughout the room. It is distracting to students if each board has a different color scheme. When students begin to produce work, it is a good idea to reserve at least one bulletin board for the display of their efforts. After class rules have been planned by you and your students, you may want to post them on one of the bulletin boards.

It is also possible to use walls and ceilings for the display of student work or for pictures or mobiles, but it is important to remember that too much in the way of "environment" can make the room look congested, and it can overwhelm students. Classrooms that are too "busy" affect the noise level and students' ability to study and be reflective.

Resource Materials and Bookcases

Resource materials in the classroom are a convenience. They save you and the students time. Bookcases should be placed where they are accessible and where it is possible for several students to obtain materials at the same time. This means there needs to be enough room around the bookcase for people to stoop to pick out what they need. The bookcase should be visible so that you can monitor behavior. You do not want bookcases in alcoves or back rooms where you cannot see the students when they are obtaining materials.

Display Centers, Aquariums, and Plants

Display items, such as pets, plants, and fish, add cheer to the classroom. They make the classroom a warm and inviting place to be. However, once again it is important to consider how much you are putting into the environment. At least for the first week or two you do not want to introduce too many distracting items. If you do decide on special display things, introduce them to the class and provide time for students to examine them. Otherwise students will try to observe them at times you may not consider advantageous.

Professional Materials

You may need to store personal teaching materials, equipment, seasonal items, or materials that you use infrequently. These materials should be labeled and stored in boxes in closed cupboards, closets, or on shelves designed for that purpose. Because you do not need these materials often, it is a good idea to label them so that you can find them quickly.

Science, music, and art materials may all be considered in this category for elementary teachers. Secondary teachers may need to store learning packets and other resource materials that are not always appropriate.

Learning/Interest Centers
The arrangement of centers in the classroom needs to be planned. The center needs to be located so that it is accessible to students, traffic patterns need to be considered, and it must be easily monitored by the teacher. The development of centers, their function, and their management will be discussed later in the chapter.

LEARNING ACTIVITIES IN THE CLASSROOM

Suppose you wanted to play the game hide-and-seek. One of the first things that you need to do is set some boundaries for the game. Remember that in the game someone is "it." This person does the seeking and must discover where the other players are hiding. Once "it" discovers someone, there is a race between the "hidee" and "it" to see who will tag "safe" first. Parents tend to get very upset when children try to play this game in the house. Furniture and people tend to get in the way of the game. Similarly the classroom would be inappropriate for this game. Action in classrooms needs to be planned with the same foresight as if you were planning a real game of hide-and-seek.

In Chapter 6 on instructional strategies it was noted that there needed to be a match between the purpose for instruction and the method of instruction. Now we need to consider that there must also be a match between the environment of the classroom and the activities that will occur. Or, another way of putting it is that the classroom setting must be compatible with the activity that is planned.

RESEARCH AND READINGS

Clark, Leonard H., & Starr, Irving S. (1986). *Secondary and middle school teaching methods* (5th ed.). New York: Macmillan Publishing, p. 98.

"If you can arrange the classroom so that it is attractive and easy for the students to work in, your classes are likely to progress more easily than in the dull drabness of an old-fashioned classroom. Many modern methods and techniques do not work as well in traditional formal classroom setups as they do in more relaxed environments."

Gump (1982) points out that physical arrangements are not necessarily "good" or "bad," but sometimes inappropriate for the instructional purpose. The hide-and-seek game was a far-fetched example, but another example would be to imagine a classroom with the desk/chairs screwed to the floor and students sitting in rigid rows. Now suppose you wanted to have a class discussion. What kind of a discussion would it be when students can only look at the teacher and not each other? In this situation all interaction would be between teacher and student and back again to teacher and the next student. The students would have no need to listen to each other. There would be no linkage or interaction among students. The students would be dependent on the teacher's responses and in fact, quite passive.

In the classroom described above, activities such as independent seatwork, viewing a film, or listening to a lecture would all work quite well. Recall that the lecture and film viewing are expository techniques. So it appears that a teacher can perform in the expository mode and have students work independently in the aforementioned classroom, but guided discussion and interaction would be impossible.

Now let's take a closer look at Figure 7.2. The E formation is a useful arrangement in an elementary and junior high school. Suppose that Julie Kramer wanted to have a whole-class discussion. The students

Figure 7.3. Classroom Floor Plan, Secondary

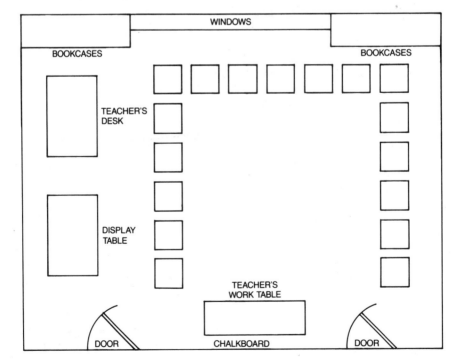

Figure 7.4. Alternative Classroom Floor Plan, Secondary

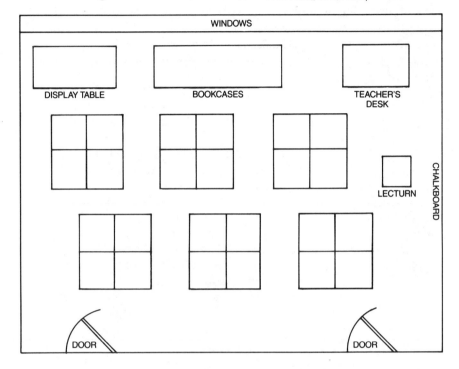

who sit on the outside of the E would all be in a good position to see everyone. The students on the inside of the E would need to move. These students could bring their chairs to the front of the classroom to form a square. Now all the students can see each other, and only half of the class needed to change position.

Consider group work in the various classrooms. In the classroom described above it would be virtually impossible to have students work in groups because the screwed-down desks would not permit a group meeting. These students would need to sit atop their desks in order to talk together. This is bound to cause classroom management problems.

In both of the high school, middle school arrangements shown in Figures 7.3 and 7.4, the desk/chairs can be moved to form small groupings in the classroom. In these classrooms although many students will need to change position, all three modes of instruction are possible. In Figures 7.1 and 7.2 there are many possibilities for small groupings, so again all three modes of instruction can be utilized by the teacher.

It is the view of some educators that there are fewer classroom management problems in classrooms where the furniture arrangement does not permit interaction. However, there is also conflicting evidence that indicates less involvement of students when lessons require passive participation throughout the day. One must remember that teachers are responsible for a wide range of instructional goals, and these goals cannot be achieved unless teachers utilize a variety of instructional modes.

RESEARCH ON ENVIRONMENTAL SETTINGS

Although there is not a great deal of research on the effect of the physical environment on the management of classrooms, some research is of particular interest. Weinstein (1979) learned that density in classrooms affects students' attitudes and conduct by increasing dissatisfaction and aggression and decreasing attentiveness. Weinstein also noted the need to design traffic aisles carefully in classrooms.

In another study Silverstein (1979) also found that students reacted to density in classrooms by acting distracted and frequently wanted to move away from others who talked or interrupted them.

In an old and classic study of the traditional classroom where the physical arrangement has students sitting in rows of desks and chairs, Adams and Biddle (1970) found that the front and the center of the classroom were the "action" zones. Students sitting in these zones were more likely to participate and be called upon by the teacher. Potter (1974) found that this occurred most frequently in low-ability elementary classrooms. In secondary schools Brooks and associates (1978) indicate that students seated in the action zone enjoy a more permissive and interactive style of communication than students seated at the sides or back of the classroom.

Good and Brophy (1986) report visiting a fourth-grade classroom where the teacher was presenting a creative writing assignment. The students were seated at individual desks in groups of six, forming rectangular tables. During the discussion phase of the lesson there was a great deal of interaction, but when the students were assigned to write their own creative endeavor, they had difficulty. These authors account for the difficulty because the students would look up and have eye contact with others sitting close to them. The arrangement of the classroom facilitated the discussion phase but inhibited the private composition phase.

Glaser (1977) studied the physical design of open classrooms and found that classroom boundaries are very important between groups of students or activities so that students and activities do not intrude upon each other.

Most of the research on the physical design of classrooms supports good common sense. Furniture arrangements must accommodate the instructional purpose and the activities to be performed. For this reason arrangements need to be flexible. Classrooms need to adjust to individual work, group work, and interaction. Space must be utilized for traffic, storage, and equipment. Open space can encourage movement and flexibility.

DEVELOPMENT OF LEARNING CENTERS

Difference between Learning Centers and Interest Centers

An interest center connotes student choice and student development, whereas a learning center tends to be teacher created and directed. The distinction between the centers is very slight—and confusing. All centers should be interesting and provide a learning experience. Both centers can be student developed. This will be discussed later. Also, both interest and learning centers can be developed by the teacher. Primarily, the interest center is designed to encourage student activity and choice during free time. The learning center is planned to meet specific objectives.

Function of Learning Centers

The learning center motivates, reinforces, and supports the students' learning. The centers approach allows the teacher to provide for individual choice, meet individual ability level needs, promote self-direction, and encourage responsibility and learner evaluation of progress. The centers approach is success oriented since it is based on the theory of differentiated instruction to meet individual ability level needs and interests and learning characteristics.

Why Should Centers Be Developed?

The centers approach encourages students to become involved in the learning process. By developing a variety of centers, teachers can recognize differences in abilities, provide for differing patterns of growth, and adjust to special learning modality needs. Short-range objectives can be efficiently planned, and students can take part in the planning and evaluation.

Sample room arrangement plans for a learning center approach are illustrated in Figures 7.1 and 7.2. Although not illustrated, a viewing center and an area for dramatic representation may also be planned in the primary classroom.

Because a center can be designed for a specific group of students or even one or two students, it is an approach that allows the teacher to focus in on individual needs. Based on the diagnosis of learning needs, centers provide a means for the teacher to develop a learning prescription. Students can self-evaluate their work at the center or evaluation can be a group task with the teacher participating. Materials at the center can extend and enrich learning to provide depth to student understanding or the center can be used to reinforce and allow students to practice a needed skill.

Are Centers Appropriate for All Subjects?

Learning centers can be developed for all subject fields. Because a center's purpose is to individualize learning as well as to provide small-group participatory activities, the centers can be used whenever instruction needs to be differentiated. Time spent at centers will differ depending on the task involved and the subject to be studied. Probably centers will not be used every day for every subject. New centers should be added to the classroom as students learn how to work using the centers approach and as they become accustomed to the routines. Centers should be changed as soon as the learning objectives have been met.

How to Develop a Learning Center

Step 1: Decide on the purpose of the center. What objective(s) do you want to accomplish? A lower grade teacher may want to extend sight vocabulary with a center that challenges students to match pictures of objects with their word labels or perhaps it is to be a science center where students try out an experiment (making a magnet) in order to develop specific concepts. A center is an environment arranged to accomplish a particular instructional purpose.

Step 2: What will the students do at the center? What activities are to be performed? Will the students group number families, classify rocks, study the developmental process of tadpoles, write a story, or what? Whatever the activity, it should accomplish the instructional purpose. If the purpose is to reinforce a skill, then the activity should provide for practice and application of the learned skill. If students need to practice research skills, then a research center should be created for students to substantiate a class hypothesis.

Step 3: Decide what materials will be needed for the students to perform the activity. Center materials can include books, paper, pictures, magazines, filmstrips, slides, records, tapes, and manipulatives materials. If students need to write, cut, paste, color, do they have the needed materials? Is there a waste receptacle nearby for discarded materials? If library books are needed, is the library center adjacent?

Step 4: How will the activity be evaluated? Some activities can be designed so that students can self-check their work. If the activity has answers, correct responses can be provided in a booklet located in the center or on the back of pictured objects so that students can verify their work. Some work should be corrected by the teacher or the aide and then returned to the student so that the student receives the appropriate feedback. Evaluation can also be a joint students-teacher endeavor and may involve a classroom discussion instead of a paper-pencil check.

A review of the steps taken to develop a center reveals four major teacher decisions.

Learning Center Developmental Steps

1. Instructional objective: What is the purpose(s) of the center?
2. Activity: How will students interact? What will students do?
3. Materials, Resources: What resources or materials are required for students to perform the activity or tasks?
4. Evaluation: How will students (and teacher) know when they have successfully completed the task or concluded the activity?

Student-Developed Centers

Students accustomed to the centers approach frequently desire to contribute to or to design their own centers. This is particularly true of junior-high-school students. Students should follow the same developmental steps as teachers. In a classroom visited recently, a student brought in her stamp collection to share. Student interest was high, and many students talked about their own collections. The teacher asked the students if they would like to develop a center using their personal stamp collections. The students were thrilled, and a group was appointed to decide how it would be handled. When the center was established, there were books about stamp collecting (one book described the origin of the first postage stamps), a magnifying glass, stamp catalogs, tweezers, envelopes, and an atlas.

At the center the students identified ways in which stamps differ; they studied cancellation marks and special stamps. Collections were displayed, and students traded their extra stamps—often obtaining long-sought-after stamps. The stamp interest center was a free-choice activity, but the teacher correlated it with social studies.

By insisting that students develop a center systematically and purposefully, the teacher avoids having centers that are meaningless or silly. Some ideas should be pursued after school, and sometimes the interests of the few are not meaningful to the many. When this occurs, the teacher should not hesitate to dissuade the students and to explain that the center is not appropriate to present class needs.

Another purpose of student-developed centers has to do with ego development and success. When teachers allow students to pursue personal interests, teachers are responding to motivating factors identified by the students. Student resistance to instructional approaches or curricular areas can often be overcome by encouraging student participation. Geographic skills and history would not have been nearly as interesting had they been presented by the teacher instead of being initiated by the students in a stamp collecting center. By capturing student interest, achievement can be assured.

CLASSROOM MANAGEMENT PROCEDURES USING LEARNING CENTERS

Organizational Considerations in Implementing a Learning Center

A center has been planned to meet an instructional need, and the teacher has made the decision about where to locate the center. Density and traffic to and from the center have been considered. The next problem is how to introduce the center to the students. Let us assume that you are Midge Brady and that your students have no prior experience in the use of a learning center. You have developed a reading center to be used as a follow-up to the directed teaching period.

Begin with one center. For the purposes of this discussion, we will assume that you have three reading groups. Two of the groups are performing follow-up seatwork, and you are ready to teach a directed lesson with the third group. Using the directed teaching time, you introduce the idea of a learning center and explain the meaning of the term *learning center*, the purpose of a center, and the activity at the center.

You walk the students to the center, where the materials are displayed. Several students are asked to demonstrate the activity that has already been discussed. The students are asked for suggestions about what they can do when they have concluded the activity. The additional activities are chosen.

Next, you take the students back to the directed teaching area and discuss the method whereby the students will move to the center. When this is clarified, standards for center work are decided upon. Students discuss individual responsibilities for use of materials and cleanup as well as for verifying success. Suggestions are made for helping others if "one of our friends has a problem." Decisions are made about how to store the materials. Since this will be the first time the students have used any center, it is decided that if there is a problem, the student will raise his or her hand, and the teacher will come over to the center to give help.

When all questions have been answered, you give the signal and the students walk to the center and begin the activity. Next you will direct the reading work of group 2. At the conclusion of group 2's directed lesson, you walk over to the center and evaluate the activity with group 1. All problems are discussed, and you praise the group's work. Group 1 is assigned to another seatwork activity and you continue the reading procedures.

When you feel that group 1 has established appropriate behavior for center work (one to three days), the development of a second center is begun, and you begin the task of introducing the existing center to the next reading group. When the students in Group 2 are introduced to the center, directed reading time is again used, and they begin work at the center during their follow-up activity period.

The third reading group is introduced to the original center just as soon as the second group is secure. The same introductory system is used.

When the students become adept at using the centers approach, the new center is introduced at the *end* of the directed reading time instead of using the entire directed reading time for the introduction.

TEACHING HINT

Summary of Introductory Steps for a Learning Center

1. Explain the meaning and purpose of a center.
2. Explain the purpose and activity of the planned center.
3. Walk the students to the center and have them demonstrate the activity; decide upon a supplemental activity, if needed.
4. Move back to the directed reading area and:
   a. Discuss standards for moving to center.
   b. Discuss standards for using the center.
   c. Clarify how students can obtain teacher help, if needed.
5. The students practice "moving" behavior and go to work at the center.
6. At the end of the work period the teacher evaluates the work done at the center.
7. When the students are working effectively using the center's approach, a new center is established and another group is introduced to the original center.

The centers approach can begin in any subject area. The teacher will need to decide whether or not to introduce more than one center at a time. Upper grade and middle school students certainly could begin several centers at the same time. The decision depends on the prior experiences of the students, their behavior, and their sophistication.

EVALUATION

Monitoring Student Progress

Both social and academic progress need to be monitored in learning centers. The purpose of the centers approach is to meet students' individual needs, and so learning must be evaluated in terms of individual progress. Students should not be compared to each other. Was a given student successful in writing a story about dinosaurs? How do you know? If the student was not successful, why not? Individual educational programming requires answers to these questions. To facilitate student self-evaluation of academic tasks the following techniques can be used:

1. For activities that require matching, the answer can appear on the back of the card. Wheel activities can contain the correct response on the back. See the center in Figure 7.11.

2. Correct responses can be written in a small booklet on the learning center table, and students can use the booklet when they have completed their work.

3. The small chart rack noted in the center in Figure 7.12 can hold the correct task responses for students to self-check their work.

4. For primary number activities, if students are to put together number, label, and manipulative objects (1, one, *), all three can be drawn on an answer sheet (note the center in Figure 7.16). Or if students are arranging number families on a flannel board, there can be a special chart on a small chart rack with the appropriate families drawn so that students can verify their own work.

5. Simple inspection of some activities, such as building a magnet or fitting a puzzle, will provide instant feedback for students. Some commercially prepared materials contain interlocking pieces so that students know immediately if they have inserted the proper letters or words.

Accomplishment Versus Closure (No Wrong Answers)

Success needs to be individually assessed when the goal is to produce a product, such as a story, a map, data related to a given hypothesis, art project, craft object, or individual or group creation. Observation of the work assignment and a private conference with the individual student or the group should determine whether or not the actual accomplishment was positive.

In the center in Figure 7.10, the teacher must decide if the problem is conceptual (problem of meanings), a problem with decoding (dead end), manipulative (inability to reproduce the picture), or another problem. Careful observation of the student at work and a conference with the student will probably be necessary to determine the nature of the student's problem or reason for failure.

In the center in Figures 7.14 and 7.15, if a student is unable to arrange the pictures in order of the polliwog's developmental stages, the teacher will need to determine if the student is having a reading problem, conceptual problem, or memory problem. Because the center is not dependent on reading skills (the bucket contains polliwogs at all stages of development), the problem may be that the student does not understand words like "first," "second," and "last." Observation of the student at work and a conference will be necessary to find out the cause of failure.

Student diaries, logs, and notebooks can be used to determine the appropriateness of a center and the students' achievement at the center. When students are gathering data for a report, their notes should verify effort, ability, and progress. Similarly, when students have a booklet for pictures or for storywriting, the results can be quickly observed by the teacher.

Keeping records of social progress can be performed by both the students and the teacher. A number of the checklists in Chapter 4 are appropriate for this task. Students can be asked to self-evaluate their learning center work habits (Tables 7.1–7.4).

Monitoring Social Progress

Thus far the centers have been observed from the perspective of individual academic progress, but centers are also used to encourage small-group work, and center effectiveness must be considered observing whole-class behavior. Student behavior walking to the classroom centers, attending to the given tasks, working with and alongside others, completing tasks and performing cleanup details all contribute to the

Table 7.1. Example of a Student Log

Center	Date
Math	October 1, 1990

Comments: I worked on the base-5 exercises but I didn't finish. I'm not sure I always understand. Maybe I need help.

Table 7.2. Student Contract

Today I Will Perform the Following Tasks:

1. Work Problems 5–11
2. Read Chapter 7 of the...
3.
4.
5.
6.

I Did Better Today	YES	NO
Tomorrow I Will...		

Table 7.3. Self-Evaluation, Work Habits

Did I...

1. Enjoy working at the _____ center?
2. Need assistance?
3. Help others?
4. Work quietly?
5. Begin work immediately?
6. Get along well with others at the center?
7. Complete my own work?
8. Do my very best work?
9. Clean up my work?

Table 7.4. Self-Evaluation, Learning

1. I did not understand that...
2. I learned that...
3. I need help with...
4. I want to learn about...
5. I enjoyed learning about...
6. I want to work with...
7. I prefer to work alone because...
8. Tomorrow I am going to...

social growth of each student. The center approach encourages self-responsibility. Students learn to assist others at the center. Prudent help as well as restraint require mature judgment; sometimes teachers need to hold their tongues and exercise a wait-and-see attitude or students do not learn when to offer assistance and when to let a peer work it out alone. To summarize monitoring and record-keeping tasks, teachers should plan the following procedures:

1. A folder or a box should be provided at each center for completed work and incomplete work.
2. When specific responses are required, there should be a system for verifying correct answers.
3. When tasks are open ended, teacher observation and individual or group conferences should be planned.
4. Planned tasks should not be too easy or too difficult.
5. Checklists can be used for student self-evaluation and for teacher evaluation.
6. A planned system to monitor center use and student progress should be developed.

Anticipating Problems

LEARNER ACCOUNTABILITY.   The concept of being accountable means that at any given time students should know what they are expected to be doing and what (within reason) their expected level of performance should be. A typical problem in classrooms arises as a consequence of forgetfulness and poor listening habits. Frequently students cannot remember where they are supposed to be working. The problem occurs particularly if teachers adhere to the concept of flexible grouping and the student's work group changes too frequently for teacher and student to remember without going to a record book to evaluate the student's progress to date. Therefore, students and teacher need to have a system that makes everyone accountable for the expected work center assignments. There are a number of very simple charting systems that can take care of this problem.

In lower grades a large pocket assignment chart can be displayed at the front of the room (Figure 7.5). The chart names or pictures all of the work centers in the classroom. The chart should be aligned according to the number of work periods and the subject(s) of each center. For each of the designated work periods, the students' names will be displayed so that at any time, individuals can look up at the chart and find their name and walk to the appropriate work center.

Another system is to number the centers on a chart and display the number at the center. Again, work periods must be designated. Once again the students' names should be displayed next to the numbered center and at the appropriate work time.

Centers can be labeled with colors and students' names can appear next to the appropriate center. Or another system uses group names or colors (Figure 7.6). The chart can then reflect the name of the children's

Figure 7.5

CENTERS	NAMES			CENTERS	NAMES		
SCIENCE	▌▌▌	▌▌▌	▌▌	1	▌▌▌	▌▌	▌▌
MATH	▌▌▌▌	▌▌	▌▌	2	▌▌▌	▌▌	▌▌
DECODING	▌▌▌▌	▌▌▌	▌▌	3	▌▌	▌▌▌	▌▌
LIBRARY	▌▌▌	▌▌▌	▌▌	4	▌▌▌	▌▌	▌▌
	I	II	III		I	II	III
		Work Period				Work Periods	

Figure 7.6

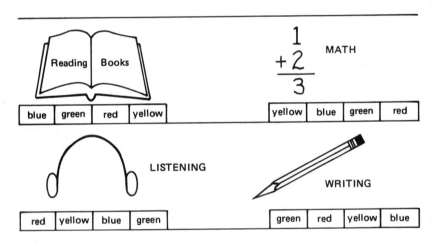

blue	green	red	yellow

$$\begin{array}{r} 1 \\ + 2 \\ \hline 3 \end{array}$$ MATH

yellow	blue	green	red

LISTENING

red	yellow	blue	green

WRITING

green	red	yellow	blue

Table 7.5. Work Period Chart by Group Name

	Time Period		
Group	(First)	(Second)	(Third)
Lynne's Group	Centers	Free choice	Directed teaching
Roberto's Group	Directed teaching	Centers	Free choice
Clancy's Group	Free choice	Directed teaching	Centers

group and the designated center instead of displaying the names of all the children in the classroom (Table 7.5).

Upper grade classrooms can use a more complicated charting system that reflects the work pattern for an entire week so that students can anticipate and plan more effectively (Table 7.6).

Table 7.6. Learning Center Chart for Entire Week

Students' Names (alphabetical)	Center Names and Days of the Week				
	M	T	W	T	F
Alan A.	1, 2, 5	6, 8, 9	Science	Research	Art
Barbara B.					
Charles C.		*(Center names can be coded.)*			
Dale D.					
Evelyn E.					
Fred F.					
Gloria G.					

Learner accountability can also be achieved by developing a system to verify that students perform work at the center (Figure 7.7). For instance some teachers have a sign-in sheet at each center so that when students go to work at the center they sign in, and the teacher can tell at a glance who has worked at every center on a given day. Another system is to use a pocket chart at the center itself and have students slip their names into the chart when they are working there. If students perform a task that requires them to do a work sheet, it is possible to have a folder at the center for completed papers. Another folder should be provided for incomplete papers.

A close look at the center in Figure 7.12 reveals that task 6 requires students to "do a guide word booklet." Students perform the required tasks in the guide word folders and then replace the folders in the wire basket. In this way the teacher can record the tasks performed by the students. Other task assignments have similar accountability measures at this center.

Figure 7.7

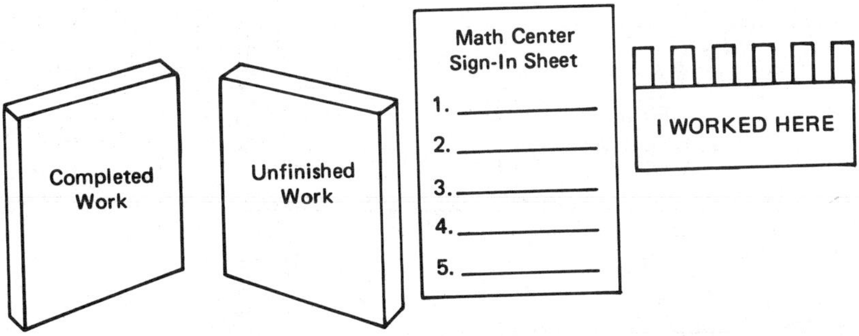

Another system is to record the task assignments at a center and have students sign their names when they complete each task (Figure 7.8).

The centers shown in Figures 7.10, 7.11, 7.15, 7.20, and 7.22 all have wire baskets available in which students can place their work papers; at these centers both finished and unfinished papers are stored in wire baskets, although the folder system would be just as effective.

ESTIMATE WORKING TIME. Differentiated work assignments at learning centers require an accurate estimate of how long it takes to complete a given task. If students at center 1 will complete their task in 10 minutes, but the directed teaching group will require 20 minutes of instruction, and all of the other centers require 20 minutes, then center 1 must have some open-ended tasks or student-developed tasks to fill up the extra time. It is extremely important to estimate students' working time for each given task requirement because the unanticipated time allotment will cause behavioral problems if students do not know what to do with themselves.

Figure 7.8

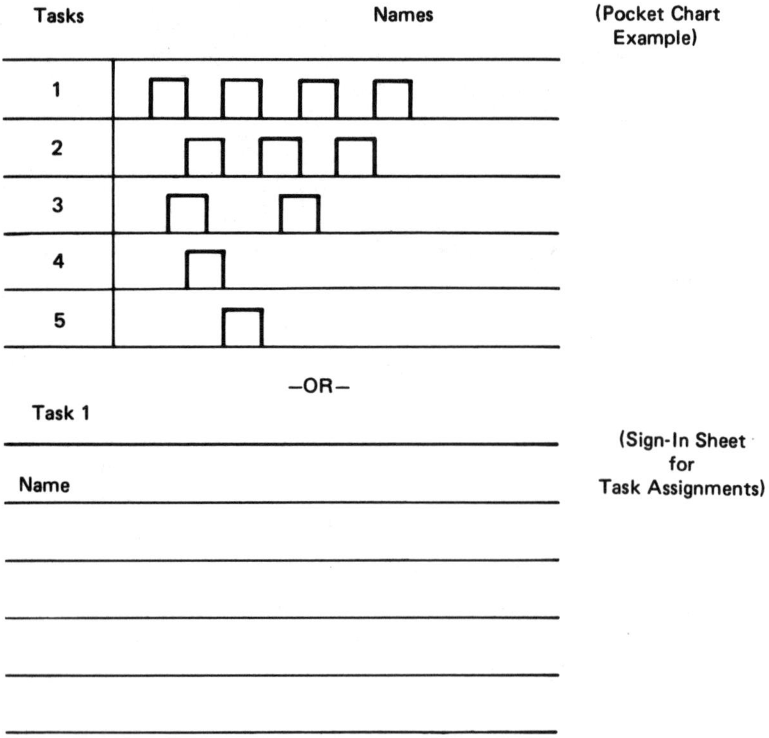

ANTICIPATE MATERIAL NEEDS. If students need pencils at the center, either tell students to carry their pencils or provide them in a pencil holder at the center. Anticipate paper, scissors, crayons, book needs as well. Anticipate the need for a waste receptacle at the center. Provide a basket for this purpose or a paper bag with its top folded back.

ANTICIPATE ABILITY LEVEL AND LEARNING MODALITY NEEDS. Both a multi-level and multimodality approach should be provided for at each center. High- and low-achievement students need a variety of instructional approaches. Text materials can be rewritten to accommodate lower reading levels, and tapes can be teacher made so that students who prefer an auditory mode can benefit from the center. The high achiever needs some open-ended assignments to extend and enrich work at the center.

TYPICAL CENTER PROBLEMS AND QUESTIONS

"If a teacher assessed students' work skills and discovered that the entire class was extremely deficient in reading and social skills, should the teacher eliminate (or not plan to use) learning centers?"

Absolutely not! The class needs motivation and encouragement. Initiate each center carefully, explain its purpose, activity involved, and develop standards for the use of the center. Evaluate center use and students' accomplishments every day. Share the instructional objective for each center with the students so that they can take part in the evaluation of growth.

"I have a student that cannot walk to a center without disturbing others and while at the center performs no work. Should this student be forbidden to use a learning center?"

Work with this student individually to improve responsibility. Set up a contract system with the student in which you and the student decide on appropriate work tasks for the work period. Evaluate at the end of the work period with the student. Have the student keep a work contract notebook. Walk with the student to the center or allow the student to walk before or after the other students. Keep the tasks simple so that the student will meet success.

"I have a student who was in a special education classroom. I have been told that the student is of average ability but cannot read and actually rejects the use of a text. What should I do?"

Plan work tasks that are conceptually the same as those performed by the other children, since the child has average ability; however, furnish resource materials that appeal to more preferred modes of learning. Use records, teacher-made tapes, pictures, and tactile experiences.

"I have a child who is disruptive at the centers. She finishes the tasks quickly and then bothers everyone else. Should I not allow this child to work with others at the center?"

Evaluate the student's work at the center. Since the student is finishing the tasks quickly, it sounds as if the tasks may be too easy. Develop some more challenging tasks for this student and see if her work habits improve. Also, have the child self-evaluate her work and find out if she is satisfied with the quality of her accomplishments (Figure 7.9).

"Should students choose where they want to work or should I assign them to centers for work?"

If there are four centers in the classroom and all four of the centers have objectives compatible with the students' needs, then students can choose where they want to work and rotate from center to center when they are ready. However, if only centers 1, 3, and 5 will meet a given group's needs, then only these centers should be used. In this case the teacher may guide the children by saying: "Only centers 1, 3, and 5 are appropriate for your needs today; choose among those three centers." If certain centers have been developed to meet multilevel needs or

Figure 7.9. Example of a Contract

I will work at these centers today: _____ (Math) _____

_____ (Science) _____

(Student identifies the centers.) _____ (Reading) _____

(Student identifies the work accomplished.)

I am satisfied with my work today because _____

_____

I am *not* satisfied with my work today because _____

_____

_____ (signature) _____

multimodality needs, then this information must be shared with the children who will benefit.

If students have alternatives in terms of choices or centers that are to be used before others are begun, then it is wise to chart this information for student use.

Students' Names	Center Assignments
Mary Sue	1, 3, and 5 or 6
Bill B.	2, 4, 7
Ron	2, 4, and 5 or 6
Lynne	1, 4, 7
George	2, 4, 7
Sylvia	1 or 3, 4, 7

Steps for Classroom Management of Learning Centers

Planning Considerations
Have you...

1. Identifiable objective(s); (purposes)?
2. Multilevel activity(ies) to accomplish the objective(s)?
3. Accumulated multimodality materials?
4. A plan for evaluation and record keeping?

Management Considerations
Have you...

1. Decided on centers' locations and traffic patterns?
2. Arranged materials to be accessible?
3. Identified each center with a name, number, or code and communicated the label to the students?
4. Communicated with students the purpose of each center?
5. Decided how many students can use each center at a given time?
6. Decided how aides or others can help (if available)?
7. Discussed with students traffic and center standards of behavior?
8. Had students demonstrate appropriate work techniques at each center?
9. Developed and communicated a system for peer assistance or other ways for students to obtain help?
10. Communicated when each center is to be used?

11. Decided and communicated whether students are to choose their working center or be assigned to them?
12. Communicated open-ended assignments to extend and enrich work for high achievers?
13. Communicated where to place work when completed?
14. Developed with students a cleanup system?

Evaluation Considerations
Have you . . .

1. Planned both individualized and group interactive centers?
2. Considered learning abilities and learning modalities?
3. Developed a system so that all know where and when they are to work at the centers?
4. Developed a learner accountability system for record-keeping purposes?
5. Developed a communication plan for learner and teacher feedback concerning successful performance and achievement?

LEARNING PACKETS

Learning packets are used in upper elementary grades, junior and senior high schools for much the same purpose(s) as learning centers. Learning packets are sometimes called learning modules or instructional packets. They are particularly useful for individualizing instruction. Each learning packet may focus on a specific skill, concept to be learned, or basic information. The major difference between a learning center and a learning packet is that the packet typically can be used at the student's desk rather than in a single study area of the classroom. Also the center may be used by a group of students, whereas the packet is usually for a single student.

Learning packets may be used in free time for extra credit; they may be used as a system for continuous progress and individualization; or they may be used as an assigned period of study much as the center is used. Often the packet is used as a laboratory assignment.

Learning packets usually consist of directions to the student and study materials. The materials may include pictures, charts, guides, maps, or whatever the student will need to perform the assignments. The packet is usually packaged in an interesting way to motivate the student. Many of the ideas for centers are appropriate for learning packets. Teacher stores often have a supply of learning packets particularly in the area of social studies. However, packets that focus on reading skills are also popular and used frequently in junior high schools in reading improvement classes.

Specifications and Procedures for Developing Learning Packets

1. Describe the activity to be performed. Explain the purpose (objective) of the module and why it is important. Remember that you are dealing with a youngster who is working alone.
2. Identify the components of the packet, assuming that it includes several items.
3. Provide step-by-step directions for performing the tasks. Remember that the packet must guide the student. If there are "use me first" materials, indicate this.
4. Include a plan for the student to evaluate how he or she is doing. There might even be a pre-test so that the student can identify how much he or she knows before beginning. If the student is to produce something, such as a report, there should be an indication of what the report should contain. If the student is working on a skill, there might be a post-test.
5. Give the student an idea about the time investment. How long should it take the student to complete the packet?

The contract identified earlier (Figure 7.9) might be used in conjunction with the learning packet. Modify the contract for older students.

Ideas for learning centers and learning packets can be found in the Appendix. Remember that learning packets may contain more than print material. Consider other visual material, audio tapes, and realia.

KEY TO CENTER PICTURES

The center in Figure 7.10 is a combination language arts and social studies center. It was designed for a first-grade classroom. Focusing first on what students will do at the center, it is apparent that each student is creating a personal "book" of environmental signs. A student goes to the center and uses the chart that identifies typical signs (wet paint, freeway, slow, danger, dead end, one way, no smoking, poison); he or she reads the word(s) and draws the appropriate sign using the pencil and paper provided. The student cuts out the drawing with the scissors and tapes it into his or her own book. Ultimately, the student will write a story about the sign. All materials are provided, and there is easy access to them. When the student completes the activity, the book is stored in the wire basket. The bulletin board and additional picture material on the table provide resource information. Objectives for the center include:

To expand comprehension skills
To increase vocabulary skills (by drawing a picture to match a label)

Figure 7.10

Figure 7.11

Figure 7.12

Figure 7.13

Figure 7.14

Figure 7.15

Figure 7.16

Figure 7.17

Figure 7.18

Figure 7.19

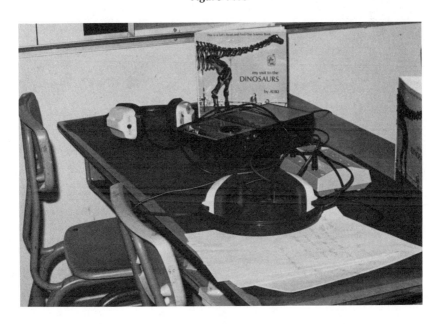

Figure 7.20

Figure 7.21

Figure 7.22

To identify social concepts that affect community life
To improve manipulative skills (drawing, cutting, taping)
To teach storywriting

The center in Figure 7.11 is a reading center where students work on decoding skills. There are a number of game materials on the table and students identify opposites (up, down; you, me), practice phonetic skills (sound-symbol relationships) using the wheel game, identify sight words by matching pictures with labels. The center is appropriate for first and second graders; it is also appropriate for students with special decoding problems.

The center in Figure 7.12 is for the middle grades. The purpose of the center is to expand library skills. The small chart holder directs the student to learn the proper use of a dictionary. Students are given eight tasks to perform. There are picture and junior edition dictionaries for the students to use, demonstrating that different ability levels have been considered by the teacher. The application of dictionary location skills is transferred to the use of the telephone directory (task 7) and a telephone directory is available for students to use.

The center in Figure 7.13, the library center, is a free-choice reading interest center. Students go to the center to choose a library book, and they sit on the beanbag cushions while they are enjoying the center. The center is appropriate for lower grades. In this particular center the students bring in their own books to share with other students, as well as using the books selected by the teacher. Similar centers for free-choice reading could be developed at any grade level.

Figures 7.14 and 7.15 are pictures of the science center. Resource information is contained in the books that are exhibited. The center also has a large magnifying glass and a bucket of polliwogs. At this center there are a number of activities for students. First, students may observe the polliwogs at different stages of development. Second, the students may read about and follow the development of polliwogs through pictures in the resource book. Third, students arrange the cutout developmental pictures in the appropriate sequence. They can evaluate their choice of sequence by referring to the resource book. Finally, there are materials with which the student can draw and paste pictures of the development of frogs and toads. This center is appropriate for primary grades.

The mathematics center in Figure 7.16 contains manipulative materials for primary children to use in developing number, symbol, and counting relationships. There are beads for counting and a plastic strawberry basket to use for counting disks; there is an abacus, a chart for resource information, and workbooks. Any youngster having a problem understanding the one-to-one relationship in math would find this manipulative center useful.

The science center in Figure 7.17 is a research center in which students study about rocks. The center encourages student observation, manipulation, and classification. At the center students can read about rocks. They are asked, "What is a fossil?" The center has progressed through different stages. In step 1 the students were asked to classify the rocks by feeling them and observing them through the magnifying glass to determine whether the rocks were hard, rough, bumpy, or whatever. Next the rocks were put in the rock tumbler and after two weeks they were again felt and observed. Again, the students were asked to classify the rocks. Although not apparent from the photograph, there are different baskets on the tables for the students to use in sorting and classifying the rocks into different groups. The students also learn the appropriate names for the rock groups.

The center shown in Figures 7.18 and 7.19 has been designed for language arts and science. The center contains pictures, books, and tape resource information. After studying at the center, the student will write a story about dinosaurs. The student can display a one-line story on the word rack on the table. Paper strips, pencils, and felt pens are available for the storywriting phase. The teacher or classroom aide assists the student as needed and checks the story after it is written. Although it cannot be seen, there is a paper bag handy so that students can throw away aborted efforts without causing a classroom mess and without sauntering across the room to a wastebasket.

The social studies center shown in Figures 7.20 and 7.21 focuses on geographic skills. The bulletin board displays maps of the world. There is an atlas and additional maps for student use. There is a small chart with task instructions. The center is designed for upper grade students who are utilizing location skills. Also, the students make maps and have their own workbooks for note taking and for performing the study skills.

The food center in Figure 7.22 should be in every classroom. The student in the picture is about to enjoy peanut butter and jelly on a cracker. Before going to the center, he had to wash his hands; he will also have to clean up to prepare the center for other students. Health rules and nutrition are emphasized, and after eating, the student will go to the other side of the center to study about the classes of food and about appropriate snack foods.

SUMMARY

The classroom environment can be consciously designed and used to promote affective and cognitive understandings. The use of learning centers and learning packets in the classroom can be an effective means to reinforce and support learning. But their use requires proactive structuring in which the teacher (1) plans the teaching concept to be reinforced, (2) organizes the physical environment for effective and safe use, (3) develops or obtains needed material resources, (4) considers alternatives and mechanical problems that invite disruptions, (5) plans and communicates rules, and (6) monitors procedures for feedback and evaluation of progress.

These kinds of tasks and prethinking for effective teaching require diagnostic techniques so that teachers can know the level of learning, decide where it ought to be, and plan how to move toward the desired target.

CASE STUDY PROBLEMS

1. Mainstreamed. Mary Sue's previous experience had been in a special education classroom. Now she was in a regular classroom. Because Mary Sue did not read at grade level, she would not be able to use the same reading centers the other students were using. Mary Sue's preferred modality is auditory. Identify a grade level for Mary Sue and design a center or a learning packet for her.

2. Nonsense. Your principal believes that learning centers and learning packets are a big waste of time. Plan to convince him or her of their educational importance.

3. Furniture Mover. Ms. Michaels likes to use a variety of activities in her classroom, but she complains that she is never very successful. Her students either will not participate in discussions or they become too noisy when they work in groups. She has invited you into her room to observe small-group work. The first thing you notice is that the students do not seem to have space for group work. They seem to sit on desk tops or they stand. Help Ms. Michaels plan a room design to facilitate both discussions and small-group work.

QUESTIONS

1. For the grade level you are teaching, design a classroom floor plan. Consider desk, storage, work table(s), traffic patterns, and demonstration area.
2. Synomorphy refers to the compatibility of learning activities and the classroom's physical environment. Why is this an important concept?
3. Describe effects of classroom environment on students' behavior.
4. What's wrong (or right) with using one seating arrangement and not having students utilize movable desks?
5. Select a subject field and design a learning center for teaching a skill or a concept. Use the instructions provided in this chapter.

CHAPTER 8

Refining Teaching Techniques
Lesson Planning, Teaching Functions

As teachers approach their third year of teaching, most become less stressful about classroom management and begin to refine their teaching skills. In this chapter we shall talk about some of those techniques that distinguish the pro from the novice.

SUCCESS IN THE CLASSROOM

Preparation for Teaching Tasks

In both the student and teacher roles we are all acquainted with what it is like to walk into a classroom unprepared. There is that feeling in the pit of the stomach and the nagging question: Can I read this material quickly in order to make sense of what is to come? Because the student role can be rather passive if one chooses not to participate, you can sometimes walk out of the classroom and say to yourself: "I pulled it off." It is considerably more difficult in the teacher role to "pull it off" if you are not well acquainted with your subject field or have not prepared your teaching strategy. Examples follow.

Student success on tasks affects their on-task behavior. Good and Brophy (1986) point out that teacher behavior is related to student achievement. Students need to be well prepared for the task they are to perform. This means that the teacher has adequately assessed what students know and what they do not know. The learning module has been broken down into components so that students will be successful and progress through the learning task. When students make errors, the teacher needs to figure out whether or not these errors are "meaningful," that is, are the errors logical and do they demonstrate being on the right track or are they illogical because of a complete misunderstanding?

Along with knowing whether students' errors are meaningful, the teacher needs to determine whether the errors occur because the work is too difficult and the students do not have appropriate background to accomplish the task.

If students become frustrated over learning, they will misbehave because they do not stay involved and on-task. We are talking about frustration that results from trying too hard on tasks that are beyond their capabilities, *not* the good frustration from a "quality" error.

When students lack preparation for the learning task, it is the teacher's fault. If students are pushed too fast or given tasks that confuse them or asked to apply information and skills they do not possess, the teacher has lacked judgment. This occurs because the teacher has not adequately prepared for the teaching assignment. The teacher did not avail him- or herself of information that is readily available:

> Information about the content to be taught
> Information about how the content should be taught (process of
>   instruction)
> Information about the learner (ability, characteristics, past
>   performance)

Information from these sources (content, process, and learner) allows the teacher to plan teacher behavior and learning tasks productively. If teachers fail to do this, then students are not successful and classroom management problems develop. The key to success is preparation.

Classroom Climate

In an ethnographic study of second- and fifth-grade classrooms during reading and math instruction, Tikunoff, Berliner, and Rist (1975) identified some key teacher behaviors that seemed to make a difference and promote more effective teaching and learning results. Results reported in Good and Brophy (1986) noted that teachers who made their classrooms *convivial* places to be, achieved warmth, familylike quality to classroom interaction, and good feelings between students and teacher and among students. The key point is that students reciprocated and radiated similar warmth to teacher and peers.

The convivial climate contributed to student *engagement*. Students were eager to participate and were productively involved in their learning tasks. Teachers in these classrooms encourage students both to participate in group tasks and to perform on independent work tasks. Tikunoff et al. (1975) report that the teachers demonstrated more spontaneity in their teaching, which probably infected the students and increased their task engagement.

Another aspect of the classroom climate noted in this study was student *cooperation*. The students were more willing to cooperate with each other and with the teachers. Students helped each other. Contrast this with classrooms in which teachers overly worried about classroom management forbid students to communicate with each other and offer assistance to each other!

Another difference in these classrooms was that teachers encouraged students to be *self-sufficient*, which means that the students needed to take responsibility for their own classwork. Psychologists have long noted that poor students typically blame others for their own failures. If we can help students take personal responsibility for both success and failure, we will be promoting self-confidence, self-respect, optimism, security, and status—in short, what this author calls ego-satisfying behaviors.

A final component of the classroom climate in successful teachers' classrooms was that *other adults* were encouraged to instruct students. These teachers were accepting of others and encouraged other adults to provide guidance to the students.

Teacher Attentiveness

The teacher "pro" is constantly aware of what is happening in the classroom and is attentive to instructional needs. Some researchers talk about teacher-led instruction, Good and Brophy (1986) refer to "active instruction." The concept really is one of teachers teaching what is needed, when it is needed, and being alert to the ebb and flow of student involvement. The teacher is constantly "on stage" teaching, *not* floating. If large-group teaching and group alerting are necessary, then the teacher performs whole-group teaching; if small-group teaching is appropriate, then the teacher is alert to systematic group-based activities.

Contextual Alertness

To review Thursday night homework on Monday morning is out of context and a terrible waste of time. To direct dramatic play on Monday morning after a vacation is a classroom management headache. To expect students to rigidly adhere to skill instruction standards the day before Christmas is burying your head in the sand, ostrich style. Contextual alertness refers to using common sense and knowledge about the students you are teaching, grade level, and subject matter in relation to the situation and even the day, week, or time of year. An elementary teacher would not want to take students out on the playground on a rainy day to teach about using the sun to tell time. Context variables are extremely important in teaching. Although it is good sense to review homework each day before beginning the current lesson, it doesn't make sense when that homework is not "fresh" in students' minds.

Teachers also need to be alert to different types of students. After a playground skirmish one group of students needs to talk about it. Another group will refuse to discuss it. This often has to do with differences in social economic status (SES). To make a mistake and refuse classroom discussion to a high-SES group is to court classroom management disaster. Similarly to insist upon the discussion with the low-SES group may be painful and time consuming.

Success Rate and Teacher Judgment

Knowing when to make tasks more difficult or easier is also a matter of judgment and relates to the students you are teaching. For some students a challenge spurs them on to accomplish more, but to other students too great a challenge destroys confidence and results in off-task behavior.

Good and Brophy (1986) note that for high-SES students, questions need to be posed to challenge the students. They need to be successful about 70 percent of the time for them to feel good about themselves and be eager to respond. In contrast to this, low-SES students seem to need about an 80 percent success rate to be encouraged to participate in learning activities.

Along with success rate differences one should keep in mind that high-SES students are typically quite competitive, and so teachers need to curb this in the classroom through activities that do not challenge students independently to "show off." Low-SES students are often quite shy about responding aloud. Cooperative work tasks and group incentives, in fact, work quite well with both the low- and high-SES groups.

TEACHING HINT

When the principal walked in the room to observe the biology teacher, many of the students had their hands in the air indicating they wanted to respond to the teacher's question. But the teacher called on a student whose hand was not raised.

At the end of the period the principal asked the teacher, "Why didn't you call on one of the students who volunteered to respond?"

The teacher responded, "I know they know the answer!"

The principal spotted one of the high school "hand raisers" and said to the student, "You didn't read the chapter last night, did you?"

The student looked stunned and said, "How did you know?"

The principal smiled.

Student responded, "Does Mr. Kendall (the teacher) know?"

Principal responded: "Not yet."

Student: "Well, I guess that won't work tomorrow, will it?"

Principal smiled in agreement.

ADAPTING INSTRUCTION

Multimodality Learning

We tend to think in one dimension—print materials—but many students respond better to a multisensory array of materials and instructional activities. So instead of providing one system for response activities, successful teachers think about all the possible ways in which students could demonstrate competence in performing a specific activity. If students are to add a simple problem, surely they can demonstrate understanding by writing the answer, by laying out on the table concrete objects that exhibit the problem and the answer, by drawing the answer, or by reciting the answer. In a sixth-grade classroom a teacher provided an electrical question-and-answer board for students to evaluate their understanding of electromagnetic principles. The students were required to wire the question to the appropriate answer. If the student was right, then a small flashlight bulb would light up next to the answer. For students who preferred to write their answers, paper and pencils were provided.

But not only do response activities need to be thought about in several dimensions, so too do instructional materials. Materials for instruction may include pictures, media, magazines, games, newspapers, brochures, advertisements, sports pictures, catalogs, maps, and directories. By varying the materials, interest is motivated.

Adapting Learning Experiences for Different Ability Levels

Effective teachers differentiate instruction to accommodate students' differing ability levels. In Julie Kramer's sixth-grade classroom students read at levels ranging from 4.5 to 10.5. This is not at all unusual in a sixth-grade classroom. When subject field reading is necessary, particularly in social studies and science, Kramer needs to provide special material for her low-ability readers. To do this she will often rewrite material herself and provide a handout. When possible she will utilize a variety of materials, such as filmstrips, magazines, and lab materials.

. Sometimes Kramer groups her students heterogeneously for work and allows the students to select their work materials themselves. Students will naturally select what they can do. Her task is to provide a variety of means to achieve the same goal.

Students also differ in their ability to process information. In Chapter 6 the concept attainment model, which helps students learn to process information, was discussed. An important strategy in that teaching model is to have students share their thinking process. By doing this, students who are slow in assimilating and integrating information will learn from those students who process more efficiently and quickly.

The work of Piaget also provides us with guidelines about stage development. Some students in the classroom, particularly in the middle elementary years, may still need many concrete materials while some of their classmates may be ready for greater abstract concepts. Classroom management problems are bound to occur if teachers ignore developmental levels.

Kohlberg's moral development stages also provide guidance for classroom management. Young students may respond quite well to adult direction; these students may be extremely sensitive to obedience and punishment. But other students in the classroom may be slightly beyond that stage and require involvement in decision making; they may be more influenced by peers than adults.

Personal Characteristics and Work Habits

When talking about success rate, we considered ego-satisfying behaviors of students; it is also important to think about different personality needs and how these needs affect assertiveness. Some students are natural "seekers." They will question, search, attempt to define, analyze, and ultimately enjoy conceptualizing and evaluating. Other students are submissive and dependent. They want everything brought to them and explained. They will be quick to say, "I don't understand. Explain it to me." These students need teacher structure, patience, and support.

Some students are naturally independent. They will enjoy initiating, creating, and making decisions. But other students will be just the opposite. In classrooms we need to help the dependent student become more assertive and independent while still offering support as it is needed.

Behavior that affects school success for students includes ego-satisfying, learner-assertive, independent-oriented, and group-satisfying behaviors. Skilled teachers arrange learning interactions and thereby develop successful learning behavior. All students cannot be treated in the same way. (See Tables 8.1 and 8.2 for school success-oriented behaviors.)

LESSON PLANNING AND TEACHING FUNCTIONS

Rosenshine (1983) reviewed a number of significant studies of teachers in elementary grades, junior high school, and high school teaching basic skills (reading and mathematics). Results of the several studies indicate that there are a number of important teaching functions that affect students' achievement. Each of these functions will be briefly discussed. These teaching functions are all related to the pattern of direct instruction discussed in Chapter 6.

Daily Review

At the beginning of a skill lesson successful teachers check students' understanding of the previous day's work. This may include checking a homework assignment. Before beginning the present day's teaching,

Table 8.1. School Success-Oriented Behaviors

Ego-satisfying behaviors	Self-confidence
	Self-respect
	Optimism
	Security
	Status
Learner-assertive behaviors	Questing
	Seeking
	Searching
	Defining
	Analyzing
	Conceptualizing
	Evaluating
Independent-oriented behaviors	Initiating
	Decision making
	Individuality
	Creativity
	Dependability
Group-satisfying behaviors	Cooperation
	Rationality
	Responsibility
	Respectfulness

From Lemlech, 1977, p. 13.

the teacher verifies that students understand the prior lesson. Because skill lessons are usually hierarchical, the previous day's lesson will be prerequisite to the present day's activity.

Presentation of New Content or Skills

The next order of business is to introduce the present day's lesson. Presentations, whenever possible, should be demonstrated or modeled. The teacher may do this first and then have students model the desired performance. If more than one skill is involved, each should be presented separately, and students' understanding should be verified before progressing. If facts or ideas are to be presented, then they too should be discussed one at a time in an organized and systematic manner. When presenting new material, it is important not to distract students with side comments or stories or peripheral information. Whenever possible a variety of examples should be presented, and students can be asked to supply additional examples to demonstrate their understanding. (Review the concept attainment model in Chapter 6.) Throughout the presentation the teacher should assess students' comprehension through questions that monitor student progress.

Table 8.2. School Success-Oriented Behaviors

Emergent Behaviors	Behavioral Goals	Means to Achieve	
		Teacher Behavior	Learner Behavior
Ego-satisfying behaviors	Self-confidence Self-respect Optimism Security Status	Define class organization, structure, requirements, constraints. Provide motivation, acceptance, clarification, reinforcement, evaluative procedures. Provide appropriate learning tasks and responsibilities.	With knowledge of class organization, structure, requirements, and constraints, develop personal goals for work, companionship, leisure. Choose activities for work, play, and leisure. Choose both independent and group activities. Act as a leader and a participant.
Learner-assertive behaviors	Questing Seeking Searching Defining Analyzing Conceptualizing Evaluating	Develop challenging tasks for independent and group inquiry. Develop problem-solving skills and social conscience skills utilizing conflict situations.	Utilize vocational, research, value clarification skills in large group, small group, and independent tasks. Participate in buzz groups, dramatics, construction, exhibits, debates, interviews, panels, reporting.
Independent-oriented behaviors	Initiating Decision making Individuality Creativity Dependability	Provide time, space, materials for independent projects; environmental, creative, skill oriented.	Define goal, decide means, develop project or specific task. Participate in cartooning, crossword puzzles, cooking, modeling, sewing, reading, picture making, hobbies.
Group-satisfying behaviors	Cooperation Rationality Responsibility Respectfulness	Develop group projects and tasks: Research, conflict problems, art projects, music making, science experiments, group roles in simulations.	Participate as both a leader and group member in small-group projects, discussions, games, simulations, art and music works, experiments, choral speaking, listening activities, puppeteering, plays, service projects.

From Lemlech, 1977, p. 58.

Student Practice

After the presentation has been completed (demonstration or model), it is time for students to practice what is expected of them. This is accomplished with the teacher providing guidance. (These functions follow the sequence of Julie Kramer's direct instruction lesson discussed in Chapter 6.) The purpose of the guided practice is to ensure that students understand and can perform correctly, to develop student self-confidence in their performance, and to check student performance as they practice. *Throughout* the monitoring during this phase, the teacher asks frequent questions to prompt students. Many students are individually called upon to respond. Group responding is also desirable. The teacher provides feedback to verify correct and incorrect performance and the teacher reteaches whenever it is necessary. The practice session is continued as long as it is functionally purposeful. Repetitions lead to overlearning, which is desirable. The teacher's guide to "how much is enough" is the percentage of correct answers (correct performance). Remember that it is desirable to have a high success rate.

Feedback

For the feedback function the teacher needs to differentiate the varied student responses. (1) If a student responds or performs in a way that tells you the student is really off base and does not understand, then it is important to reteach; giving incremental hints will seldom correct the problem. However, if the error leads you to believe that a hint will help, try it! (2) If the student is correct but appears to lack conviction about his or her correctness, then verify the response and explain again to help the student feel more confident. It is also appropriate to make a response such as "good," "OK," "right," "right on." (3) If the student appears to understand but gives an inappropriate response that leads you to believe the student was thoughtless, then correct the response, but do not make a big deal of it. Finally, (4) if the student provides a correct response quickly and obviously with confidence, then go on to the next person. Provide a smile or wink but do not allow the student to "show off."

Independent Practice

Before independent practice is commenced, the teacher should have determined that students are really ready to work alone without much assistance. This means that the material has been presented and retaught, if necessary. The purpose of this stage is for students to become so accurate and quick in their performance that they almost "automatically" perform the task. However, it is important to realize that often at the beginning of the independent practice period students are unsure of themselves and need to think through each step. During reading this stage is called the seatwork period or "follow-up" period. Classroom management problems arise during this period (1) if students do not understand their task sufficiently to perform alone and (2) if teachers have not provided a means for students to obtain help, if needed. Students who are well prepared for this phase will not cause management problems. During reading instruction, as teachers change groups, it is wise to circulate briefly to monitor independent practice; scanning the class during reading instruction is also a good way to anticipate potential problems.

Review Procedures

Periodic reviews of learned skills and needed information should be performed weekly and monthly to verify students' understanding and to provide needed information for future lesson planning. The review helps students recognize the importance of what has been taught and ensures continuity and fit of new information and skills with what has been taught in the past.

TEACHING HINT

Time Use for Direct Instruction Using Basic Teaching Functions

	Reading: 1 Group	Mathematics
Daily Review:	5–8 minutes	5–8 minutes
Presentation:	10–12 minutes	8–10 minutes
Guided Practice and Feedback:	8–10 minutes	8–10 minutes
Independent Practice:	20–25 minutes	15–20 minutes

VARIATIONS ON THE THEME

Earlier in the chapter we talked about multimodality learning and differences among students. There is absolutely no reason for basic teaching functions to be performed in the same way every day without consideration of personality differences and learning styles. Research cited in Chapter 3 indicated the value of students working together. Cooperative practice, with students helping each other learn, is a viable way for students to perfect performance and learn automaticity. Co-operative learning can be an alternative to independent practice.

Oral participation can be another alternative to the solitary practice session. Oral participation should be guided by the teacher through repeated questions that are specific and narrow in scope. All students should be given the opportunity to respond.

Drill and game activities in small groups may also be used to help students develop speed and confidence in what has been taught.

Still another means for practice is achieved through the learning center and learning packet approach. At the learning center students may work alone or cooperatively with others to practice the desired skill. The learning packet is most typically an individual, programmed approach (training manual) to help students achieve mastery of a given skill.

There are also a variety of ways that review tasks can be accomplished. For example, students may be placed in charge of the review. They can develop questions to ask others. They can write summarizing statements. They can be asked to develop short quizzes. The trick is to keep students motivated and on task.

Teachers can provide time for working with individual students through utilization of these varied activities that do not require complete teacher guidance.

Other Goals and Other Means

Comprehension and application of basic skills are not the only goals that teachers are responsible for teaching. Some teaching tasks require that teachers vary the cognitive level of questions. Instructional objectives that require problem solving and creativity necessitate different teaching behaviors. Let's look at some different goals and the required teaching behaviors.

Suppose that you want your students to engage in creative writing. You would probably begin by motivating students' interest. This might be done by reading a stimulating selection to them. Let us observe Midge Brady and her primary students. She has just read to them a story about jungle animals and shown them pictures from a book by Sendak. Next she turns on the record player and asks the students if they recognize the sounds and footsteps of the animals. She has groups of students perform some rhythms imitating the animals. Then she asks them to plan a story about jungle animals incorporating the sounds they have imitated. She elicits ideas from the students. She tells the students that their stories should only be about four sentences long and that while they are writing she will help them if they need assistance.

At the end of the writing period the students work in groups of three and share their stories. Then Midge tells them that tomorrow they will get a chance to illustrate their stories. It is important to realize that the purpose of this lesson is to allow students to invent, imagine, and express. Now let's look at the teaching functions.

MOTIVATION.   Midge motivated the students by reading a story to them.

EXPLORATION.   Midge had the students explore the story through rhythms, "acting out."

PLANNING.   Midge elicited ideas about stories from the students. The ideas are shared and guide the students' thinking.

WORK PERIOD.   Students write individual stories, and teacher monitored and provided assistance when requested.

EVALUATION.   Students shared stories in groups of three and planned pictures about stories for the next day.

◆   In Julie Kramer's classroom the students see a filmstrip on space travel. Then Julie shares her objective to have students write creatively. She recalls the fine work they did on a prior occasion. She reads to the students a poem about space travel.

She engages the students in talk about the varied types of writing they could perform: short story, poem, composition. They discuss the differences in approach. She expresses confidence in their ability to do something interesting.

Students begin to work and Kramer monitors the different forms their creativity takes. She provides assistance to several students who ask her questions. Several youngsters obtain books to look at for ideas. Now and then, Kramer offers encouragement.

When most of the students have finished Kramer asks them for attention and inquires, "Who will share?" Most of the students are eager and they share their writing. Kramer encourages them and students appreciate the different styles and approaches to the assignment. She compliments the students on key tasks in writing: opening, development, and closure.

Kramer's key behaviors included:

- Motivation—filmstrip, reads poem.
- Shares objective.
- Recalls past performance which reviews creative efforts.
- Engages students in discussion about writing forms.
- Encourages student performance.
- Monitors and provides feedback during students' independent work.
- Synthesizes and integrates learning through student sharing of writing.

Once again the reader is urged to review Chapter 6 for different instructional purposes and different teaching models.

Lesson Plan Formats

There are a variety of formats for lesson plans. Some school districts have prescribed plans that you will want to follow or adapt. The purpose of the plan is to help you think through your lesson procedures. Most plans include the following: general objectives or purposes, instructional materials, procedures for motivation and development of the lesson, and evaluation or conclusion of the lesson. Some sample plans are presented to provide you with ideas for adapting your plans (Table 8.3–8.6)

Table 8.4 shows a plan that is particularly useful for secondary teachers.

Table 8.3. Lesson Plan 1

Subject:
Date:
General Objectives:
Materials:
Procedure:
   Motivation:
   Development:

   Conclusion:

Table 8.4. Lesson Plan 2

| Subject: | Grade: | Date: | Period: |

Topic:

Textbook, Other Materials:

Objectives:

Procedures

Key Questions:

Students' In-Class Assignment:

Review:

Homework:

Table 8.5. Lesson Plan 3

Subject: American History   Grade: 11   Period: 5   Date: 3/17/89

Concept: Separation of Powers

Topic: Reconstruction

Objectives: Students will explain the constitutional purpose of separation of
powers.
Students will discuss the disagreements between the Radical
Republicans and President Andrew Johnson.

Materials: Reconstruction Map of States in 5 military districts; 14th Amendment
Constitutional Rights Foundation Newsletter Vol. 3, No. 3 (Winter,
1987).

Procedure:

1. Introduction. "President Lincoln was assassinated on April 14, 1865. Vice-
President Andrew Johnson became president and began a program of
reconstruction. Johnson was sometimes called King Andy by the Radical
Republicans in Congress. We're going to read about King Andy and then
talk about it in small groups."
2. Students read "King Andy vs. the Radicals."
3. Students work in small groups with each group responsible for one question
to discuss.

Use following questions (*write on board*):

How did President Johnson's reconstruction plan differ from the plan of the
39th Congress?

Which plan do you think was better in its treatment of black people in the
South?

Why did Congress try to impeach President Johnson? Do you think the
Radicals were right in trying to impeach him? Why?

Who should have planned for reconstruction—the president? the Congress?
Why?

4. Have a whole-class discussion with each group leading the discussion for the
question they prepared.
5. Conclusion and Evaluation: Discuss:
What does the separation of powers have to do with the disagreements
between the 39th Congress and President Johnson?

Homework:
Read about reconstruction in your text and prepare to discuss:
What should have been the purpose of reconstruction?

Midge Brady's creative writing lesson plan would probably have looked like this:

Table 8.6. Lesson Plan 4

Objectives: To create individual stories; to enjoy creative writing

Materials: Story book, record player and record, writing materials

Procedure:
1. *Motivate* writing by reading a story about jungle animals.
2. Encourage students to "act out" animal rhythms and sounds.
3. Elicit ideas about stories from students.
4. Provide about 10 minutes for students to write individual stories. Monitor and provide assistance.
5. *Evaluate* by having students share stories in groups of three; have students plan pictures about stories for tomorrow.

RESEARCH AND READINGS

Schrag, Peter (1986). What the test scores really mean. *The Nation*, p. 312.
   Beginning in the late 1960s, children's scores improved on achievement tests "at a rate of roughly a grade per year as those birth cohorts aged, reaching the senior high schools in the late 1970s."
   Children born in the late 1970s are now scoring higher than children have for the last thirty years.

KEY CONCEPTS FOR LESSON PLANNING

Sequence

We have considered the concept of sequence in many different ways throughout the text. For example, when teachers consider developmental levels for selecting appropriate learning experiences there is consideration of "sequence." Beginning with concrete experiences and moving to abstract concepts is an example of developmental sequence. For young children we often talk about beginning with what is familiar before introducing unfamiliar ideas. Using the advance organizer model, we demonstrate a structure for students to facilitate assimilation of new ideas. Here again, this is an example of sequencing. Social studies programs are sequenced to begin with the child's family, teach about the community, the city, the state, the nation, and the world.

   In professional education we talk about the sequence of a lesson and the sequencing of content for instruction. Both are important for teaching and impact upon classroom management. When content has not been carefully sequenced, students will be confused and frustrated. This of course can lead to management problems. When teachers skip key elements of a lesson, this too can cause a classroom problem. For example, if students fail to understand the purpose of a lesson and are asked to perform in ways that are "out of sequence"—performing independent practice before they understand the learning task—they tend to rebel. Sequencing content and methodology are important professional responsibilities.

Continuity

This concept has to do with the linkage between what was taught on Friday and what will be taught on Monday. Each learning experience should be based on what happened in the past and what ought to happen in the future. Learning experiences are dependent on preceding experiences and prerequisite for subsequent efforts. Learning is developmental. Experiences that have continuity allow the student to build on prior skills and produce in more complex ways. Continuous skill development is dependent on the vertical reiteration of skills in the curriculum. But skill development is not the only area of the curriculum dependent on continuity of planning.

Student behavior is also dependent on teachers at a school emphasizing similar behaviors from year to year and room to room. There needs to be continuity related to school standards and school and teacher expectations.

Students who have gone through several years of never working in small groups will have poor group process skills. This occurs because of a lack of continuity. Developmental experiences are lacking. Similarly in subject fields there can be disregard for needed experiences that are developmental. Students who are never asked to create in writing, certainly will have difficulty. If subjects such as social studies are not taught in the elementary grades, students will miss key concepts and ideas necessary for understanding social studies in junior high school.

Integration

This concept emphasizes the application of knowledge and skills from one subject to another. For example, mathematics skills may be related to the understanding of time periods in social science. Or graph reading is related to social studies when students need to read graphs to understand unemployment trends. When an elementary teacher teaches about key body functions, nutrition, and exercise, the teacher is integrating science, health, and physical education. This kind of teaching is logical, efficient, and maximizes the opportunities for students to learn.

Where continuity has to do with the vertical reiteration of key concepts in the curriculum, integration has to do with the horizontal relation of curriculum experiences across subject fields.

Curriculum and lesson planning affect classroom management in very important ways. If teachers neglect to integrate subject fields, they are losing important instructional time that should be used for the application of knowledge and skills in a variety of contexts. When teachers fail to plan for sequence and continuity, confusion is often the consequence; when students are confused, they typically cause management problems.

ACHIEVEMENT CONTROVERSY AFFECTS INSTRUCTION

"Trends in Educational Achievement," a report from the Congressional Budget Office (1986), indicates that achievement tests have been generally ignored by both the educational community and the public. Attention has been geared to looking at SAT scores and not how students perform on their yearly achievement tests. This report, based on data from major elementary and secondary testing programs across the nation, indicates that scholastic performance has drastically improved, and the recent emphasis on "basics" may have nothing to do with the trend.

The report makes it clear that neither academic relativism nor parental permissiveness caused the decline in SAT scores. Instead, the cause of lower SAT scores (Schrag, 1986) *may* be demographic, related to the baby-boom and the large family syndrome. School reforms and the back-to-basics movement did not reverse the decline in SAT scores. Instead, higher scores on the achievement tests may really be the consequence of smaller families and a larger age span between siblings.

But the real impact of this report is the fear that the improvement that occurred in elementary grades will never reach the high school and SATs because thinking skills are taught so rarely in the schools today. Rote learning, drill, and drill-type homework predominate and do not prepare students for sophisticated thinking. Although the pattern of direct instruction is good for teaching basic skills and good for classroom management, it is not sufficient or effective for teaching students to inquire and problem solve.

SUMMARY

In planning instruction teachers need information about the content to be taught, instructional processes for teaching content, and information about the learners' ability, personal characteristics, and work habits.

Ethnographic research indicated the importance of the classroom as a convivial place to be. The classroom climate contributes to students' being self-sufficient and responsible. This research also cited the importance of "active instruction" and the need for teachers to be alert to context variables related to the situation, time, and calendar.

Six teaching functions were discussed in relation to the pattern of direct instruction. These functions have been found to relate to higher achievement by students in the basic skills. Additional teaching functions were discussed related to higher cognitive and affective goals.

The concepts of sequence, continuity, and integration are key concepts in lesson planning. Effective use of these concepts facilitates classroom management and affects the academic program.

A new controversy concerning higher test scores in the elementary program indicated that family planning rather than educational reforms and a return to the basics may be contributing to higher achievement.

CASE STUDY PROBLEMS

1. Feedback.   Teacher Mary Brown is teaching reading to her fifth graders. She is questioning the students after silent reading to determine their understanding of events in the story.

TEACHER: Why was Penelope angry at Boris? Tom.
TOM: Because Boris was thinking about his football game?
TEACHER: Absolutely not. Jennie.
JENNIE: I think it was because Boris hadn't helped Penelope do the dishes.
TEACHER: Very good, Jennie. Now who knows why Caldwell was barking? William.
WILLIAM: Well, Caldwell was sympathetic to Boris, and he was barking at Penelope because she hit Boris.
TEACHER: William, I don't think you even read the passage. What a silly idea. Jean, you answer.
JEAN: I think Caldwell heard something, and he's afraid.
TEACHER: Hmm, Jerry, you tell us.

Critique the teacher's responses to students and compare Mary Brown and Bill Symes in the following incident.

Bill Symes is teaching English Composition at a junior high school. The students have just finished reading a paragraph written on the chalkboard. Their task is to critique punctuation.

SYMES: What's right or wrong with the first sentence? Sheila, help us.

SHEILA: I don't see anything wrong with it, Mr. Symes, it's OK.

SYMES: Does everyone agree? [There's a chorus of noooo.] William.

WILLIAM: An apostrophe is missing where it says, "students diverse problems."

SYMES: Yes, Sheila, what confused you?

SHEILA: I guess it was the word "diverse" in between "students" and "problems."

SYMES: OK, good observation. Is there anything else wrong?
[No responses] OK, let's go on. . . . Jim?

JIM: I didn't raise my hand.

SYMES: I know you didn't. [Other students smile.] Jean, can you help us with the second sentence?

JEAN: Well, there's a capital missing and there needs to be an exclamation mark at the end.

SYMES: Why do you think so?

JEAN: It just seems to need one. It feels right.

SYMES: Bill? What do you think; what bothers Jean about the sentence?

Why did Symes call on Jim? How are these two episodes alike? How are they different?

QUESTIONS

1. Responses by students to teachers' questions provide an indication of students' understanding. Discuss what the various responses mean and the importance of successful responses.
2. The teaching functions discussed in this chapter are utilized in the direct instruction model; what are the strengths and weaknesses of this method of instruction? Identify when this model is appropriate for use.
3. If several students are raising their hand indicating that they want to respond to a question, which one will you select? Why?
4. Describe the differences in teaching functions in the creative writing lessons as compared to the direct instruction model. Why are the differences important?
5. In the grade level you are teaching, provide an example of sequence, continuity, and integration.

CHAPTER 9

The Missing Link
Parent-Teacher Relations

CHAPTER HIGHLIGHTS

Communicating with parents

Sharing education records

Writing notes to parents

Back-to-school night

Requesting parent help

Sending papers home

Parent conferences

Student-teacher-parent conferences

COMMUNICATION

Some parents hesitate to participate in school affairs because they recall unpleasant experiences from their own youth. Conflict as a consequence of differing cultural priorities also affects parents' motivation to participate in school affairs and articulate personal goals. Sometimes a teacher's note elicits the following reaction:

> "Harry, we have a note from Billy's teacher. She wants us to come to school for a conference. Billy has misbehaved again."
>
> "I went last time, Mabel. It's a big waste of time. There's nothing the teacher can tell us about Billy that we don't already know. Tell her we can't make it."

Frequently parents are unwilling to attend school conferences because of preconceived ideas about the purposes of the conference or their feelings about teachers and schools. Teachers have commonly been characterized as little old men and women in sneakers and as ivory tower dwellers or historically stereotyped as schoolmarms and masters. Recent characterizations have portrayed teachers as unfeeling, militant unionists. When teachers are wearing their professional hats, they too are subject to stereotyped thinking and often characterize parents as hostile, apathetic, and unwitting humans.

Meetings between parents and teachers seem to occur most often during moments of stress; for this reason relations between parents and teachers are often impersonal and strained. To alleviate tense and nonproductive interactions, school districts have attempted to involve parents in the school program by forming parent advisory committees. Working together, sharing advice and decision making, and trading banter, teachers and parents begin to develop mutual respect and warmth. Interaction on these committees has facilitated healthy, friendly relationships as parents discover that teachers have families, responsibilities away from school, and problems similar to their own.

But these committees do not go far enough. The majority of both parents and teachers are not committee members, and the benefits do not accrue to all members of the school community. A teacher's ability to control environmental experiences during the school day is often hampered by the student's out-of-class and after-school experiences. The homework reinforcement assignment can be spoiled by misinterpretation of it or by Dad's "system" versus teacher's system, with the student's loyalties severely tested. Planned intervention strategies and accountability measures may go down the drain because teachers and parents do not communicate.

To fulfill instructional role tasks and to be an effective model of desirable behavior, the teacher's professional responsibilities must be broadly interpreted to include seeking out others, and guiding and coordinating the efforts of others, to achieve the student's best interests. Bronfenbrenner (1970, p. 154) considered the teacher's role potential for social action and theorized that teachers must "organize, develop, and coordinate the activities of other appropriate models and reinforcing agents both within the classroom and outside." To do this, of course, means that teachers exercise leadership capacities in organizing group and team work within the classroom and involve others in tasks to assist students in the home and the community.

Teacher Initiative

Breaking down the barriers that impede effective communication involves initiative on the part of teachers to solicit parent involvement. The American school system is responsible to the public. It is the public that defines educational goals and the professional that implements policy. In too many communities there is widespread dissatisfaction with students' achievement; yet rarely do parents take the responsibility to inquire about the educational program or take part in defining what kind of program they want for their own children (Fantini, 1975). In these communities the feeling seems to be that the schools belong to the teachers when in fact they belong to us all. The Gallup Poll of the Public's Attitudes toward the Public Schools (1986) revealed the biggest problems confronting the public schools as perceived by parents:

1. Lack of discipline
2. Use of drugs
3. Poor curriculum/poor standards
4. Lack of proper financial support
5. Difficulty getting good teachers
6. Teachers' lack of interest
7. Parents' lack of interest
8. Integration/busing
9. Pupils' lack of interest/truancy

Asked to grade their local schools, national totals indicated that 11 percent of the respondents graded their local schools A, 30 percent graded the schools B, 28 percent C, and 11 percent D.

Parents were asked to rate schools on success characteristics. Parents whose oldest child is in elementary school are more likely to rate their school safe and orderly than parents whose oldest child is in high school.

Concerning the goals of education, parents' reasons for desiring education for their children included (in descending order):

Job opportunities
Preparation for life
Education as a necessity of life
More knowledge
Financial security/economic stability
To get a better paying job
To become better citizens
For a successful life
To learn how to get along with people
For better/easier life than parents
Specialized training profession
Teach people to think/understand
To contribute to society
Personal development/self-realization

To become self-sufficient (independence)
To learn basic skills/fundamental learning skills

Parents need to know what teachers are trying to accomplish and how they are going about it; teachers need to know what is going on in the home and community that affects the student's growth and development. If parents are dissatisfied with the educational program or if teachers are dissatisfied with parental cooperation, quality education is impossible. Communication is a process of talking *with* people and involves listening as well as speaking. The Gallup poll clearly indicates that the public is concerned about quality education, but it appears that teachers must take the initiative to elicit parental involvement in the schools.

DEVELOPING A PARENT-TEACHER PARTNERSHIP

School-Parent Relations

Prior to the initiation of steps to involve parents in school and class-rooms, it is important to examine factors that affect relationships between teachers and parents. Although most successful teachers and administrators do not feel that it is essential for teachers to live within the school community, knowledge of and familiarity with the community are crucial.

One of the best ways to become knowledgeable about the community is to use neighborhood services. For instance, if there is a local cleaners, bring your clothes in for cleaning and chat with the proprietor. Buy your gas in the school neighborhood and while you teach, have your car serviced. Make it a practice to stop at the market and buy food items; talk with the clerks and the store manager. Shop at the community bakery, fresh fish market, and drug store. In each of these places identify yourself as a teacher at the local school. Ask the store owners and employees if they have children attending the school. Find out if they ever come to visit. If they do not, find out why. When teachers use community services and resources, they demonstrate respect for the community, and the community develops respect for the teacher.

In order to appreciate the conflict sometimes felt by parents about school, pretend that you are a visitor and even someone who does not speak perfect school English, rather than a teacher. Are there *physical barriers* such as guards or locked gates that inhibit parental passage into the school? As a visitor how do these restraints make you feel? If you do not know your way around the school, how will you find the room that you want? Is the school office easily recognized?

Are there *social barriers* that will make visitors feel ill at ease? In the office do the school clerks leave their desks and greet you promptly? Do the clerks speak a language other than English? If your school English is not perfect, will you be embarrassed? If you are dressed in working person's garb, will you feel out of place?

School-parent relations are also constrained by the working hours of parents. Working mothers and fathers who are hourly employees can rarely take time to attend school functions or to participate in school conferences. Even when these affairs occur during the evening hours, child-care problems, meal planning, and physical well being may interfere. Middle-class professional parents may have client appointments that prevent their attendance at unexpected school conferences or meetings.

Teachers' assumptions about the socialization process may also interfere with good school-home relations. For instance, primary teachers may expect young students to know their ABCs, how to write their names, and perform other simple cognitive tasks. Teachers expect students to be able to sit still and "behave" *and* be interested in whatever the teacher presents. When students do not exhibit these assumed home socialization tasks, teachers are often disappointed. Teachers' disappointment may be communicated to children, then to the parents via the students; thereby a chain of misunderstanding begins.

Fuchs (1969) provided an apt example of an all too frequent case of school-parent cultural conflict. An unremorseful Mexican boy is banished from the classroom for swearing. To gain readmittance his mother is required to come to school to confer with the teacher. At the conference the mother appears to accept her son's swearing without concern. The result is conflict between a super-sensitive teacher, a machismo-oriented boy, and a parent.

In summary, school-parent relations are affected by preconceived notions of both teachers and parents about each other, teachers' understanding and knowledge about the community, physical and social barriers, and assumptions about the socialization process that interfere with the acceptance of responsibility for helping the child.

When school-home relations are nonexistent or poor, the first step is to get acquainted and to communicate an "I care" attitude. The second step is the acceptance of responsibility for the development of an appropriate individual educational plan for each student. The plan must be communicated to the parents so that they may become involved partners in the process. Evaluation should be continuous with communication between parent, teacher, and student.

IMPROVING COMMUNICATION

Sharing Educational Records

In November 1974 parents gained the right to view their children's educational records. The Buckley Amendment required that parents be allowed access to all educational records maintained by a school district that pertain to their child. School districts must establish a policy that explains how parents may go about seeing their child's educational records. School districts must also inform parents of their rights under the amendment, about district policy concerning school records, and where that policy can be read. Parental permission must be sought before the school district can identify the student to others outside of professional personnel within the district. Certain aspects of the law are particularly important.

Two key terms in the law are *educational record* and the word *maintained*. An educational record is any record—handwritten, film, tape, and so on—that is kept by an educational agency and that is related to a specific student. A maintained record is one that is in the possession of a school employee for the purpose of sharing with another school district employee. A teacher who keeps notes about a student but does not share them with anyone is not maintaining an educational record on that child, and therefore is under no obligation to share those notes with parents.

An example of the implementation of the law follows: Suppose a research study were to be proposed in a particular classroom or for a specific group of children. Parental permission would have to be sought, if "personally identifiable information" were to be given to the researchers. This information is defined as any of the following: (1) name of child or parents or other family member, (2) address, (3) social security number or any other identifying number, and (4) personal characteristics that would enable the student to be identified by others. If a student cannot be identified by the information disclosed, then parental permission is not necessary. Figure 9.1 demonstrates the type of letter that should be sent to parents if students' records are to be used.

If parents do not read English, then the letter must be sent in the primary language of the family. The letter should provide information to parents about the purpose of the project, the name of the test(s) involved, how test information will be used, where and when the research proposal may be read.

Since parents have the right to see their children's records, school-home relations can be improved when teachers assume the responsibility to share and interpret the records to parents. For instance, teachers

Figure 9.1

June 5, 1990

Dear Mr. and Mrs. Parent:

Your (daughter, son) along with other members of (his, her) class has been asked to participate in a research project. The purpose of the project is to learn more about ways in which students' learning styles differ.

To take part in the project, members of the class will be tested using the _____ of the _____. Results of the test will be available for you to see.

The research project proposal is on file in our school office, and you are invited to read it.

Students' names will not be used; however, birthdates and achievement records are needed by the researchers.

In order to participate in the project, parents' permission is requested. Please indicate your approval or disapproval.

Sincerely,
T. Teacher

. . . .

_____ (may, may not) participate in the project.

Date	Parent Signature

can explain what tests have been administered, what the tests measure, how test results are used, the student's scores, and what they mean. If the child has had a psychological test, this should be shared along with the counselor's notations and teachers' notations. If parents feel that the information contained in the school record is incorrect, misleading, or harmful, they have the right to have their child's records amended, corrected, or expunged. Regulations by the U.S. Department of Education specify the means whereby parents can protest a school record if they feel that their child's privacy has been violated.

Notes to Parents

A personal note to parents provides an excellent opportunity to develop a positive relationship with the home. Teachers can use a note to request assistance, suggest a conference, inform parents about progress, offer suggestions, or discuss future plans. Too often in the past notes to parents were written only to inform parents about a discipline problem or failure in a curriculum area. Figures 9.2–9.4 should provide some ideas for school-home communication. The note in Figure 9.2 was intended as an initial welcoming message to parents. Some teachers like to include information about their own professional specialties, personal

THE MISSING LINK **229**

Figure 9.2. Welcome Letter

Date _____

Dear Mr. and Mrs. _____:

I am (Jan's) teacher. I am very pleased to be working with (her) this semester. I am hoping to get acquainted with you because I have found in past years that children perform better when their parents and teacher work cooperatively together.

At different times during the semester I will write you a note about our activities and (Jan's) progress. I will also plan some conference time so that we can meet privately.

Next Thursday night is a special back-to-school night for parents. At that time I will be talking to all of the parents in my classroom about our activities this semester. I do hope that you will be able to attend.

You are welcome to come and visit the classroom at any time, and I want you to know that I am looking forward to meeting with you.

Sincerely,
T. Teacher

Figure 9.3. Progress Notes

Date _____

Dear Mr. and Mrs. _____:

I am very pleased with Roy's progress. We have been doing small group work in social studies. Roy's group has been working on a time line. He has been a cooperative group member. He has accepted responsibility and he has helped other students. Please ask him about the research that he has been doing.

Sincerely,
T. Teacher

Figure 9.4

Date _____

Dear Mr. and Mrs. _____:

We are working on decoding skills in reading. Henry has been doing extremely well identifying the beginning sounds and letters of familiar pictures. During the next couple of days we will continue to select pictures with key sounds and select letters representing beginning sounds. If you would like to help Henry, you may have him read letter names such as Mm, Pp, Dd, Tt.

Sincerely,
T. Teacher

---

interests, and personal information about themselves. All are appropriate and of interest to parents and children.

Students should be told the purpose of any note that they are asked to carry home to parents. The note should be written in a manner that students can understand and read. If students are too young, then the note should be read to them by the teacher before they are asked to deliver it. Children's fears should be alleviated; otherwise the note is bound to end up in a wastebasket. If a note is really personal, then it should be mailed rather than delivered by the student.

Students should also be informed about the teacher's hidden agenda. If the real purpose of the note is to involve parents in classroom life, students can help if they understand the importance of parent-teacher cooperation. Students can also be asked to obtain a return message for the teacher. Some teachers ask students to record their parents' response or some notes may have a tear-off for parents to sign. Parents often appreciate being able to dictate their response to their child rather than signing a form letter.

In the note in Figure 9.5 the teacher is still writing a "progress" note but communicating that there is a classroom problem requiring some assistance. The teacher is subtly suggesting that the parents visit and observe. Another letter idea (Figure 9.6) that communicates a classroom problem could explain how the teacher is handling the problem. The teacher let the parents know that Jed is restless and does not pay attention. The teacher also suggested a conference and asked the parent to take the initiative to confirm it. It is important to remember that parents need encouragement as much as students. Even though growth may be infinitesimal, if it can be recognized as growth, it may be worthwhile to brag about it (Figure 9.7).

The note in Figure 9.8 is a no-nonsense request for a parent conference.

Notes to parents need not be long. They should focus on specifics, such as the instructional approach (what the teacher will do/is doing to help the student), parental assistance (suggest techniques or suggest a

---

Figure 9.5

Date _____

Dear Mr. and Mrs. _____:

After a long summer vacation at home, it is always difficult for students to settle down to classroom routines. We are working on our listening skills and following directions. I would appreciate it if you could spend some time helping (Sylvia). It often helps children when we listen very carefully to what they are saying and then follow up their conversation by asking them a question about it. In class we need to remind students that only one person can speak at a time. Please encourage (Sylvia) to talk at home and let her see how carefully you listen to her. Please feel free to visit our classroom at any time.

Sincerely,
T. Teacher

Figure 9.6

Date _____

Dear Mr. and Mrs. _____: .

Reading is extremely difficult for some children because it requires longer periods of attention and sitting still. I have noticed that Jed has some difficulty remembering some of the words that he has been taught and that he does not seem to enjoy reading. I am using the following techniques to help him: flash cards to review words, word games, listening to stories at the listening post, and reading with a partner.

If you would call the school office for an appointment, I would be happy to meet with you and suggest some home techniques to assist Jed.

Sincerely,
T. Teacher

Figure 9.7. Progress Note

Date _____

Dear Mr. and Mrs. _____:

I am pleased to let you know that Jed is making real progress in the fourth grade. Yesterday he voluntarily assisted another student during mathematics. He is learning to evaluate his own work and correct his own behavior. I am very pleased and I know that you will be too.

Sincerely,
T. Teacher

Figure 9.8. Conference Request

Date _____

Dear Mr. and Mrs. _____:

Lately Jan has been having a classroom problem that requires our assistance. She has not been finishing her classroom assignments and does not take responsibility during her group assignments. She appears to have difficulty working with others. I know that Jan has home responsibilities, too. I am trying to encourage Jan to finish the tasks that she begins. Will you do the same at home? I would like to tell you about some other ways to help Jan. I am able to meet with you on _____ at _____. If this is not convenient, please call the school office _____ for another appointment.

Sincerely,
T. Teacher

I am able to attend. _____ I will call for another appointment _____.

conference), conference (suggest day and time or suggest a parent call the office to confirm an appointment), student progress (reinforce positive progress by praising child to parent), classroom activities (just a report to establish contact between school and home). Notes should be carefully written and edited to ensure that there are no spelling or sentence errors. Read your note aloud to yourself before sending it or have the note read by a colleague. When teachers make errors, the whole community knows about it!

Telephone Conversations

Some teachers prefer to talk to parents on the telephone rather than writing a note. It is possible to call twenty to thirty parents in about three hours, and parental reaction is usually quite positive. Telephone conversations should be limited to positive contacts versus reporting problems. Because telltale nonverbal reactions cannot be used on the telephone, it is wise to talk about classroom activities and ways in which children have demonstrated growth; a negative comment by the teacher may cause a child to be punished unnecessarily as a consequence of a misunderstood comment.

The value of telephone communication is that it frequently saves the teacher's time and provides instant appreciation from parents because the teacher cared enough to call. Students normally feel flattered. Bilingual teachers really reap appreciation from their non-English-speaking parents when they telephone and speak to parents in the primary language of the home.

Back-to-School Night

This is often the first occasion of the school year for parent-teacher communication. Parents will be observing the room environment and "looking the teacher over." Students have already described their teacher to their parents, and the parents will be verifying the child's observation. One of the first preparatory tasks is to invite parents to visit and learn about the school program. A welcoming letter similar to the one in Figure 9.2 may be used or a special letter of invitation may be issued (Figure 9.9).

Some teachers make the mistake of talking to parents at back-to-school night in the same manner they talk to their students. There is nothing wrong with talking to students in an adult fashion, but for those individuals who use a special style for talking to children, it should be modified for an adult audience. Parents want to be assured that their child is supervised by an adult, and nothing turns them off faster than histrionics or "teacher as buddy" approach.

Figure 9.9. Back-to-School Night

Date _____

Dear Mr. and Mrs. _____:

On Tuesday, February 12, 1990, at 7:30 P.M. we will be having our annual back-to-school night for parents. At that time I will discuss our plans for the semester, display our textbooks and other learning materials, and answer questions about our program. I am really looking forward to meeting you and getting acquainted.

Sincerely,
T. Teacher

I will be able to attend _____.
I cannot attend, but I will call the office to make an appointment with you for a conference _____.

At the meeting parents should be seated as comfortably as possible, and the teacher should begin immediately with an overview of the curriculum for the school year. Goals, plans, and the teacher's philosophy should be explained simply. The teacher's instructional approach and priorities should also be discussed. Some typical problems of children at this grade level can be mentioned briefly, but generally the parents are more familiar with their children's foibles than the teacher.

If special materials or an innovative program is to be tried, this should be explained carefully to the parents. The new program should be contrasted with the old, and the explanation should include why it has been chosen, teacher expectations, the philosophy of the program, and expectations for progress. It is pointless to introduce a new curriculum and then say, "I haven't read the teacher's manual yet so I can't tell you about it tonight, but we are very excited about it."

Parents want to know what steps the teacher will take if a student does not make expected progress. This is a good time to tell parents your system for communication. Will you call? Write? Tell the child? Will student work samples be sent home? What ought parents to look for on the work samples? Are parents expected to visit? How can parents help students?

The environment of the classroom should be explained to parents. If there are special learning centers in the classroom, discuss their purposes and when and how they are used. If children's work is displayed, include work samples of all children. If there are resource and environment needs in the classroom, talk briefly about them. Parents may be motivated to help or at least to vote positively to help schools obtain needed improvements or resources.

If parental assistance for tutoring or other classroom activities will be needed, this is a good time to mention it. Perhaps a volunteer list could be established with one of the parents coordinating it.

If students are absent for an extended period of time (three days? five days? more?), should parents contact the school? Will you send work home?

Try to focus the discussion time to questions about the school program rather than a discussion about an individual child's personal problems. If a parent persists in asking personal questions, suggest a private conversation where full attention can be directed to the child's specific case. It is wise to have a conference request sheet handy for parents to write down their names and telephone numbers.

Teachers often have parents sign a sheet upon entering the classroom for a back-to-school night. If this is done, follow it up with a thank-you note for attendance or a sorry you couldn't make it for the parents who were absent. For the absent parents, suggest a conference at their convenience to discuss the school program and their child's progress.

Request for Parent Assistance

Parent assistance will be discussed in Chapter 10 in greater depth; our purpose here is to suggest ways in which parent assistance can be sought for both classroom and school-wide programs. The best way to elicit help from parents is through their children. If students understand the need and use of parental help, they will seek parental involvement in a most enthusiastic manner. Parents can help in the classroom by tutoring, storytelling, taking/writing dictation, arranging an environment, supervising a learning center, and teaching a mini-course that involves the use of a special skill. School-wide activities that benefit from parent involvement include supervising lunch and game activities, library assistance, clerical work, school beautification projects, sewing costumes and uniforms, set design for school plays or musicals, fund-raising activities, club programs that cut across grade levels, field trip supervision.

Normally parents are flattered when they are asked to participate and help. In most cases parents do not volunteer because they believe that their services or attendance are not desired. Therefore, it is important to tell parents how they can help and why their assistance is needed. The effects of parent involvement can be remarkable. For instance, a Los Angeles high school principal curbed Friday night football fights by asking parents to attend the games free of charge. A junior-high-school counselor cut down on student absence by asking parents to check out whether or not their children actually boarded the school bus that carried them to school. An elementary school faculty did away with weekend vandalism by visiting parents living across from the school and asking them to call teachers or principal personally if they detected anyone entering the school grounds for suspicious purposes.

A teacher's personal note addressed to parents for assistance is the second best technique for obtaining parent involvement. The note requesting help should be specific, telling what is needed, why, time constraints involved, and how to volunteer. The note shown in Figure 9.10 was written by a teacher to request assistance for a field trip.

Parent Visitations

Parents should always be welcome in the classroom. Usually when a child's parent comes to visit, the student feels self-conscious yet exhibits a glow of pride. The parent may be slightly uncomfortable because of the strangeness of the classroom environment. Often parents do not know where to station themselves once inside the room; nor do they know what to observe. If parent visits are anticipated by teacher and students, provisions can be made to welcome them to the classroom and orient them to what is happening at that particular time.

In some classrooms there is a student assigned to the task of welcoming strangers and directing the visitor to an empty place in the classroom for the visit. Sometimes it is wise to have the parent's own child serve as a guide, thus helping both parent and child feel less self-conscious. Many teachers prepare an observation checklist for visitors to use (Figure 9.11).

Students' Work Samples

The work students produce is evidence of what is happening in the classroom. Individual contributions to group work, creative writing, art

---

Figure 9.10. Request for Parent Assistance

Date _____

Dear Parents,

During the next three weeks we will be studying a unit on communication. The telephone company has a historical display about communication and many interesting exhibits and demonstrations on the subject. The students would like to go and visit, but as you probably know, the use of buses for field trips has been curtailed because of inadequate funds. In order to make the trip, we will need private automobiles and adult supervision.

We are hoping to make the trip on Thursday, November 12. We will plan to leave school at 9:30 A.M. and return at 12:00 P.M. for lunch.

Please let us know whether you will be able to drive us to the telephone company on Thursday, November 12.

Sincerely,
T. Teacher

I am able to drive _____ students to the telephone company field trip.

Figure 9.11. Observation Checklist for Visitors

Dear Visitor:

The students and I welcome you to our classroom. We are very pleased to have you visit. You may sit in any empty seat in the classroom or you may move about to watch or listen to us work.

Because I am unable to answer questions during class time, please write down your questions or comments, and we will discuss them during a conference time.

The classroom is a very busy place. Usually there is a hum as students work with others. (We do not have an old-fashioned classroom that is absolutely quiet!) Sometimes I am teaching individuals or sometimes the whole class, but more often I am teaching a small group of students with other groups of students working together and waiting their turn for guidance. To make your visit meaningful, I have prepared this observation checklist:

Observation Checklist for Classroom Visitors in Elementary Classrooms

Room Environment
Do you notice that each bulletin board is related to a different subject?
Can you detect the purpose for each interest center?
Are the textbooks, supplies, and resource materials accessible to all students?
Are the students' tables and chairs grouped to accommodate group discussion and
        group cooperation?
Is the room too hot or too cold?
Is the room messy or is it too neat?

Student Behavior
Do the students appear interested?
Do the students seem to be comfortable and relaxed?
Do the students seem to be meaningfully involved in work activities?
Do students work cooperatively together?
Do students seem to understand what they are to be doing?
Do students ask for help when needed?
Do students seem to know what to do with their work when completed?
Do students know what to do with their time when they have completed their work
        assignment?

Teacher Behavior
Does the teacher seem to guide students' learning?
Does the teacher answer questions and offer suggestions?
Does the teacher appear to diagnose learning problems?
Does the teacher change activities with a minimum of lost time?
Does the teacher maintain a reasonably quiet and disciplined classroom?
Is the teacher friendly to all students?
Does the teacher encourage all students?
Does the teacher circulate and observe all students?

projects, outlines of oral presentations, map work, time lines, science experiments, nature study exhibits—each is unique and each tells a story about classroom life from the perspective of the individual student. When students bring an interesting sample of classroom work home and explain it to parents with the enthusiasm typical of the inventor, creator, or author, then parents, too, will be enthused and delighted about their child's progress. The work sample is a link to the classroom, and parents' interest will be sparked if students can tell them what it is about, why it was produced, and in what ways it is important.

Drill work, such as arithmetic practice papers, handwriting practice sheets, and spelling papers have not been included in the preceding discussion because in most cases they are *not* unique or interesting. Parents do need to know how students are progressing in computation skills, handwriting, and spelling, but in some classrooms these papers seem to be the only ones that do go home, and they are not particularly interesting for parents to view or for students to discuss. A student's progress in basic skills should be a subject for a parent conference; viewing an isolated paper brought home by a child will not clarify learning needs and problems or suggest techniques for remediation.

Should Test Papers Go Home?

If a test is designed so that it is self-explanatory, then it may be of real interest to parents as an indication of what the teacher considers important for students to know and as an indication of what a child has learned. For instance, a multiple-choice test that includes the entire question and all the possible choices can be evaluated by parents in terms of content, objectives, and student outcomes. Short-answer tests that include the test question can also be evaluated by parents.

But when students respond with a single word or phrase on a test, and the test paper does not include the test question, it is not particularly helpful to send it home because it cannot be interpreted by anyone but the teacher. When a parent is asked to sign a test paper that has maybe twenty true/false responses and is graded 13/20, their reaction may very well be—so what!

Teacher's comments on work samples or test papers are extremely important and revealing about classroom priorities. Comments are zealously read by both students and parents. Notes of praise from teachers are found in every child's scrapbook of memories or pinned up on the kitchen bulletin board. Reading the comments, parents evaluate both teacher and their child. When teachers write suggestions, praise, or encourage specific behaviors on papers that go home, they are communicating to both students and parents. The teacher's remarks can help parents learn how to assist their child and how a teacher feels about the child's progress.

The comments can relate to the student's performance of the required task or test items. Remarks can also relate to the teacher's perception of student effort, use of basic skills (handwriting, spelling), creativity, work habits, or interest in the subject or project. Some teachers like to use nonverbal symbols such as smiles and frowns, but a frown should be followed up with encouragement or a suggestion for improvement.

PARENT-TEACHER CONFERENCES

The personal and intimate conversation between teacher and parent is the very best way to communicate concerning student progress. Some important guidelines about the conference may facilitate communication.

1. Teacher and parent should sit somewhere in the classroom so that they are both seated at the same level. (Avoid sitting at the desk.)
2. For interaction to occur, teacher and parent must talk *with* each other; this involves speaking and *listening*.
3. The conversation should be at the adult level. (Avoid a teacher's style of speaking to children; avoid school jargon.)
4. Remember that preconceived (and sometimes stereotyped) notions about each other will hinder communication.
5. Prepare for the conference by accumulating work samples, test scores, and any other evidence that will facilitate understanding about growth and development.

A parent is almost always the child's advocate and this is as it ought to be. The teacher must convince the parent that she or he is also the child's advocate. This means that a conference between parent and teacher will be (and cannot avoid being) at the affective level. Feelings are involved. It is often a good idea to get these feelings out front, first. The beginning chitchat and getting acquainted prelude to the conference are very important in order to set the tone and to develop some rapport between teacher and parent. The following conference between teacher and parent may serve as a demonstration.

Conference between Parent and Teacher

(This excerpt represents an "unplanned" conference. The parent suddenly appeared at the classroom door.)

What Was Said?	*The Interpretation*
P: Mrs. Downey, I am Janet Peters, Sylvia's mother. I am very concerned about some of the things that are happening in this class.	Parent is angry.

T: Please come and sit down and tell me about it.

Teacher needs reflection time and must "cool" the interaction. Teacher does not know what is troubling parent.

P: Why was Sylvia told to sit by herself at the back of the room?

Parent states immediate concern and the reason for her visit.

T: Are you upset because I asked Sylvia to work alone?

Teacher is courteously accepting parent's statement and reflecting.

P: I'm upset because it seems that Sylvia is always being picked on by you and the class.

Parent states real concern and purpose of visit.

T: Can you give me some examples of ways in which Sylvia has been picked on?

Teacher needs to gather more information and specifics.

P: You are avoiding my questions. I asked you why Sylvia was sent to the back of the room.

Parent is still angry and believes that the teacher is putting her off.

T: Mrs. Peters, I'm sorry that you are upset. I am trying to understand what is the matter.
Sylvia was asked to work alone, yesterday, so that she would complete her work. Lately she has not been finishing her assignments, and I suggested that there would be fewer distractions if she sat by herself.

Teacher responds to parental need and proves that she is "attending."
Instead of defending own actions, teacher provides information.

P: Is that the reason? Has this been happening often?

Parent is interested; anger is abated. Parent requests additional information.

T: Frequently in the last several days. I was about to contact you to find out if there is anything happening at home that I should know about. Is Sylvia getting her proper rest?

Teacher expresses personal concern and again asks for information.

P: Well, as a matter of fact her younger brother has been in the hospital, and we have been going back and forth. Sylvia has been up late and has been upset.

Parent provides information and probable explanation for child's problem.

T: I'm sorry that your son has been ill. Is there anything I can do to help?

Teacher reiterates concern; expresses willingness to help.

P: He has had pneumonia, but he is coming along OK now. Thank you. I'm sorry if Sylvia has been a lot of trouble in the classroom.

Parent provides additional information and apologizes for child's behavior.

т: I wish I had known about Sylvia's brother. I would have been able to help her more. I have been concerned that Sylvia is getting into some bad work habits.	Teacher focuses on problem.
p: What can I do about it?	Parent expresses willingness to help teacher.
т: Sylvia has been restless and fidgety in the classroom. I would suppose that she needs more rest. Also, now that we know that her feelings about her brother are affecting her work, I think that you should talk to her and assure her that her brother will be fine.	Teacher theorizes about ways in which parent can assist.
p: Yes, now I can see what she must have been thinking. And, we will stop taking her to the hospital with us and get a sitter so that she goes to sleep on time.	Parent accepts teacher's suggestion.
т: I am going to talk to Sylvia about taking responsibility for her own work and see if we can plan some goals for her to work toward.	Teacher explains her own approach to correct the problem.
p: Will you let me know how she is doing?	Parent requests continued feedback.
т: Yes, I think we should plan another conference and this time invite Sylvia to sit with us. But first let's see how she progresses during the next week.	Teacher agrees that there is a need for continued communication and suggests a three-way conference.
p: Thank you very much.	Parent departs reasonably contented.
т: Thank you for coming in and sharing what is happening.	Teacher acknowledges satisfactory conclusion to conference.

When conferences can be planned, teachers can arrange the interaction to begin with a get-acquainted and get-comfortable stage. Second, the conference is an opportunity to learn about the child through the parent, so the teacher must approach the session with the idea of obtaining as much information as is possible. The teacher should also provide time for the parent to ask questions and obtain information from the teacher. If the teacher has reviewed the student's work record before the conference, then it will be possible to answer the specific questions of parents.

Because many conferences represent unplanned happenings,

teachers need to think about the basic conference components and ways to avoid the typical pitfalls.

Suggestions for Planned and Unplanned Conferences

Planned Conferences

1. Get acquainted. Relax and get comfortable. Share interests; develop rapport. Put the parent at ease.
2. Focus on the purpose of the conference. If the student is having problems, focus on the difficulties.
3. Focus on your instructional approach: how you will remediate, motivate, and so on.
4. If you are reporting progress (no problems), interpret test scores, growth, and development. Share student's work.
5. Listen to parent's observations and questions.
6. Respond to parent's questions.
7. Ask for additional information from parent. Focus on student's social development and responsibilities in the home. Remember that the parent knows more about the child than you do.
8. Make suggestions for the future. Share decision making. Establish goals and commitment for continued communication.
9. Summarize and thank parent for attending.

Uplanned Conferences

1. Try to establish neutrality. Sit down and get comfortable.
2. Allow parent to explain purpose of visit, to explode, to get the heat out!
3. Listen, reflect, and gather information. Demonstrate by your comments that you are listening and are concerned.
4. Do not allow yourself to speak defensively. Do not accept blame.
5. Ask questions to gather information. Respond without heat if parent questions you.
6. Avoid use of professional jargon.
7. If the conference was motivated by a student problem, describe the student's difficulties.
8. Explain your instructional approach.
9. Ask for parental suggestions.
10. Develop a plan with the parent; share decision making. Suggest home techniques.
11. Summarize, set future goals and commitment for future communication.

The most important point to remember at a parent conference is that both you and the parent care about the student and are interested in ways to assist the child. The parent and student need to learn that the teacher is the child's advocate as well as the parent.

The Three-Way Conference

The teacher-student-parent conference is most typical for secondary students and their parents/guardians, but it can also be used for elementary students. The major purpose of the three-way conference is to improve teaching and learning by gathering information about student effort. Typically, the student discusses ways in which he or she has tried to achieve instructional goals and estimates own progress. Teacher and parent should share how they perceive the student's efforts and how they assess progress. The conference should end with goal setting and commitment for future actions.

There are several advantages achieved by the three-way conference:

1. The student does not wait for parental interpretation of the conference; the student hears the evaluation firsthand and can recognize the "truth."
2. There can be no mistake about student effort, progress, and future goals. Each participant hears what the others are saying.
3. The student perceives the interest and involvement of both teacher and parent in his or her behalf.
4. The student sees parent and teacher working together cooperatively and respectfully.

Parent Evaluation of Student

Teachers work with students approximately six hours per day. The majority of the teacher's contacts with students relate to academic skills. The parent, on the other hand, sees the child adapt to environmental problems. Many adaptive skills and personality and behavioral characteristics may be more apparent to the parent than to the teacher. The parent has specific information that can be useful to the teacher. Usually the parent does not know how to share this information or that the information can be used to good advantage. Therefore, it is the teacher's job to request the information at the parent-teacher conference. When teachers work with mainstreamed children, information from the home is particularly important. For instance, teachers need to know about the child's level of independence: Does the child wash self? Can the child dress without assistance? Tie shoes? Does the child choose own clothing for school? Does the student need to be reminded about home responsibilities or schoolwork?

Parents are also knowledgeable about a student's academic progress. It is advantageous to find out how much help the parent needs to give the child at home to complete homework assignments. Does the child require assistance to write a personal letter? In what subject areas does the parent feel the child has done particularly well? In what areas does the parent think the child needs to improve? What evidence does the parent have? What are some parental suggestions to improve academic and social skill performance? As the teacher receives parental suggestions and feedback about the child's performance, it is a good time to contribute professional information, suggestions, and assessment.

Parent Tutoring at Home

There are many very simple techniques that teachers can suggest to parents so that they may give assistance at home. Teaching techniques and intervention strategies may go astray if the home or after-school environment does not support and reinforce the planned program. This is the reason why teachers should seek out parents, provide guidance concerning appropriate measures for help, and coordinate the learning activities.

◆   Bill was a newly mainstreamed child in the third grade. He was having difficulty learning to read. Some of his problems included mixing letters and words (teh for the, saw for was, bad for dad), poor auditory discrimination (hour for our, were for we're), and confused directionality.

The teacher's techniques for working with Bill included the following: tracing words written in manuscript on large cards; listening to taped stories and directions, then repeating them to an adult aide; playing games that required knowledge of left and right.

Because Bill required a great deal of personal attention and practice time, the teacher contacted the parents and made the following suggestions:

Bill should be given very simple and clear directions about any task he is to perform. After he listens to the directions, he should be asked to repeat them. Bill should be encouraged to write very short stories of two or three sentences about his experiences at school or at play. When Bill needs help with a word, he should immediately be given the word written in manuscipt on a sheet of paper; he should trace the word with his preferred hand and then use it in his story. In addition, Bill should play outside games or exercises that require the use of directions.

The teacher's responsibility includes reteaching and trying out different instructional approaches. Assuming that the teacher has assessed Bill's problems accurately and has discovered ways to facilitate learning, the teacher must encourage the parents to participate in the process so that Bill receives consistent motivation, support, and reinforcement. Bill's teacher must provide some instruction to the parents so that they will know how to help him. Bill's teacher would have to explain the kinesthetic method for remediation so that the parents would have a clear understanding of the purposes of tracing words. The parents may even need help in learning to write the words using manuscript. Each of the teacher's techniques must be carefully explained and provision should be made for a future conference date to evaluate growth.

School-Wide Meetings and Social Events

If schools are to be responsive to community needs and goals, then parents must be encouraged to become involved in school activities. Parents are more likely to be action oriented if the school is candid about school-community problems. Principal and teachers should speak honestly about problem situations. Professionals need to accept probing and questioning about problems, causes, and consequences. If parental (community) assistance is really desired, then suggestions need to be listened to and thoughtfully considered. If parents discover that their advisory capacity is a mere formality and that professionals will make all the decisions without regard for community desires, they are turned off and future contact becomes negative.

As a school advisory council chairperson, the author observed a community directed to take part in decision making about curriculum priorities and goals. After members of the community worked hard and contributed time and ideas, their wishes were disregarded without explanation. Attendance at the advisory council meetings decreased; parents refused to volunteer to assist the school.

Communities learn to take care of and care about their school when they perceive that the school belongs to them. One Los Angeles elementary principal frequently went over to the school on Saturdays along with some of the faculty to garden and make simple improvements in the school environment. Curious neighborhood residents came to observe the activities and stayed to participate. The Saturday gardening chores became regular weekend activities with refreshment and companionship as added inducements.

Some inner-city principals fear night programs and Saturday festivals. In the aforementioned elementary school, parents and older brothers and sisters were invited regularly to school programs. Teenaged visitors were told, "If you rip off the school, you will be hurting your brothers and sisters." (No rip-offs occurred.) In this school parent and teacher rapport was excellent because communication lines were open; teachers and parents shared mutual respect.

There are an endless number of activities to solicit parent involvement. When children are involved in school programs, parent attendance is almost assured. But sometimes it is interesting to have a program in which only adult community members and faculty take part. A school musical or play provides a vehicle for joint faculty-parent involvement. The cooperation and friendship that develop during the rehearsals and enactment stages are never forgotten, and the closing night's party is memorable. These amateur productions attract the entire community, raise funds for student activities, and provide opportunities to exchange information and insight about school-related problems.

PARENT INVOLVEMENT AND CLASSROOM MANAGEMENT

Children work and play in three environments: school, home, and neighborhood. Their work involvement at school is influenced by the capability of their classroom teacher and their peer group. In the home the child is influenced by parents (adults) and in the neighborhood by the peer group. The decreasing influence of the family has been a source of societal concern; research has indicated that children are more influenced by a *lack* of parental attention than by the attractiveness of the peer group. In addition, peer-oriented children participate more frequently in antisocial behavior (Bronfenbrenner, 1970).

Parents and teachers are concerned about quality education, but neither teachers nor parents alone can bring it about. Classroom life is affected by the school, the family, the neighborhood, and society at large. Children bring their out-of-school experiences, behaviors, and needs to the classroom. In the classroom children are also affected by the teacher's competence to plan curriculum, organize procedures, arrange the learning environment, monitor progress, and anticipate problems. Leadership along with instructional competence determines the teacher's success with students.

Students' needs continue beyond the classroom and so the questions are: Should the teacher's influence as a model and as an instructional leader be bounded by the classroom door? Should the teacher use professional expertise and leadership potential to influence other adults, including parents, in the child's behalf?

The theme of this chapter has been parent involvement in schools because without a positive relationship between parents and teachers, students' perceptions of adult models is bifurcated. Family and school, parents and teachers, must support one another respectfully in mutual endeavors; each must accept full responsibility and expect increasing levels of responsibility from the child so that growth, development, and self-identity assume a natural progression.

SUMMARY

Elementary teachers have more contact with parents than teachers of older students. Perhaps this occurs because of greater concern about basic skills instruction and in part as a consequence of the security needs of the young child. However, both elementary and secondary teachers need to communicate with parents concerning student progress. Parent conferences provide a fine means to convey information to parents and to attain information about students' out-of-school behavior, interests, and motivation. The conference also provides a means to elicit parent support for schools.

In preparing for the conference, the teacher can gather student's work samples as evidence of classroom progress, data on student behavior in class and during the school day, and data from specialists if it is available. The teacher can also prepare both student and parent for the conference through a preconference with the student to alleviate fears and a friendly note to the parent(s).

Unplanned conferences must also be dealt with in a friendly and calm manner. Most experienced teachers have had occasions when they had to talk with parents who were angry and critical. By listening carefully and communicating fully in a nonemotional tone, confrontations can usually be cooled. It is important to be a respectful and active listener, to respond as completely as possible in a nondefensive manner.

School life is enhanced through parental involvement. Activities to solicit parent involvement include school programs in which students participate and school programs in which adult community members and faculty take part.

CASE STUDY PROBLEMS

1. Poor Grades.   Ms. Betts received a letter from Tim Ferris' father. Tim's father was angry because his son received a D as a midterm grade in science. As a consequence Tim will not be able to participate in any extra-curricular programs including athletics. Tim had really been a borderline case; she could have let him squeak by with a low C, but somehow it seemed advisable to give Tim the lower grade to emphasize his need to work harder. Mr. Ferris wants a conference to discuss the grade. Prepare for the conference. What evidence will you need? How will you "cool" Mr. Ferris? Plan an imaginary dialogue.

2. Adviser.   You are the faculty adviser for the School Advisory Committee. Parents on the committee are upset that more faculty do not attend the committee meetings. Most faculty do not live in the community. Faculty are upset that parents do not attend back-to-school night programs or pay attention to conference dates. How can you sensitize both groups to be more active? How can you develop a parent-teacher partnership?

QUESTIONS

1. You have been approached by a university professor to allow a research study to be conducted in your classroom. The study is primarily observational but will involve some interviews with your students. You feel it is a worthwhile study. Identify the steps you will need to go through to ensure that the study is conducted properly. What will be the "permissions" procedure?

2. It is the beginning of the school year and your principal has suggested that teachers write an introductory letter to parents. In this letter you are to communicate a little bit about your learning goals, instructional methods, and classroom procedures. You will want, for example, to explain whether you will be doing group work or projects. You will also want to communicate something about how you will handle disruptive behavior should it occur. The letter will be typed in the school office and mailed to parents. Plan the letter.

3. You have just had conferences with most of your students' parents. Plan a conference evaluation form to be given to parents to "rate" the success of your conferences.

4. Use the visitors' observation checklist in Figure 9.11 and develop your own observation checklist for your classroom.

5. How can you improve parent contacts throughout the school year?

6. Write a checklist of what you want to say to parents at back-to-school night.

Management and Leadership in the Classroom

Research performed by individual scholars, corporations such as the Rand Corporation, and research centers at universities reveals that the education system, the curriculum, and the teacher's role will change as we approach the year 2000. By the mid-1990s the teacher will manage an educational program that is broader and more versatile than any program designed in the past. The traditional classroom will change as a consequence of a number of factors:

Greater variety of teaching resources
Emphasis on instructional components (language development, mathematics, reading, total curriculum planning)
Emphasis on early childhood
Increased emphasis on individualized programming
Emphasis on normalized classrooms
Formal evaluation of achievement
Teacher accountability

Use of parent volunteers and aides
Paid paraprofessionals
Differentiated teaching roles
Team teaching
Cross-age tutors
Consultant services
Need for continuing professional development

These factors have contributed to the need for teacher planning, class-room organization, leadership, and guidance. Perhaps the real impetus for classroom teacher leadership began in 1965 with the passage of the Elementary Secondary Education Act. Title I of the act, dealing with compensatory education based on the number of poor families in a school district, initiated the utilization of community aides in the classroom. The legislation required the hiring of low-income people from the school community in order to lower the student-teacher ratio in the classroom, to provide tutoring services for students, and to bridge the cultural gap that sometimes occurred between teacher and community.

It is quite common today for the elementary classroom teacher to be responsible for coordinating the efforts of community aides and volunteers, teacher assistants, cross-age tutors, and collegial consultants. It is even possible for all of these individuals to be in the classroom at the same time, thereby testing the ingenuity, coping skills, and guidance of the regular classroom teacher. Working with other adults in the classroom poses problems not usually dealt with in teacher preparation. However, a number of continuing education programs have been developed to assist teachers in the new role as classroom leader of a teaching team.

School personnel and education writers use terms interchangeably to describe individuals involved in helping the classroom teacher. Parent volunteers, teacher aides, paraprofessionals, and teacher assistants are some of the current terms. Because different meanings are conveyed, in this chapter the following role distinctions will be made:

Parent volunteer: An unpaid adult who has volunteered or who has been recruited to assist in the classroom or school, usually a community resident.

Teacher aide: Paid adult, usually a community resident with a high school degree.

Teacher assistant or paraprofessional: Paid adult, usually enrolled in a college preparatory program in education.

The first section of this chapter discusses the purpose and responsibilities of auxiliary personnel and the responsibilities of the classroom teacher working with other adults in the classroom. The second section of the chapter deals with team teaching, the use of consultant personnel in the classroom, and collegial leadership and support.

MANAGEMENT OF AND RESPONSIBILITY FOR AUXILIARY PERSONNEL

The Parent Volunteer

When school faculties and administrators are able to share responsibility with parents for planning and evaluating the school program, the children benefit because school and community develop a positive relationship. In these schools parent volunteers abound. However, if parents are *not* allowed to share in the decision-making process, they hesitate to contribute time and effort, and as a consequence the school not only loses their help, but the community does not perceive school needs, functions, and goals,.

Purpose of Parent Volunteers
The prime purpose in having parent volunteers is to involve the local school community in the education process. In the classroom children benefit by working with an adult community model. At the Denker School in Gardena, California, the adult-child ratio was lowered to 1 to 10 as a result of parent volunteers. Teachers benefit because they are relieved of many nonprofessional chores, for instance, clerical duties, thus enabling teachers to spend more time individualizing instruction.

Recruitment of Volunteers
The section on parent involvement and recruitment in Chapter 9 is relevant here. Parents can be recruited through the PTA, advisory councils, a parent coordinator, or a resource teacher. Children can ask parents. Teachers can telephone or ask parents before or after school in an informal manner for specific help such as sharing a particular skill or performing a particular chore. If parents are asked to share a skill or perform a specific job, they should be given a definite date and time. Ethnic cooking and sewing band costumes are examples of specific jobs that parents can fulfill.

In some schools the parents are surveyed to determine parental interests. Then a parent coordinator assumes the responsibility to call parents about specific tasks related to the parents' interests. Sometimes parents feel uneasy about working in classrooms. These parents can perform other tasks outside the classroom such as typing, duplicating materials, or making games.

In neighborhoods where there is a community newspaper, ads can be written to attract parental and senior citizen attention. Senior citizen homes can be canvassed. By inviting senior citizens and other members of the community to a school program or tea, it is possible to interest them in helping out at school activities.

A school coordinating chairperson for volunteers could develop a form similar to the one shown in Figure 10.1.

Volunteer Responsibilities
In the classroom the volunteers can be used to tutor individual students. They can demonstrate a specific skill (needlepoint, surveying) or personal interest (stamp collecting, numismatics) to a small group or to the class as a whole. Volunteers can set up and supervise special labs for reading, math, or science. Often, parents can make special equipment needed in these labs. Parents can be leaders of mini-units in which the parent's special skills, job, profession, or interests are displayed or demonstrated for children. Some schools have mini-units or club programs once a week; children sign up for the program that appeals to them and take subjects such as ethnic cooking, folk music, jewelry making.

Figure 10.1. Volunteer Request Form

Name _____ Telephone _____
Address _____
I have a car available for use. _____
I do not have a car available for use. _____
I speak the following languages: _____.
I have achieved the _____ grade level in school.
I am available to help on the following days: _____ and during the following hours: _____.
I am willing to help students in:
   English language skills _____
   _____ language skills _____
   Reading _____
   Art _____
   Music _____
   Library _____
   Mathematics _____
   Social Studies _____
   Science, Health _____
I prefer to work with students in the _____ grades.
I prefer to work in classrooms. _____
I prefer to work in the office. _____
I prefer to work at home preparing educational materials. _____
PLEASE RETURN THIS FORM TO YOUR CHILD'S TEACHER.

Special Program Designed by Parents

At a number of Los Angeles schools, parents have developed psychomotor testing programs for kindergarten and first-grade children. The parents equip and run these centers. In recent years educators, clinicians, and psychologists have theorized that there is a relationship between motor development and the child's ability to perform academic tasks. Some researchers have found that as children improve in perceptual-motor activities, they are able to concentrate for longer periods of time in the classroom, their self-concept is affected, and tensions are relieved. It is believed that motor activities may constitute another learning modality.

Psychomotor skills testing can detect poor serial memory. If a child cannot remember two or three body movements that are to be performed consecutively, then the child will also have difficulty spelling simple three-letter words or arranging events in a series.

While the testing program can detect problems, practice may alleviate them. Teachers can work on shape recognition through tactile and visual modalities in the classroom, and parents can help children outside the classroom through hopping and jumping exercises on squares, triangles, and half-circles drawn on the playground. Pattern recognition practice can help students recognize letters and words required for reading skills.

At the Denker School, parents, under the supervision of a school psychologist, tested students in body awareness/perceptual spatial relationships, fundamental movements, and the use of objects and equipment. The program was developed under an early childhood education grant.

The Denker perceptual skills program attests to the fact that parents can perform meaningful activities to improve the educational program. In summary, parents can help teachers by performing the following activities:

1. Tutoring
2. Sharing interests and hobbies
3. Performing clerical tasks: typing, duplicating materials
4. Making games for classroom use
5. Supervising playground and classroom games
6. Assisting on field trips
7. Supervising a special lab
8. Story telling
9. Assisting students in story writing
10. Sharing personal experiences (useful for oral history)
11. Recording cultural folktales
12. Testing and remediating psychomotor skills

Parents can also assist in the total school program by collecting items needed by many teachers in the school (jars, rags, egg cartons, etc.), by working on school beautification projects, by running office machines, by typing school-home bulletins, and by evaluating the total school program.

Teacher Aides

Before federal and state funding facilitated the use of teacher aides, Bay City, Michigan, presented a plan to the Ford Foundation for funding teacher aides in their schools. They began their program in 1953.

RESEARCH AND READINGS

Morse, Arthur D. (1960). *Schools of tomorrow—today*. New York: Doubleday, p. 62.

"Physicians, lawyers, engineers and architects utilize the services of secretaries and clerks to handle their paperwork and nonprofessional duties. Teachers, overburdened by the number of their pupils and the magnitude of their responsibilities, are required to waste precious hours in nonprofessional activities."

The Bay City program was originated by Superintendent Charles B. Park. Park studied and timed teachers' duties during the school day and discovered that 26 percent of the teachers' time was spent on non-teaching chores.

Teacher Aide Responsibilities

The Michigan teacher aides were required to have a high school education. They performed chores such as arranging bulletin board displays, writing assignments on the chalkboard, forwarding school messages, obtaining library books, accompanying music lessons, collecting papers and milk money, supervising the distribution of supplies, and checking attendance. Teacher aides also conducted drills and reviews with small groups of students, but they never introduced new, unfamiliar work to children.

The Bay City project demonstrated that, with the use of teacher aides, teachers were able to spend more time making assignments, monitoring progress, and listening to students recite. Teachers had more time to individualize instruction and give personal counseling to students. The teachers also spent more time developing important lesson plans.

The Los Angeles Unified School District defines typical duties of their education aides as follows: Assists a teacher or other certificated employee by performing paraprofessional duties such as

1. Reading to pupils, drilling them in materials presented by a teacher to maintain or improve learning skills, assisting pupils in library activities, correcting work papers and scoring tests, and supervising a group while the teacher is busy elsewhere in the classroom.
2. Collecting and distributing materials; monitoring classes during tests; helping to set up or arrange furniture, audiovisual, and other equipment; and storing or disposing of materials.
3. Monitoring or checking assigned areas to assist in enforcing safety and disciplinary rules.
4. Making home contacts or visits to review school or center programs with parents or community groups, to assist in establishing or maintaining favorable relationships, to resolve problems related to attendance or behavior, and to encourage parental involvement.
5. Posting information on records, filing materials, storing supplies, running errands, operating simple office equipment, and performing other miscellaneous duties.
6. Preparing instructional, display, and work materials.
7. Accompanying pupils on bus trips as needed.
8. Performing related duties as assigned.

Teacher Assistants and Paraprofessionals

In most cases the teacher assistants are enrolled in teacher preparatory programs. In choosing the teacher assistant, the local school often gives priority to the community resident. Similar to the aide program, the teacher assistants are partially funded by federal or state grants to the school district. The TA (teacher assistant) usually works in the school two to four hours per day and attends college in the late afternoons. Sometimes TAs are supervised by college coordinators, sometimes by a school or district coordinator.

The duties of the TA are similar to those of the aides; however, there is an effort to "teach" the TA proper classroom technique through constant feedback and evaluation of the TA's performance. The TA is more likely to be entrusted with small groups of children for drill and review exercises or library research lessons. The teacher assistant may be asked to prepare an occasional lesson, and the classroom teacher evaluates it carefully before it is presented; after the lesson the teacher assistant and the classroom teacher evaluate the performance.

How Do Teachers Feel about Auxiliary Personnel?

In the mid-1960s there was some hostility and opposition to the use of paraprofessionals or aides in the classroom. Teachers feared the competition of the nonprofessional; they were concerned about the value judgments of community residents when they observed and worked in classrooms and many felt that the aides did not appreciate the skills needed to diagnose learning problems and prescribe appropriate activities.

But as teachers discovered that the new workers actually freed them to work more with students and to develop their own creativity more, their opposition decreased. In 1970 the American Federation of Teachers in New York organized the paraprofessionals and obtained higher pay, a salary schedule, and benefits for them.

Teacher Responsibilities for Auxiliary Personnel

> "Teachers need to anticipate the work needs of their aides or else both teacher and helper's time is wasted."
>
> *Los Angeles City School Administrator*

Parent volunteers, teacher aides, or paraprofessionals can perform many chores that relieve the teacher of nonteaching tasks, but the teacher must preplan meaningful assignments for the auxiliary personnel (Table 10.1). In addition the teacher is responsible for explaining how tasks are to be performed. The teacher's management

---

Table 10.1. Checklist of Management Responsibilities for Working with Volunteers, Aides, Assistants

1. Have you discussed with your auxiliary personnel the classroom program and your room standards?
2. Do you preplan the activities to be accomplished by your assistants?
3. Have you explained emergency procedures and duties?
4. When you give a work assignment, are you specific in your directions? (Does the aide know what is expected?)
5. Are you careful not to assign more tasks than can be accomplished?
6. Do you assign enough work to keep the volunteer busy?
7. Do you monitor the accomplishments of your aide(s)?
8. Do you give positive as well as negative feedback?
9. Do you encourage businesslike attitudes (punctuality, finishing tasks, appropriate comments to students)?
10. Do you help your auxiliary personnel feel welcome in the classroom and in the school?

responsibilities are extended with the use of auxiliary personnel in the classroom. These responsibilities include (a) preplanning of work assignments, (b) explanation and guidance, and (c) evaluation and feedback concerning performance.

Preplanning tasks for the classroom helper can be difficult for teachers who have never worked with another adult in the classroom. Some experienced teachers keep a list of chores handy so that the classroom aide can move from one assignment to the next without disturbing instruction. One experienced teacher commented, "You need to anticipate all of the organizational details for a day of teaching. If you do that then you can see clearly all of the nonteaching aspects that are a part of every lesson. These nonprofessional chores are extremely time consuming and can be performed by an aide."

Planning conference time with the aide(s) is crucial for success. At the Heschel School in Northridge, California, the classroom teacher and the assistant confer every morning. The "master" teacher explains the day's objectives, including how children will "move" from activity to activity. If special learning centers are to be used, they are explained to the assistant so that appropriate help can be given to the students when requested. If special supplies will be needed at the centers, the assistant is told about them so that during the day materials and resources will be ready for the students. During the conference time the classroom teacher asks for ideas from the assistant. Sometimes the assistant will note organizational details that have been forgotten. At the Heschel School the two adults work as a team.

Just as it is important to explain what needs to be accomplished, it is equally important to evaluate results or performance. At the end of each day at the Heschel School the teacher and the assistant go over the day's happenings in order to facilitate planning for the next day. Because the aide often works individually with students, it is important to offer guidance about child growth and development. If a child has a special problem, the paraprofessional will do a better job with knowledge and understanding about the nature of the disability or problem.

Leadership for Auxiliary Personnel

The classroom aide expects the teacher to be the leader. In some cases the parent volunteer or the community teacher aide may be older than the teacher; however, when it comes to instructional competence, it is the teacher who has had the training and experience. Teacher leadership must be exercised in terms of defining and guiding what needs to be done in the classroom, interpersonal leadership must be provided, and forethought must be given to the continuing education of the assistant.

Failure to provide appropriate work tasks for the aide or volunteer means that teacher and children lose the value of classroom assistance. Also, the teacher will probably lose status and respect. The real purpose for having auxiliary personnel in the classroom is the individualization of instruction; therefore, the tasks designed for the paraprofessional should free the teacher to spend more time with students *and* to provide additional tutoring time for students through the use of the adult tutor.

When teachers are displeased with auxiliary personnel in the classroom, the problem is usually a lack of communication. The following are suggestions for improving communication between teacher and aide.

1. Encourage the exchange of ideas by accepting feedback about the task performed or an observation of a learning activity. Listen and ask questions to clarify own and aide's understanding.
2. Develop trust and respect between you and the volunteer or aide. Correct performance as needed when children are not within sight. (Do not "save up" corrections for a rainy day!) Provide positive feedback as well as negative feedback.
3. Develop a system whereby the paraprofessional will always know what to do and be able to find new tasks to accomplish, but do not overload the person with more than is possible at a given time.
4. Be careful about the use of professional jargon that will not be understood. Exercise care that "loaded" or emotional words are not used.
5. Do not identify really personal information about any of the students unless the information is necessary in order to facilitate the teaching of the child.

Suggest interschool and interclass visitations to parents and aides and suggest attendance in education classes designed for parents and paraprofessionals. There will be occasions when the teacher will notice educational deficiencies or particular learning needs of the paraprofessional. As the classroom leader, the teacher should suggest appropriate continuing education for the assistant. The teacher may learn about area workshops or discussion groups or resource personnel that are available. Every opportunity should be used to improve the performance of auxiliary classroom personnel. Many schools invite the paraprofessionals to attend faculty in-service programs.

School District and University Continuing Education for Paraprofessionals

Federal and state programs usually provide funds for staff development and continuing education of the paraprofessional. In most cases these individuals represent their community, and they are a source of pride for school and students. Most programs mandate a comprehensive training program designed specifically to meet local community needs. The University of Southern California in conjunction with two school districts developed a training model for continuing education of the "para-educator."

The program objectives follow:

1. Examine responsibilities of the paraprofessional in classroom and school
2. Identify concepts in psychology of learning, child development, personality, socialization, and dynamics of behavior
3. Improve skills in interpersonal and intergroup communication
4. Improve ability to work with individuals and groups in planning, problem solving, and decision making
5. Improve understanding of multicultural variables
6. Develop positive working relationships in the school community
7. Develop accommodative knowledge and understanding in the implementation of basic skills
8. Provide a base for continuing teacher-paraprofessional in-service programming

The core curriculum for the program focused on five components: role clarification and communication, child growth and development, multicultural studies, basic skill techniques for reading and math, and classroom management. The underlying purpose of all staff development programs for the paraprofessional is to encourage continuing education and career advancement.

An assignment sheet (Figure 10.2) for elementary school aides, volunteers, or teacher assistants provides a written record of tasks and achievements. The assignment sheet can also be used for evaluation purposes at the end of the day.

COLLEGIAL TEAMING, MENTORING, AND SUPPORT

Team Teaching

Team teaching or cooperative teaching is a way of combining the efforts of two or more teachers in order to use their abilities to the best advantage. The teachers pool their respective classes of students, and in schools where there are teacher aides or assistants, they too are included as members of the team.

The team meets together to plan cooperatively, to instruct, and to

Figure 10.2. Assignment Sheet for Aides, Volunteers, and Teacher Assistants

Name _____ Date _____

Work Assignments:
1. Meet children at playground and walk to classroom.
2. Supervise cloakroom area.
3. Take attendance.
4. Reading: Tutor _____, _____,

   _____, _____,

   _____, _____.

5. Prepare a paint center.
6. Duplicate materials for math.
7. Cut papers for art lesson.
8. Handwriting: Assist _____,

   _____,

   _____.

9. Correct math test.
10. Record spelling scores in grade book.
11. Supervise cleanup after art lesson.
12. Walk children to lunch area.
13. Gather materials for a science center, magnetism.

Evaluation of Personal Work Assignments:

_____

evaluate teaching and learning performances. Team teaching allows students to be grouped flexibly for large- and small-group and individualized instruction. An effective team pools the resources of teachers so that each instructor provides specialized input in the area of greatest personal strength and interest.

The Franklin School

One of the first team teaching plans was begun in 1957 at the Franklin School in Lexington, Massachusetts. The children were grouped in "families" of 75 to 150 students. The faculty was divided into three teams. Each team had an experienced, superior teacher as team leader, senior teacher(s), and regular teachers. The team teaching plan allowed the children to move from one group to another depending on the subject and the student's individual ability in each subject area. The plan recognized that children do not have the same ability in all subjects. Teaching improved at Franklin because there was more planning time. Learning improved because the students were never subjected to a bad teacher because each teacher was a lead teacher in an area of strength.

Montebello, California

At the Macy Intermediate School in Montebello, California, classrooms have flexible walls and teachers open up their rooms for cooperative teaching. Students move between teachers for specialized instruction to meet specific instructional needs. The math teachers at the junior high level find this approach particularly advantageous. Some days students select a favored math strand, such as geometry, and work with the teacher expert in this strand. Teaming does not necessarily occur on a daily basis, but teachers plan together for teaming several times a month.

Teaming at Macy Intermediate School also occurs in the social studies. Teachers group students for special activities; for example, a large group is used for films and video, while small groups receive more teacher attention. The teachers choose to work together because they feel they have a talent that they want to share with team members. Students enjoy the diversity of teaching styles and the enrichment they gain as a result of the teaming.

Team Planning

Planning may occur formally at set times among team members or informally on an ad hoc basis. At the Heschel School an eighth-grade social studies teacher and an English teacher discussed a common problem related to grading students' papers. The teachers taught the same students, and the English teacher found it difficult to grade composition papers in which she felt the content was inaccurate. The social studies teacher commented that he was troubled grading social studies content when students' work was grammatically wrong, composed poorly, and had misspelled words. As a consequence the teachers decided to collaborate on a term project with the social studies component providing the content for the project and the English component the necessary composing skills. The students would work with both teachers, and the assignment would be jointly assessed. The teachers planned and coordinated on a regular basis after making the decision, and the students worked during both class periods on the project.

Observations about Teaming

There are no set rules for teaming; its implementation can be different in each situation. However, teaming must be a matter of choice for the participating teachers. The professional rationale for teaming should be to refine curricular content so that teachers lead in an area of strength and have an opportunity to learn from colleagues. For students, the advantages include greater motivation, individualized instruction, and delabeling of ability.

SPECIALIST TEACHERS

Both elementary and middle school teachers specialize in a number of different subjects and program areas. There are reading, math, bilingual, early childhood, and special education specialists. Some schools have a teacher who specializes in music and/or art or physical education. The term *resource teacher* may designate a special education teacher or a teacher who provides resource materials and ideas to other teachers. Some schools have a resource teacher at every grade level.

In some schools the specialist teacher maintains a classroom where students receive special instruction at scheduled times. In other schools, it is the specialist teacher who travels from room to room. Whichever system is used, the specialist teacher is available to consult with the regular teachers, and together they form a teaching partnership.

Math Specialist Teacher

The following is an example of a math specialist teacher consulted about a behavioral problem by the student's regular teacher:

◆   "Janice seems to have special problems during math. She doesn't finish her work, she moves about and bothers others. Actually she is really impossible at that time. I decided to test her to find out whether she is working at the right level. I checked her computation skills and found that she can add and subtract three digits with renaming, but that she had difficulty with four digits. I also found that. . .so I put her in a different math group, but she has not improved. What do you think I should do?"

"First, let me come in during math and observe her work."

The next school day Janice was observed by the math specialist teacher who verified that Janice appeared frustrated and unhappy during the math period. Again the two teachers discussed the problem and decided to ask Janice's parents to come to school for a conference. The parents told the teachers that recently Janice had complained about school and pleaded to stay at home. The math specialist teacher decided to retest Janice in order to verify Janice's functional level in math since it appeared that Janice was only unhappy at that time of the day.

The math specialist verified that the regular teacher had indeed found the functional level for Janice, but that Janice became agitated when she was pressed to work at her functional level. The specialist teacher suggested an individualized program for Janice in which she would work slightly below her functional level at a "proven" success level.

Both teachers observed the child and found that she became less frustrated and more willing to work. It appeared that Janice's functioning level in mathematics was also her frustration level, and so she had seemed to be a behavioral problem in the classroom. Together the two teachers were able to work out an appropriate learning program for the student.

Reading Specialist Teacher

It is extremely difficult for an elementary teacher to keep up with all subject fields, and so it is particularly helpful when there is a colleague who specializes and can give some instant advice or assistance.

◆   Mr. Peterson taught fourth grade, and he had a class of identified gifted children. With these children he believed that he should teach reading through the content fields, and so he used science books, social studies, and health texts to teach reading. In order to grade the children in reading, he tested their comprehension skills by asking study questions about their work. Their responses and their written work allowed him to assess their level of comprehension. However, one day as he was working with a small group of students, he realized that they were having difficulty decoding some unfamiliar words. He conferred with the reading teacher at his school: "Should I teach decoding skills to gifted children in the fourth grade?"

The reading teacher shared a continuous progress profile in reading with Mr. Peterson. The specialist explained that the language and vocabulary development of gifted children certainly assisted them in comprehension and that gifted children were especially adept at using contextual clues. Mr. Peterson's use of the content areas for reading was motivating and helpful in teaching comprehension skills but even gifted children needed some assistance with phonetic analysis and structural analysis. Therefore, Mr. Peterson needed to assess his students' development by testing a variety of comprehension strategies. Mr. Peterson's approach had been too narrow.

Mr. Peterson had confidence that his colleague was a specialist in reading. Although Mr. Peterson did not need the services of his colleague in the classroom, he received assistance when needed by conferring with the reading specialist.

Special Education Resource Teacher

◆   Marty was a first grader at the King School, and he was severely testing the abilities of his first-grade teacher. His language skills were poor; he was not learning to read; he disturbed others whenever possible. His teacher began an anecdotal record about Marty; but after several days she decided she had better begin a testing program and get some assistance. With the help of an aide Marty was tested for motor development. Next Marty was sent to the school nurse where his sensory functioning was tested. The teacher used the anecdotal record to provide information about socialization factors, independence, and personality factors. The teacher tried to test cognitive development and tried to pinpoint particular learning characteristics, but she felt she was not successful.

The teacher developed an assessment record with as much information as she was able to gather about Marty's skills and abilities. Next she contacted the parents in order to gather additional information and to let them know about Marty's school progress. Although the teacher had determined that Marty was almost unable to work alone at any task at school, she wondered about his independence at home.

The parents were able to furnish information about dressing, bathing, eating, and playing. Marty was able to ride a tricycle but not roller skate or jump rope. He brushed his teeth and dressed himself but often had difficulty buttoning his shirt. The parents did not feel that Marty was doing well at school, and they said that he rarely wanted to listen to a story and never chose a book for his own pleasure. They also said that Marty was taking Ritalin. The teacher's information alerted the parents that the Ritalin dosage was not right. The teacher had not known before the conference that the child was on medication.

Marty's teacher arranged a three-way conference for herself, the parents, and her special education colleague. The teacher's assessment records were shared with the special educator. Together (teacher, parents, and resource teacher) they decided that Marty should have some additional psychological tests. The psychologist determined Marty's cognitive level and provided information about learning characteristics. Then the special educator was able to develop an instructional prescription and suggest specific methods and materials. The special educator would monitor Marty's progress by observing him in the classroom in order to verify the accuracy of the treatment. If problems developed, then new procedures would be tried.

The classroom teacher is the leader of the team. The regular teacher knows more about the student's learning behaviors and therefore is in the best position to decide what kind of help the student (and the teacher) needs. The regular teacher must call on other experts: physician, parents, special educator, reading teacher, and so on. The classroom teacher is responsible, legally, for coordinating the efforts of all involved—the experts, the aides, tutors—in order to achieve the best individualized program for the student.

COLLEGIAL COMMUNICATION

In Chapter 9 teacher-parent communication was emphasized with a discussion about stereotyping problems, cultural misunderstandings, and poor interrelationships. But teacher-to-teacher relationships are rarely discussed in professional books. It is apparently assumed that teachers talk with one another. Teachers do talk in lunchrooms and offices, and there is plenty of small talk concerning professional problems. New cooperative teaching plans have encouraged collegial planning and evaluative conferences. New interrelationships are being established, but there are times when there is a real communication gap. The following example is illustrative.

◆   Mrs. Rivers, a sixth-grade teacher, expressed a willingness to accept an emotionally handicapped child into her classroom. She was told that the child was considered "rehabilitated."

James had attended a special class for two years, but now that he was a sixth grader it was felt that he should attend a regular class before going on to junior high school. Since James was almost two years behind in reading, he would continue to receive reading instruction in his special classroom.

The cumulative record provided test score information, for instance, James' scores on the Wide Range Achievement Test (WRAT). Although Mrs. Rivers enthusiastically accepted James, she discovered after three days that he could not work with other children; he would invariably have difficulties when standing in a line, and he was unable to play a team game such as soccer, volleyball, or baseball.

After school on the third day, Mrs. Rivers [holding her head!] began to think about James and realized that there were a number of things that she did not know about him.

The Communication Gap

Mrs. Rivers does not know what academic tasks James can or cannot perform. Even though James has a fourth-grade reading level, does that mean that James can be expected to perform reading follow-up tasks that most fourth graders can do? Will James be able to fold an arithmetic paper and write math problems within the space provided? What is James' frustration level? What is his attention span? Can James sit in a small group with other students and carry on a conversation? Can James participate in group planning tasks? Will James accept responsibility?

If the class is told to outline an oral presentation, will James have had any experiences with outlining? Public speaking? Is James affectively mature? Does he get angry quickly? What type of reinforcement is effective with him? What are *his* expectations? Does *he* understand what is expected of him?

Mrs. Rivers and her special education colleague had exchanged information about their daily schedules. What time was reading? When should James go to the resource room? Mrs. Rivers was a strong, experienced teacher and that was why she accepted James in her classroom, and her colleague, knowing this, felt comfortable about James' program change. The special educator expected Mrs. Rivers to be knowledgeable about James' prior program experiences, but Mrs. Rivers had not known enough to ask questions, and she certainly did not anticipate all of the things that she would need to know.

Mrs. Rivers failed to think about the fact that in the resource room James worked only with about nine other students. Almost all of James' instruction for the last two years had been tutorial and individualized. He had not worked on any group tasks. His social participation skills were about nil. Since James became upset easily, his test taking in his special classroom had been oral. (In Mrs. Rivers' room he would need to tape record his responses—probably at home.) James' physical coordination was poor, and his writing was still illegible. He would have a difficult time containing his work on sixth-grade lined paper. He would have a similar problem when he tried to do his math problems. Special education students at the school were allowed to go to the cafeteria five minutes sooner than other students; therefore, James had not had to wait in a line—for anything—for two years.

Anticipation of possible problems is basic to good classroom management. Perhaps Mrs. Rivers was naive, but her colleague could have taken the responsibility to initiate a discussion about the differences in program orientation between a special resource room and a regular classroom. Mrs. Rivers should not have been allowed to be surprised. Also, she should have received a written report about James' social, emotional, and academic performance, including information about what kinds of work assignments James could do. A record, such as the one shown in Table 10.2, would have bridged the communication gap.

When teachers perform reciprocal collegial services, communication and interrelationships become more important, and detecting a col-

---

Table 10.2. Performance Information for Mainstreaming

1. What is the functional level of the student in
   Reading?
   Mathematics?
   Spelling?
2. What kinds of work tasks can the student perform successfully in
   Reading?
   Mathematics?
   Handwriting?
   Social studies?
   Science?
   Art?
   Music?
3. To what extent can the student interact successfully with other students in

	Great deal	Little	Not at all
a. Small-committee/group work?			
b. Class discussions?			
c. One-to-one relationships?			
d. Team sports?			
e. Large-group games?			

4. To what extent will the student accept/respond to

	Average	Poor	Not at all
a. Waiting?			
b. Praise?			
c. Criticism?			
d. Touching?			
e. Questioning?			
f. Responsibility?			
g. Student-directed work activities?			
h. Self-directed work activities?			

5. How can the student be tested?

	Yes	No
a. Paper and pencil?		
b. Orally?		
c. Using cassette tapes?		

Table 10.2. *(Continued)*

6. Does the student tend to respond easily/quickly to

	Yes	No
a. Anger?		
b. Laughter?		
c. Embarrassment?		
d. Fear?		
e. Helpfulness?		
f. Nonverbal communication?		

7. Does the student have special material/resource needs?   Yes   No
   a. Paper (extra large, lined, unlined)
   b. Pencils (primary, regular)
   c. Books (large print, pictures)
   d. Workbooks
   e. Cassettes for taping
   f. Seating accommodations (hearing, vision)
   g. Other

8. Does the student have physical coordination problems?
Can the student

	Yes	No
a. Dance?		
b. Jump?		
c. Run?		
d. Skip?		
e. Hop?		
f. Throw a ball?		
g. Write on lined paper?		
h. Write within small spaces?		
i. Use puzzle materials?		
j. Saw?		
k. Hammer?		
l. Button clothes?		

9. Does the student have speech problems or atypical mannerisms? If yes, describe

10. Does the student dress appropriately?

11. What skills should be stressed with the student?

12. Are there some instructional approaches that are more effective than others with the student? Describe.

league's problem will become less difficult and less painful. Traditionally, elementary teachers did not communicate with each other, and there were no specialists or consultants to give assistance. If an elementary teacher made the mistake of requesting assistance or services, supervisory personnel would come out to observe and quite often "snoopervise." Today there is a recognized need for cooperative teaching, and it is more typical for classroom teachers, specialist teachers, preservice teachers, aides, and volunteers to work together as a team. Opportunities for professional growth and contact are unlimited.

MENTOR TEACHERS

By definition a mentor is a close, trusted, and experienced counselor or guide. Mentors are considered to be teachers, tutors, and coaches. In schools mentor teachers provide one-to-one coaching to colleagues who may be beginning teachers or experienced teachers. Professionally, the mentor helps other teachers recognize opportunities to improve performance. The mentor teacher challenges other teachers while at the same time providing "protection" and "sponsorship." Psychologically the mentor befriends, counsels, models, and assures.

In the Charlotte-Mecklenburg school district mentors assist provisional teachers one-half day each month. The mentors are selected by the principal of the school and typically teach at the same grade level or subject area as the novice teacher. Mentors are supposed to be able to apply principles of effective teaching, communicate effectively, and be an adviser to the provisional teacher (Hanes and Mitchell, 1985). The mentor teacher needs to establish rapport and trust and should be insightful in providing feedback and evaluative judgments to the beginning teacher.

RESEARCH AND READINGS

Gray, William A., & Gray, Marilynne M. (1985). Synthesis of research on mentoring beginning teachers. *Educational Leadership*, 43(3), 37–43.

Successful mentors are people oriented, share power and expertise, help protégés develop self-confidence.

The protégé needs to progress from prescriptive acceptance of mentor judgment to function as an autonomous professional.

Beginning teachers need help with classroom management, lesson planning, and school routines.

In California, mentors are appointed for one to three years. They must be full-time permanent teachers, and they must continue to teach 60 percent of the time in their own classroom. The mentors assist and guide both new and experienced teachers. They may also help develop curriculum for the school district. Mentors may *not* evaluate the teachers they assist (California Commission on the Teaching Profession, 1985).

In 1985 California had 5100 mentors in 740 school districts and county offices. Mentors are paid by the state and receive $4000 per year for mentoring. Districts receive $2000 to pay for administrative costs of the mentor program.

Wagner (1985, p. 26) reports that the mentor teacher program in the

ABC Unified School District in California is particularly successful. Mentor applicants are assessed by their ability to:

Communicate well in writing
Model exemplary teaching
Prepare and deliver workshops for adults
Lead others
Build trusting relationships
Complete mentor tasks

Coaching

The mentor's role as a coach usually provides the following services: companionship, providing technical feedback, analyzing application, adaptation to students, and personal facilitation. These functions are discussed by Joyce, Hersh, and McKibbin (1983). Companionship is particularly important because classroom teaching is so lonely and can be frustrating to the beginning teacher. The "coach" provides reassurance that what the beginning teacher is experiencing is "normal."

Technical feedback is provided as the beginning teacher or coaching team member practices new teaching behaviors. The coach identifies omissions or misplaced emphases to help the teacher polish his or her teacher performance.

Analyzing application occurs as the coach observes whether or not the teaching model is used appropriately. (Does the model match the instructional purpose?) Whenever a new model is being adapted there is the temptation to use it frequently, and so the coach helps to determine whether the use is applicable to the situation.

When teachers learn models of teaching, their first concern is with their own performance. The coach needs to observe students' reactions and help the teacher adapt the model to students' needs. During the beginning stage of practice it is hard for the teacher to judge student reaction, and so the coach must provide this special insightful assistance.

Personal facilitation occurs when the coach helps the teacher develop self-confidence and repeatedly assures the teacher to "keep trying." An unsure performance can cause students to act out, and the teacher needs to recognize this and not become discouraged.

Mentoring and coaching provide different leadership experiences than those reported at the beginning of this chapter. The mentor and coach are responsible for facilitating others' performance. The mutuality and collegial relationship necessary for improving professional performance will be discussed in Chapter 11. Classroom leadership as a mentor or coach requires subtle person-to-person responsibilities. These will be discussed in greater depth later.

SUMMARY

The use of auxiliary personnel in the classroom complicates classroom management because teachers need to spend time organizing the instructional program to include other adults in instructional activities, housekeeping chores, and clerical tasks. However, most teachers who plan in advance for the work of auxiliary personnel and include them as "members of the team" find that it is well worth the effort. Many time-consuming nonteaching tasks can be performed by paraprofessionals (aides, volunteers). In planning for the work of auxiliary personnel, the teacher needs to accept leadership responsibilities and provide training for the paraprofessional, if necessary. Teachers are responsible for maintaining the morale of auxiliary personnel in the classroom.

Team teaching can be a formalized arrangement among teachers (and auxiliary personnel) or simply an ad hoc decision to team for specified subjects and activities. Team planning allows professionals to collaborate and coordinate responsibilities for "who" is doing "what" and "when." Teaming allows teachers to take advantage of teaching strengths.

The mentor teacher role expands leadership opportunities for teachers. As a helping teacher, the mentor provides situational leadership. Role functions include advising, counseling, modeling, demonstrating, promoting, and encouraging. Mentoring has the possibility of meeting the special needs of new teachers, improving skills for experienced teachers, and increasing professional esteem and satisfaction for mentors.

CASE STUDY PROBLEMS

1. Aide. Mr. Duncan was teaching mathematics to a group of students. Another group was working independently. Roger, the new student, was waving his hand and gesturing frantically for help. Mr. Duncan was trying to ignore him and finish with his lesson. He figured that when his aide, Mrs. Jenkins, arrived, she could help Roger. Soon it looked like several other students also needed assistance.

Mrs. Jenkins arrived and immediately went to work cleaning up miscellaneous papers and paints at the back of the room. The room was getting somewhat noisy, but Mrs. Jenkins didn't appear to notice. Mr. Duncan left his group and went over to Mrs. Jenkins and in a not too subdued voice said, "Don't you see that some of the students need help?"

Mrs. Jenkins responded, "I didn't know it was my responsibility to help students in math. I thought you wanted me to clean up the paints."

Critique Mr. Duncan's classroom management and suggest ways to help both Mr. Duncan and Mrs. Jenkins.

2. Mentor. The new teacher was extremely embarrassed to teach in front of another adult. When you arrived at her classroom to "be her mentor," she seemed extremely shy. You sat down and observed her teach, but it was almost too painful to watch. If you were the mentor, how would you put this new teacher at ease? What would you tell her about mentoring?

3. Seniors.   You are teaching junior-high-school social studies, and the grandmother of one of your students has approached you about helping in the classroom. After talking with the woman, you realize that she was born in Russia in approximately 1914. She is extremely interesting, but her English is not always perfect.

How could this woman contribute to your social studies program? Or is she too old to be in the classroom? Will students be receptive? Why?

QUESTIONS

1. Plan a science lesson at your grade level and discuss ways this lesson could be teamed with one or more other teachers and aides.
2. Make a list of classroom tasks that an aide could perform.
3. You are a new teacher and a mentor teacher has come to help you. Make a list of problems for assistance.
4. If you were given the choice by a mentor teacher, what would you ask the mentor to demonstrate for you?
5. You are supervising several new teachers. How could you provide feedback to these teachers in an encouraging supportive manner? Be specific and identify proposed improvements.

CHAPTER 11

Improving Teaching Performance

> *CHAPTER HIGHLIGHTS*
>
> Evaluating teaching
> Self-improvement
> More about coaching
> Improving questioning skills
> Improving classroom management
> Improving subject matter competence
> Helping colleagues
> Preparing for the substitute teacher

This text has attempted to pinpoint some personal and technical aspects of teaching that affect successful performance in the classroom. Much of teaching is a matter of habit. We develop certain ways of doing things and dealing with problems, and then we utilize these systems over a long period of time. For a teacher to change teaching habits, it is necessary to analyze personal weaknesses and technical errors. This requires a great deal of time and dedication, but professional growth and change will not occur without personal effort.

Classroom teachers must spend hours preparing challenging tasks, making learning centers and learning packets, arranging the classroom environment, and correcting papers. The true professional also spends hours learning subject field knowledge, translating that knowledge for instructional purposes, and learning pedagogy. For example, to teach controversial issues in a way that allows students to confront the values on both sides of an issue requires more knowledge and preparation by the teacher than does lecturing or a textbook assignment. The uninformed and the novice may not recognize the effort and time it takes to perform in a professional manner.

To change a habitual pattern of teaching requires analysis of where you are and where you want to be. If heretofore you have been a highly structured teacher utilizing in the main input strategies, and you want to develop a more complete repertoire of teaching strategies, then you will need to identify your skill deficiencies just as you would do for students. You must also remember to work on one skill at a time. It is suggested that you work with a colleague to identify your personal style and to develop a plan for change.

HOW IS TEACHING EVALUATED?

Parents evaluate teaching performance every morning when their son or daughter says, "I can't wait to get to school." *Or*, "I'm not feeling so good today; I think I better stay home." Parents can also evaluate teaching performance by examining the papers that come home and by questioning their child's understanding about what was taught. The examination of homework papers is another way to learn about teaching. The child's feelings about school and teacher provide affective evidence about teaching performance. The child's understanding and the homework assignments provide cognitive evidence of teaching. It should be noted that to evaluate teaching performance using the afore-mentioned evidence, parents do *not* have to step into the classroom.

Some principals evaluate teaching performance by the number of telephone calls, notes, and visits that are motivated by the classroom performance of a particular teacher. Again, the administrator does not personally have to observe the classroom scene. Consequently, teaching can be evaluated by what students reveal in terms of learning performance and by their feelings about school and teacher. Other ways to evaluate teaching, of course, include observation of what a teacher does in the classroom, what students do while the teacher "does," and by observing the classroom environment.

What Is Evaluated?

There are three components that can be judged: the teacher's personal and professional behaviors, the teacher's subject matter competence, the teacher's methodological skills. These three components often become enmeshed as the teacher implements personal teaching style. For instance, when Johnny awakened and told his parents that he did not want to go to school, his parents were soon able to make a number of inferences about Johnny's classroom.

1. Children cannot get out of their seats and move freely around the classroom. (Parents learned about the organization of the classroom.)
2. Children may not interrupt the teacher. (Parents learned about classroom rules.)
3. Children cannot go to the bathroom because of the preceding two rules. (Parents learned about teaching style.)
4. Johnny does not want to go to school because he fears he will need to go to the bathroom. (Parents learned about the affective climate of the classroom.)

Johnny's parents have learned about the socioemotional climate of the classroom, and this information revealed additional evidence about the teacher's personal/professional relationships and teaching methods. Table 11.1 illustrates what Johnny's parents learned.

Who Evaluates?

Students evaluate, consciously and unconsciously; parents and other adults evaluate; colleagues evaluate; *you* evaluate. (Administrators evaluate, too, and decide whether or not the teacher will remain at the school, but administrative evaluation is not the concern of this textbook.) Because *you* are the most important person, the chapter will begin with the process of self-evaluation.

Teacher self-evaluation is similar to student self-evaluation; it can occur by using checklists, rating forms, accountability forms, or a more sophisticated system using tape recordings of actual teaching lessons so that the teacher can use an observation form to listen for very specific lesson components. Each of these items will be described or exhibited for personal use.

PERSONAL AND PROFESSIONAL COMPETENCE

The Visible Dimension

Interrelationships with students, colleagues, staff, and parents can be considered the visible dimension that is evaluated constantly. This

Table 11.1. Structure of Classroom Environment

High Structure	*Low Structure*
Subject-centered curriculum	Student-centered curriculum

Authoritarian teacher behaviors
   teacher makes rules and decisions
	Democratic teacher behaviors
	   teacher and students make rules
	   and decisions

dimension is usually considered the personal and professional side of the teacher. Students evaluate as you say "Hi" to Billy and nod at Jennifer. Or, when you answer Jennifer's questions but send Billy back to his seat. The following checklists provide some self-appraisal means to evaluate your personal and professional relations with students. Another means is to sit down and make a list of every student in your classroom. Next to the child's name, write something about him or her that you remember. Now evaluate yourself. Did you remember every child in the class? Did you remember only the "smarts" and only the "nuisances"? Did you write something positive about each child? If you wrote negative statements, would you write them on a cumulative record? Now think about whether you treat each of the students consistently and with equity. Are your negative statements or your lack of recall indicative of your treatment of the student?

The appraisal instrument in Table 11.2 uses the term "all students." This means boys and girls, high-ability students and low-ability students, minority and majority students. Think about each of these students as you answer.

The appraisal form in Table 11.3 deals with your personal and professional relations with other members of the school staff and faculty.

Personal and professional relations must also be extended to parents. Evaluate your parent communications and your conference manners in the form in Table 11.4.

DO YOU WANT TO IMPROVE?

If you have been frank with yourself and have identified areas of strength and of vulnerability, it is time to decide whether you really want to change. Changing teaching behavior is hard work, but if you really improve your performance, you will discover that life is considerably more comfortable.

Choose One Skill to Improve

A textbook cannot do the work for you, but it can suggest some plans. You will have to choose the plan that will work for you. In order to provide you with some ideas for improvement, one specific behavior has been chosen to illustrate the plans. Pretend that one of our fictitious teachers was inconsistent in developing and encouraging students' participation and involvement. The teacher's first task is to gather some evidence about participation and involvement. The teacher, Stewart Jackson, will use an evidence card (Table 11.5).

Table 11.2. Personal/Professional Relations with Students

Do you...?	Consistently	Occasionally	Rarely
1. Extend greetings to *all* students			
2. Provide encouragement and praise to all students			
3. Acknowledge the viewpoint of all students			
4. Provide assistance to all students			
5. Treat all students respectfully			
6. Provide nonverbal support to all students			
7. Establish rapport with all students			
8. Assist all students to set personal goals			
9. Allow all students to assist each other, foster cooperative behavior			
10. Subject all students to the same criticism when misbehavior occurs			
11. Favor all students similarly in seating arrangements			
12. Allow all children the opportunity to choose work and leisure activities			
13. Encourage student-to-student interaction			
14. Focus on positive behaviors			
15. Monitor student work and attention			
16. Encourage participation and involvement			
17. Move frequently around the room			
18. Verify students' understanding of assignments			
19. Control voice and manner			
20. Answer all students' questions			
21. Attend to problems without disrupting students' concentration			
22. Provide a system for students to request help			
23. Provide a system for students to leave room when necessary			
24. Characterize each child			

Table 11.3. Personal/Professional Relations with Staff and Faculty

Do you...?	Consistently	Occasionally	Rarely
1. Acknowledge divergent views			
2. Work harmoniously with colleagues			
3. Attend meetings			
4. Meet deadlines			
5. Establish rapport with staff and colleagues			
6. Communicate with staff and colleagues			
7. Act with poise in all situations			
8. Seek new information and insights for professional growth			
9. Use constructive suggestions			
10. Contribute information and insight			
11. Accept faculty responsibilities			

Table 11.4. Personal/Professional Relations with Parents

Do you...?	Yes	No
1. Develop rapport		
2. Communicate both positive and negative information		
3. Focus on the purpose or problem		
4. Describe your instructional approach		
5. Interpret test information		
6. Listen		
7. Make suggestions		
8. Summarize		
9. Ask for additional information		

Table 11.5. Evidence Card, Accountability

Objective: To encourage students' participation and involvement
Date 11/13/88
Subject: Social Studies, Period 5
Evidence:
1. Almost all of the students talked at least once during discussion.

Not bad. Stewart Jackson has some evidence that there was some class participation in one subject, but he feels dissatisfied. Perhaps he is aware that the students did not participate too willingly and that the discussion was mostly student-to-teacher-to-student rather than student interaction. It is time to plan. The accountability planning guide (Table 11.6) will illustrate the next step.

The next step is to try it out. Then record how you feel about it. Turn your accountability planning guide over and evaluate:

I accomplished the objective because:
I did not accomplish the objective because:

At the end of the chapter you will find a blank evidence card and a blank accountability planning guide for you to duplicate for your own use. If your plan did not work, replan and try again. Remember that good teaching is hard work.

ANOTHER PLAN.   Using the same objective, Midge Brady devised the following scheme:

1. Gather more evidence. Talk to each child in the classroom privately for at least 3 minutes during a one-week period.
2. Ask questions; listen to the student in order to learn more.
3. Find out "what turns the student on."
4. Plan specifically for each child using the information gained.

Now evaluate whether it worked. Did your personalized plan achieve participation from each child? If it did not, get more information; have another talk with the student.

Try again. Did you find a way to encourage the student's involvement? Do you feel you know the student better? If you are still not successful, get some help. Ask a colleague for some ideas. See one of the student's prior teachers. Ask a colleague or your principal to visit and watch what you do, and what the student does.

Table 11.6. Accountability Planning Guide

Objective: To encourage participation and involvement
Subject: Social Studies
Plan:
1. Rearrange discussion circle so that students face each other
2. Motivate and use role-playing
3. Plan small-group research.

Methodological Competence

The line that separates professional expertise and methodological skills is arbitrary. Typically the term *methods* signifies teaching procedures, and so methodological competence deals with the management of lesson components and the teacher's ability to project plans and procedures over a period of time. Lesson components are the same in almost all subjects though they may vary in sequence depending on the teaching strategy. It is, however, possible to generalize about lesson components. Some lesson components, such as diagnostic tasks, differ depending on the subject, but the necessity to perform diagnosis exists at all times; for this reason it is included under "methods." Table 11.7 provides you with a checklist to evaluate some basic teaching skills.

Table 11.7. Methodological Competence

Do you...?	Consistently	Occasionally	Rarely
1. Promote student attention			
2. Arouse interest at beginning of lesson			
3. Focus on the concept			
4. Provide instructional materials at varied levels			
5. Provide activity to appeal to different ability levels			
6. Individualize instruction			
7. Adjust lesson to students' needs			
8. Pace activity and instruction to challenge students			
9. Encourage students' creativity			
10. Provide appropriate reinforcement			
11. Share teaching objectives with students			
12. Evaluate students' progress at the end of each lesson			
13. Diagnose needs based on variety of data			
14. Encourage individual goal setting			
15. Ask questions at varied levels of thought			
16. Develop short- and long-term planning goals			

TEACHER-TO-TEACHER COACHING

Suppose you are aware that you are a one-strategy teacher; you do not have a repertoire of approaches that you can call upon to diversify instruction and to match instruction with desired outcomes. You and several colleagues are acquainted with Joyce and Showers' (1982) training model used to develop models of teaching. You have decided to use the elements of the model. The model includes the following components:

1. Theory or rationale of the teaching model
2. Observation or demonstration of the model
3. Practice and feedback using the model with colleagues
4. Coaching while using the model with students

The effects of these components indicate that although all of the elements are desirable, the model only works if all of the components are put together. Studies by Joyce and Showers indicate that during the practice and feedback phase (element 3) it is important to first practice in a safe environment with colleagues, then transfer the model to a small group of "well-behaved" students before trying the model with an entire classroom of students.

The coaching element is extremely important for several reasons. First, it is relatively easy when trying a new strategy to take shortcuts and to improvise on skills that you have really not mastered. The consequence is that you may destroy the desired outcomes. Second, you may not perceive that you are not following the model, and as a consequence you habituate teaching errors. Third, a coach in the room when you practice can make suggestions on adapting the strategy to the particular students in your classroom. Typically, when you try a new strategy, you are so concerned with your own teaching behavior, you are unable to "see" students' reactions.

So it appears that there needs to be continuous practice, feedback from peers, and coaching until one is really comfortable in using a new model of teaching and has developed executive control. This means that you have mastered the skills involved in the teaching model and can adapt the model across subject fields and with different groups of students and different classroom settings.

Joyce and Weil (1986) believe that the real difficulty teachers have in learning new strategies relates to the problem of transfer. They feel that a new skill must really be mastered before it is attempted with students. The skill should be practiced in the training setting before *transferring* the skill to the classroom where it needs to be adapted to students.

You and your colleagues will attempt one new model of teaching at a time. You will not hurry the process because you are aware that during learning you will be feeling uncomfortable and classroom management may be more difficult. This will occur because your transitions and pacing of instruction may not be as smooth as you are accustomed to, but you are *forewarned* about the importance of practice in order to master the necessary skills and attain control of the teaching model.

The team you have formed for improving performance needs to be considerate of each other's goals, and as peer coaches you need a respectful and trusting relationship acknowledging each other's knowledge and skills. It is important that you dialogue together using common terms to describe teaching and refine methodology.

IMPROVING THE QUALITY OF QUESTIONS

Questions need to be purposeful. Sometimes teachers find themselves asking several questions because they failed to ask the "right" question. This usually occurs when teachers are not well prepared for conducting a discussion.

Studies of teacher questioning reveal that approximately 80 percent of teachers' questions are "low-level" questions. The cognitive and affective level of questions refers to the Bloom taxonomy (1956) and the Krathwohl et al. taxonomy (1964). The cognitive domain consists of the following classifications: knowledge, comprehension, application, analysis, synthesis, and evaluation. Low-level questions usually refer to the knowledge and comprehension levels. The affective domain uses the following classifications: receiving, responding, valuing, organization, and characterization. (Refer to Chapter 5 for examples of the taxonomies).

Since questions should include both lower level and higher order questions in order to challenge students' thinking, teachers need to analyze whether their questions are clear and purposeful, thought provoking, and directed at the desired level of thought. Table 11.8 provides a way to analyze questions by classifying their level. List your questions and then tally them. Are the questions all low level or do you have a good mix? Are your questions challenging and provocative? Do your questions encourage spontaneous as well as reflective responses?

Another way to improve questioning skills is to tape-record a teaching episode. Then listen to the tape recording, record your questions, and listen to students' responses. You may want to analyze the level of thought of the questions as well as the level of thought of the responses.

Listen for the purpose of your questions. Do your questions and comments relate to the content you are teaching or do they relate to

Table 11.8. Question Analysis

List Questions	Knowledge	Comprehension	Application	Analysis	Synthesis	Evaluation	Valuing	Characteristics
Total								

classroom management? It has been found that teachers make several types of comments when they are teaching. These comments (or questions) usually relate to (1) lesson organization, (2) behavior reminders, (3) instruction, and (4) motivation and encouragement. By listening to a short teaching episode on the tape recorder, it is possible to identify most of your questions and comments to students. Tally your questions and comments using the underlined letters as a code. If too many of your comments relate to behavior and lesson organization you may want to analyze the problems you are having.

RESEARCH AND READINGS

Shavelson, R. J., Winkler, J. D., Stasz, C., & Feibel, W. (1985). Patterns of microcomputer use in teaching mathematics and science. *Journal of Educational Computing Research, 1*(4), 395–413.
Studies of teachers' use of microcomputers in elementary and secondary schools for teaching mathematics and science reveal that the computer is used for drill and practice, tutorials, simulations, and games.

CLASSROOM MANAGEMENT

The competent teacher manages strategy, variety, group changes, material organization, and environmental organization smoothly and automatically. Beginning teaching is characterized by abrupt movements of groups within the classroom and studied changes; however, as teachers become experienced, their competence develops primarily because they learn to think ahead, plan in advance, anticipate the possible and probable. The checklists in Tables 11.9 and 11.10 are aimed at goal setting so that you can identify some specific areas for improvment.

Evaluate your classroom environment (Table 11.11). Examine the bulletin boards, arrangement of furniture, learning centers, equipment and storage centers, and instructional materials. If you are not satisfied with the way your room looks, decide how you will change it. It is sometimes rewarding to allow students to offer suggestions about the room arrangement.

Frequently teachers feel that their room environment inhibits group work. The only time this author has ever found that to be true has been in a high school where the chairs were permanently attached to the floor, and there was absolutely no way for students to be seated and look at each other. As long as it is possible to rearrange furniture, the environment will support group work. The checklist in Table 11.12 evaluates group management procedures.

Table 11.9. Classroom Management

Do you...?	Consistently	Occasionally	Rarely
1. Manage change smoothly from large to small groups or small- to large-group instruction			
2. Manage input strategies			
3. Manage output strategies			
4. Manage change from input to output strategies			
5. Manage without delay to get students' attention			
6. Manage transitions without disruptions or delays			
7. Manage to attend to overlapping incidents			
8. Manage to scan and monitor the classroom			
9. Maintain student concentration during task assignments.			

Table 11.10. Planning Components

Choosing a subject field, can you...?	Yes	No
1. Identify appropriate goals		
2. Identify concept(s) to be taught		
3. Write behavioral objectives		
4. Write a question focus		
5. Sequence learning experiences		
6. Write multilevel materials for instruction		
7. Choose multilevel materials		
8. Define a variety of means to evaluate students' learning progress		

Table 11.11. Classroom Environment

	Yes	No
1. Does the furniture arrangement consider traffic patterns?		
2. Does the furniture arrangement provide flexible grouping centers?		
3. Is there an area for directed teaching?		
4. Do you change the bulletin boards frequently?		
5. Do the instructional materials meet varied needs and interests?		
6. Do you have learning centers?		
7. Do the centers appeal to varied needs and interests?		

Table 11.12. Group Work

Did you remember to...?	Yes	No
1. Assign each group a working space		
2. Suggest choosing a group leader and group recorder		
3. Verify understanding of group task		
4. Provide appropriate materials		
5. Provide a system for obtaining help		
6. Communicate time constraints		
7. Communicate a system for class attention		
8. Provide a system for free time choice activities		

Subject Matter Competence

One of the best personal ways to assure yourself that you have subject matter competence is to test yourself using the planning components in a specific subject field. If you want (or your district tells you that you should) to teach a unit about the environment at your grade level and you are unable to identify appropriate concepts, then you need to do some reading and perhaps some coursework to provide you with the knowledge components. Similarly in a skill area, if you review a skill continuum in reading or mathematics but are unable to provide examples of the components to be taught or unable to think of appropriate learning experiences, then you may need some professional preparation.

The public believes, and rightfully so, that students' learning progress is a measure of their teachers' subject matter competence. By measuring students' learning gains, teachers can determine their own teaching effectiveness. Begin in a skill area, such as reading, and use a skill continuum to assist you. As an example, let us assume that Midge Brady believes that she has taught her students a number of different ways to analyze the structure of words. In order to discover how effective she was *and* to discover individual student skill deficiencies, she will test her students' structural analysis skills (Table 11.13).

Comprehension skills could be tested in a similar fashion by developing a test to provide information about the effectiveness of your instruction in certain skills (Table 11.14).

Table 11.13. Structural Analysis Skills

Skill	Barry	Cary	Mary	Sarah	Howard	B. J.	Ramsey
1. Discriminates variant endings (*s, es, d, ed, ing, er, est*)							
2. Discriminates compound words							
3. Discriminates root words							
4. Identifies contractions							
5. Identifies possessives							
6. Identifies prefixes							
7. Identifies suffixes							
8. Can change word forms by dropping final "e" and adding "ing" or by adding a "d" to the final "e"							
9. Can change singular forms to plural forms							

Students' Names

Table 11.14. Comprehension Skills

Skill	Barry	Cary	Mary	Sarah	Howard	B. J.	Ramsey
					Students' Names		
1. Identify characters and speakers							
2. Interpret characters' feelings							
3. Identify cause-and-effect conditions							
4. Sequence the order of events							
5. Explain figurative language							
6. Identify colloquial expressions							
7. Interpret descriptive passages							
8. Explain author's purpose							
9. Suggest alternative conclusions							
10. Compare characters' problems with personal problems							

Using social studies materials the teacher can test skills such as critical thinking (Table 11.15).

Skill tests can be devised in all subject areas, and there are many commercial tests available for teachers' use.

Thus far in this chapter a number of ideas have been presented to assist teachers in identifying their areas of strength and areas of weakness. Most of the suggestions can be used by a teacher working alone in a classroom; however, when colleagues work together discussing mutual problems and planning goals for improvement, professional growth is more rewarding. The next section will deal with collegial tactics.

COLLEGIAL TEACHING

A number of years ago while teaching in an elementary school, the author recalls sitting in the teachers' room with four other colleagues at recess time. We were having a fierce debate about teaching methods. The bell rang, but we were too involved to hear it. Not until a passing student concerned about the "shouting" within opened the door did we become aware that we needed to go to class.

Table 11.15. Critical Thinking Skills

Skill	Barry	Cary	Mary	Sarah	Howard	B. J.	Ramsey
			Students' Names				
1. Uses guide words in a dictionary							
2. Uses reference books							
3. Arranges events for research							
4. Sequences events or facts							
5. Differentiates between fact and opinion							
6. Recognizes value biases							
7. Recognizes stereotyped expressions							
8. Chooses acceptable source materials and states reasons for choices							
9. Distinguishes between relevant and irrelevant facts							
10. Uses evidence to make a decision							

At lunch time the five of us returned, and the discussion continued. Our principal wandered in and joined the debate, remarking that she couldn't understand how we could manage to proceed in this way day after day—and enjoy it so much. Today, although each of us has changed, we are steadfast friends. Our mutual respect is undiminished, but our contentions continue.

True professional growth ensues because professionals are interested enough to disagree with each, offer suggestions, criticisms, support, ideas, and take the time to say, "Let me show you." Improvement occurs as a consequence of "being shown," attendance at professional conferences, readings, in-service class attendance, *and* a never-ending debate about what works.

Some Ways to Begin

Share something special that you have created such as a skill game that you have made or an unusual bulletin board display or an idea for a learning center. Invite a neighboring teacher or another teacher at the same grade level to your room to see what you have prepared. Exchange materials with this colleague and suggest a reciprocal arrangement so that you can begin enriching your classroom environment while making life easier for yourself at the same time.

Exchange unit teaching plans. Critique each other's plans in terms of the concepts identified, the level of questions to be asked, and the sequence of learning experiences. Make suggestions. Offer instructional materials. Assist in the development of resources. Plan a joint trip to a district, county, or commercial center to borrow, beg, or buy materials.

Talk about what works, what would be *more* effective. Invite other colleagues in to discuss teaching methods, evaluation of instructional materials, homework assignments, and evaluation of learning gains. Do not be afraid to disagree with each other.

Visit each other's classrooms *during teaching moments* by arranging supervisory tactics for students with other colleagues, or use parent volunteers or teacher assistants to relieve one or several teachers. Plan what is to be observed. (If it is the classroom environment, then you do not need children present.) Teaching style, classroom management, student interaction, specific teaching techniques (role playing) are all appropriate for colleague observation and evaluation.

Plan with your colleague a system for recording information so that you will have feedback. Tables 11.2, 11.3, 11.7, 11.9, and 11.12 are appropriate for a collegial observation. In addition, there are some elements of personal behavior that can only be recognized by someone else. For instance, your colleague can evaluate voice quality, dress, poise, and nonverbal mannerisms (Table 11.16).

Lesson evaluation can be accomplished by a colleague using the form shown in Table 11.17; however, it should be accompanied by collegial suggestions.

APPRAISAL BY STUDENTS AND PARENTS

An astute teacher can manage student appraisal using a number of subjective techniques. For instance, the primary teacher can use a calendar and have students draw a picture or keep a diary about how they feel each day. The pictures can describe their emotions. The diary can be more specific and students can record "what went best," "what I did not like," "how my teacher helped me," "what I would like my teacher to do." (Better be careful with that last one!) Some primary teachers hang a picture of a thermometer in the room, and at the end of the day students record the temperature in terms of a great day, average day, fair day, bad day.

A form could be devised for older students to check how they feel about the teacher's responsiveness, preparation, motivation, enthusiasm, interest in students, fairness, consistency, assignments, and

Table 11.16. Evaluation of Personal Qualities

	How Ineffective or Effective
Voice	
Too low, too high	_____
Slow, pauses, slurred	_____
Monotone, screech	_____
Non-verbal	
Eye contact	_____
Enthusiasm	_____
Poise	_____
Hand gestures	_____
Posture	_____
Movements	_____
	How Inappropriate or Appropriate
Dress	_____
Language	_____

Table 11.17. Lesson Evaluation

	Effective (5)	Improvement Needed (Suggestions) (1)
1. Objectives, purpose		
2. Motivation		
3. Responsiveness to students' needs		
4. Task presentation		
5. Use of resource materials		
6. Encouragement of self-discipline		
7. Encouragement of participation		
8. Management of organizational routines		
9. Clarity of task assignment		
10. Appropriateness of task assignment		
11. Monitoring of student attention		
12. Evaluation of student work		
13. Overall preparation		

Observer's Suggestions:

examination procedures. Students should also be asked whether they feel comfortable about coming to the teacher for help.

The observation checklist in Figure 9.11 for classroom visitors would be one way to have parents evaluate what is happening in the classroom. In addition, parents can be asked to fill out a take-home survey about classroom teaching and/or letters personally addressed to parents can ask them to respond to items such as the following:

1. Appropriateness of homework assignments
2. Length of time needed by students for homework
3. Assistance from parents with homework
4. Students' feelings about work assignments, classroom environment, teacher's responsiveness, teaching methods

PREPARING FOR A SUBSTITUTE TEACHER

Consider what it would be like to walk into your classroom not knowing school rules, classroom standards, students' names, or where supplies are located. A substitute teacher often feels "deaf," "blind," and "dumb" instead of comfortable, creative, and important. Studies of student achievement indicate how important it is that students receive as much instructional time as possible. Therefore, it is certainly essential that when substitute teachers are replacing regular teachers, classwork should proceed without too much variation or loss of time.

To effectively manage the classroom the substitute teacher needs to know:

Students' names, seating chart(s)
Daily time schedule indicating recess, lunch time, dismissal
Daily subject schedule
Classroom rules/standards
Generalized lesson plans indicating precise starting point for a given lesson and the approximate amount of material to be covered
Location of audiovisual equipment if it is to be used
Special information (where should the substitute meet the students—on the playground, in the classroom?)
Location of teacher's manuals and other text materials

One of the first chores a classroom teacher must undertake is the preparation of a "substitute folder" with all of the information mentioned above except the lesson plans. Since one can sometimes recognize the beginning of an illness, the plan book or lesson plans can be left in plain sight on the desk top the night before an absence. Many teachers use a semester plan book to record their daily plans. It is a good idea to leave this out for the substitute. In this way she or he can study the sequence of instruction and provide better lessons for students.

If you are writing lesson plans for a substitute teacher, do not make them too involved. Remember that the substitute teacher is probably a creative professional who would like some free time to teach a special lesson to the students. Although it is important for students' work to progress in an orderly manner, it is also desirable for them to learn to appreciate other adults; substitute teachers usually bring along several creative lessons with which to challenge and motivate students.

Teachers are also responsible for preparing students to receive substitute teachers courteously. Students should recognize that no matter how good a substitute teacher may be, the school day will progress somewhat differently than usual. No matter how carefully the substitute teacher attempts to follow written plans, routines will vary, communication will be different, and students' behavior will not be the same.

Suggestions for the Substitute Teacher

Hopefully you were notified early about your assignment and you have arrived in the classroom with time to spare. Your first task is to find the "substitute folder." With luck it is on the desk top or in the upper right-hand drawer of the teacher's desk. Check for the seating chart; then study the daily schedule. Locate the teacher materials and texts you will need. Remember that you want the curriculum to be as close to normal as is possible so that students do not have to accommodate too many changes.

Place the seating chart at the location where you will be most often. If you are teaching young children, you might check to see if they have name cards to place on their table tops.

When the students arrive, introduce yourself. Let the students know that you will try to maintain their normal schedule of activities; however, there are bound to be some differences, and you expect them to adjust and accept some changes in their normal program of studies. Be sure to write your name on the chalkboard.

Begin work quickly; keep class business to a minimum. Try to set a fast pace of activities. Remind students that you expect courteous, respectful behavior and that you will reciprocate. Do not threaten the students; this usually backfires.

If you are an elementary substitute teacher, plan at least one unusual, creative lesson to challenge students. You want students to remember you for something that you have taught them. Make them think rather than just keep busy.

At the secondary level plan something intriguing within your area of expertise. Remember that it is always better to provide depth in an area of specialization than to try to teach something you know little about.

Survival Kit
Bring with you one whole day's plan, just in case! Keep it uncomplicated so that you do not need too many materials. Prepare one lesson with duplicated materials for instant use. Prepare mentally for unexpected happenings like audiovisual equipment that does not arrive, assemblies that are canceled, and speakers that do not appear.

Good Sense
If students ask to leave the room, verify the need and purpose. For the student who claims to be ill, send him or her with a classmate to the nurse. Write a note to the nurse and ask for a written response from the nurse. This will usually flush out anyone who is faking an illness.

At the end of the school day leave a note for the regular teacher. Leave students' work papers for the day corrected, if possible. Tidy the classroom and be sure to lock the door when you depart. Finally, remember to check out in the school office before leaving school grounds.

SUMMARY

Improving teaching performance depends on assessing the disparity between what you want to accomplish and what you have accomplished. The variance between these two points identifies improvement goals. Effectiveness is a developmental process; teachers become more proficient in their technical skills because they isolate a specific skill in order to analyze its characteristics so that form and style can be mastered.

Professional growth never has to cease. As one goal is achieved, another should be sought. Professional growth is a very private, individual concern. It cannot be programmed for the individual nor will it occur without active participation. Each individual must define personal priorities and decide how to accomplish them.

If you are concerned about the improvement of teaching, then consider ways to achieve the following:

Bridge the gap between school and home.
Listen to each child and develop sensitivity to individual differences.
Expand teaching methods.
Develop a repertoire of teaching techniques.

Master organizational routines.
Assess learning behaviors.
Evaluate learning outcomes.

Best wishes, good luck!

CASE STUDY PROBLEMS

1. Cooperative Development. You have attended an in-service class and learned about the concept attainment teaching model. You tried it with your students but you were not too successful. Your neighboring teacher also learned about the model. The two of you want to cooperate to improve each other's skills using the model. To focus your observations of each other, develop an observation form to gather data.

2. Nonevaluative Assistance. You have agreed to collaborate and observe informally in another teacher's classroom. You have discovered that your colleague has many classroom management problems. You do not want to be "evaluative" with your colleague. How can you offer assistance to improve instruction?

QUESTIONS

1. Develop a plan for professional growth for yourself. Make a list of activities to perform and/or academic course work.
2. Plan for an observation with your supervisor/principal. Decide what data you want your supervisor to gather when observing in your classroom.
3. Why do teachers have a problem of "transfer" when learning a new skill?
4. You are a substitute teacher. Plan a "generic" lesson to take to your next assignment.
5. Prepare a rating scale for your students to use to evaluate the clarity of your explanations, presentations, or some other aspect of your instruction.

APPENDIX

IDEAS FOR LEARNING CENTERS AND LEARNING PACKETS

The learning suggestions should be considered "seeds." When the seed is transplanted into a classroom, it must meet the needs of real students; therefore, the objectives, materials, and basic activities will need to be adjusted. The ideas should not be considered sacrosanct. Every teaching experience and every textbook about instruction should provide a basis for creative thought, and every idea should be considered in terms of "how can I use it?" Consequently, the ideas presented here should be thought about, extended, adapted, and modified to fit a specific group of students.*

The center ideas are presented using the following format:

Subject field or integrated areas
Intended grade level
Objective(s)
Activity
Materials
Evaluation
Procedure (if it is not obvious)
To extend (suggestions for enriching)
To simplify (suggestions for making an activity easier)

---

* Many of the ideas for learning centers can be modified for the development of learning packets.

WORD GAME

Language Arts

Lower, Middle Grades

Objective:

To reinforce sight word vocabulary.

Activities:

Students play a word game to practice their reading vocabulary.

Materials:

Game board constructed of tagboard, reading vocabulary words on small cards, chance cards, spinner, playing pieces.

Evaluation:

Word recognition.

Procedures:

1. Construct a game board in any shape on a piece of tagboard.
2. Use reading words written on small cards.
3. Write a number of "chance" cards for motivation:

> Go ahead 1 space.
> Go back 2 spaces.
> Move to the next chance space.
> Turn back to _____.

4. Make a spinner on a paper plate from 0 to 4 moves.
5. Develop rules, such as: Take the top word on the word pile. Say it. If you do not know it, ask others. If you said the correct word, spin the spinner and move the number of spaces directed by the spinner. If you land on a "chance" square, select the top chance card and do what it says. If you needed help with your word, you may *not* spin the spinner and you may *not* move. The first person to reach the end, wins. Always place your word cards and chance cards on the bottom of the pile.

To Extend:

Use more complicated words. In other subject fields concepts or facts may be presented instead of words, and students must respond with appropriate knowledge in order to proceed.

To Simplify:

Use easier words.

FIGURATIVE LANGUAGE

Language Arts

Upper Grades

Objectives:
Students will use figurative language; improve comprehension skills.

Activity:
This is a group activity. Students will take turns choosing an expression from the expression box; then each student will pantomime the expression while the others in the group try to guess the phrase.

Materials:
A box of expressions:

He got in my hair.
She put on the dog.
I fed her a line.
My check bounced.
I died laughing.
Some of my friends were hanging around.
I hotfooted it out of there.
He was born with a silver spoon in his mouth.
She spoke with forked tongue.
Stop horsing around.
She went out with an old flame.

Evaluation:
Observation.

To Extend:
Students may write their own favorite expressions and add them to the expression box for others to act out.

To Simplify:
Students may work in teams to act out the expression.

PICTURE ANALYSIS

Language Arts, Social Studies, Science

Middle, Upper Grades

Objectives:
Students will use picture clues to analyze climate and way of life, improve comprehension skills.

Activity:
> Varied climates and ways of life are depicted in pictures used in social studies and science textbooks. The students can use the text pictures or other pictures furnished by the teacher to analyze where the picture was taken and how the climate would affect the way of life of the people living in that region of the world.

Materials:
> Pictures reflecting varied regions and ways of life. Paper for recording ideas, pencils, tape recorder for children who need to tape their responses.

Evaluation:
> Group evaluation through discussion.

To Extend:
> Capable students can write or tape a report about ways in which people adapt to their environment.

To Simplify:
> Team students for group consensus about each picture.

PICTURES AND STORIES

Language Arts

Lower Grades

Objective:
> Students will extend comprehension skills by illustrating a given story.

Activity:
> Students draw pictures to illustrate teacher-written stories.

Materials:
> Paper folded in four with a story in each square, crayons.

Procedure:
> Each child chooses a paper containing four stories. After illustrating the story, each child reads stories to others at the center.

Evaluation:
> Appropriateness of the pictures.

To Extend:
> Use more complicated stories. Use the same technique with numbers and have students draw the correct number of objects in each square.

six	five
four	three

To Simplify:
>Limit the vocabulary.

Example:

Mother is baking a pie.	The boy is flying a kite.
Zoom, zoom, zoom. I can fly.	Run, run. I can run.

COMIC STRIP

Language Arts

Lower, Middle, Upper Grades

Objective:
>Students will compose a comic strip conversation.

Activity:
>Students write a comic strip conversation. Lower grade students may dictate their conversations, if necessary.

Materials:
>Comic strip for motivation, teacher-made comic strips or commercial comic strips with the conversation eliminated, pencils, crayons

Procedure:
>Students choose a comic strip and write a conversation for the characters.

Evaluation:
>Enjoyment, discussion, creative expression.

To Extend:
>Have materials available for students to draw their own comic strips and write the dialogue.

To Simplify:
>Students may dictate their conversations.

THE RIDDLE CENTER

Language Arts

Lower and Middle Grades

Objective:
>Students will use context clues to identify the object of a riddle.

Activity:
>Students choose several riddles each to read and draw the object of the riddle.

Materials:
>A box of riddles, paper, pencils, crayons.

Evaluation:
>Students can share their pictures and read the riddles. Riddle answers can be given in an answer book and students can self-check.

Example:

>I tell you when to go to school.
>I tell you when to go to bed.
>I make a noise to wake you up.
>What am I?

>I carry many people.
>I go fast.
>I travel to many cities.
>I have wings.
>What am I?

>I wear a uniform.
>I go from house to house.
>I carry messages.
>Who am I?

>I wiggle and wiggle.
>I move inch by inch.
>I am brown.
>I live in the ground.
>Who am I?

To Extend:
>Write some complicated riddles and have the students make up their own riddles to be solved by others.

To Simplify:
>Limit the number of riddles students work with and write simple ones.

STORY MATCHING

Language Arts

Lower Grades

Objectives:
>Students will extend interpretive skills and demonstrate comprehension.

Activity:
> Students will choose pictures from a picture box and choose an appropriate story about the picture from a story box. Children can draw from the picture box in turn and then take turns to locate the appropriate story. Each child reads to the others the story that is placed in front of him or her.

Materials:
> Interesting pictures of animals and people playing, working, performing some activity, and two boxes to contain pictures and stories.

Evaluation:
> Self-evaluation as students read stories to each other.

To Extend:
> Additional pictures can be used and students can write an appropriate story; additional stories can be given to the students, and they can be required to draw the picture that demonstrates the story.

To Simplify:
> Make the pictures obvious and the stories simple.

Examples:
> Picture: Fireman at work.   Boys playing basketball.
> Story: The fireman helps us.   The boys are playing.

VOCABULARY CENTER

Language Arts

Primary Grades

Objective:
> Extend vocabulary skills.

Activity:
> Students match opposites.

Materials:
> "Game" materials, teacher-made chipboard games

Evaluation:
> Students self-check by looking at back of game.

Procedure:
> The chipboard game has opposites for students to match. Beside each word is a string or shoelace. Student can turn card over to check work.
> > Suggested opposites: big-small; light-heavy; up-down; day-

night; wet-dry; short-tall; fat-thin; lost-found; boy-girl; inside-outside; few-many.

Example

◯ big	◯ outside
◯ boy	◯ many
◯ inside	◯ girl
◯ few	◯ small

Student strings the lace through the holes on the card. Each word on the left has a string.

To Extend:
Use numbers and have students match the numeral to the word.

"HELP"

Language Arts, Social Studies

Lower Grades

Objectives:
Students will develop communication skills. Using the telephone, students will summon help. Students will recall important telephone numbers.

Activity:
Students will use a play telephone to dial the police and the fire department. They will practice communicating important information. They will make personal telephone directories.

Materials:
Two play telephones or real ones, modified telephone directories (teacher made), flannel board and numerals, chart with key numbers of police and fire departments.

Procedure:
1. Students should use the chart to find the telephone number of the police and then the fire department.
2. Students should take turns and pair off with one student practicing summoning help and the other playing the role of the police and fire department. (Students should exchange roles.)
3. Students should exchange telephone numbers by attaching numerals to the flannel board, and then each child writes the other group members' telephone numbers in a small private directory.

Evaluation:

Group evaluation of telephone manners and whether or not important information was conveyed quickly, efficiently, concisely. Important information needed by the police or fire department may be charted for the students to refer to in the future.

REAL OR MAKE-BELIEVE?

Language Arts, Art

Primary, Middle Grades

Objectives:

Students will differentiate between real and make-believe. Students will categorize real and make-believe pictures. Students will draw real and make-believe pictures.

Activity:

Students will use pictures from old fairy tale books to sort and categorize pictures into two groups: real and make-believe. Students will also draw their own pictures and label them either real or make-believe.

Materials:

Pictures from old fairy tale books, pictures from magazines, labeled sorting baskets, crayons, paper, pencils.

Evaluation:

Students will share their pictures and identify them as real or make-believe.

To Extend:

Students should write stories that are real or fanciful and share them with others.

STORY LISTENING CENTER

Language Arts

Primary Grades

Objectives:

Students demonstrate comprehension by identifying and ordering events. Students demonstrate ability to recall events. Students arrange events in the proper sequence.

Activity:

Students listen to a story at a listening post and then arrange related pictures in the proper sequence of the story.

Materials:

Listening post with a tape or record of a children's story, cut-out pictures of the story at a work table, chipboard or tray on which to place the pictures.

Evaluation:

Pictures can be numbered on the backs so that students can self-check.

To Extend:

Children can be asked to tell the story in its proper sequence. Children can draw story in proper sequence. Children can draw cartoon pictures to tell a story.

To Simplify:

Use a *familiar* story and have students arrange pictures on a flannel board. Check their work, then have them use the cut-outs and the tray. Students can also hold the pictures and arrange themselves (holding the pictures) in the appropriate order.

DATA GATHERING

Social Studies, Language Arts (Science, Health)

Lower, Middle, Upper Grades

Objectives:

Students will categorize concept attributes. Students will develop problem-solving, decision-making, and research skills.

Activity:

Students seek evidence to support and disprove the hypotheses. Lower grade children and the visually or audio-oriented child can use pictures, slides, filmstrips, taped materials. Middle and upper grade children can use, in addition, printed materials. Hypotheses should fit study and age group.

Materials:

Pictures, media, text materials.

Evaluation:

Discussion of the evidence that proves or disproves the hypotheses.

Hypotheses

E V I D E N C E	All African people are poor.	Few African people are educated.	Most Africans are religious.	
				For
				Against

Lower grade children can accumulate picture evidence that can be placed under the hypothesis in a pocket file chart.

TRUE? FALSE?

Social Studies, Language Arts

Middle and Upper Grades

Objective:

Students will distinguish between facts and opinions.

Activity:

Students will read teacher-prepared articles, text materials, or newspaper advertisements and discuss what they are reading or observing with a small group of peers. They must decide which statements are true and which statements are based on opinion. As a group or individually they can list the factual statements and those that are false or based on opinion.

Materials:

Articles and advertisements, paper, pencils.

Evaluation:

Teacher-prepared answer sheet; self-check.

To Extend:

Students can write reasons why manufacturers of products sometimes make misleading statements. Students can write their own list of true and false statements.

To Simplify:

Use advertisements in which the product is pictured and have students discuss how pictures can be misleading or precise.

NEWSPAPER CENTER

Social Studies, Language Arts

Upper Grades, Junior High School

Objectives:
> Students will perform the role of a newspaper reporter, observe an event, listen to an event, record data, synthesize information, editorialize.

Activity:
> Students will use information data cards, a story, or a tape recording of an actual incident. The students will take notes about the event, write an account of what happened, and editorialize about why it happened.

Materials:
> Tape recording (teacher made) about an animal escaping from the zoo, the birth of an animal, a problem, a conflict; information cards about an event; pictures of an event; paper, pencils, newspaper bulletin board.

Evaluation:
> Students read their articles and compare their stories with others. Students analyze why events are not described similarly. Students generalize about historical interpretations.

To Extend:
> Allow some students to be actors in an event and other students to be the reporters. The actors meet together and decide on an enactment. The reporters meet together and decide on the questions they will ask. The reporters must choose a spokesperson. After the press conference each reporter writes up the story and interprets why it happened.

MAP CENTER

Social Studies

Lower, Middle, Upper Grades

Objectives:
> Students will identify land sites; locate specific places; interpret map symbols, codes, and keys.

Activity:
> Students will be given a list of places to find. They will use an assortment of maps and globes and an atlas.

Materials:
>   Materials and activity will depend on the age group involved.
>   Lower-grade students may identify important neighborhood sites
>   using pictures of the supermarket or the fire station and place
>   them on a neighborhood map. Older students will need maps of
>   the city, state, or world depending on their task assignment.

Procedure:
>   Decide on specific places to be identified. Students can work in
>   groups of two for the assignment. Students can fill in a blank map
>   or (for young children) place a picture (market) in the appropriate
>   location.

Evaluation:
>   Group agreement concerning the location of specific places.

To Extend:
>   Number of items to locate can be increased as can the complexity
>   of the search.

To Simplify:
>   Pair students so that they can assist each other. Control the
>   number of locations to be identified.

THE IMMIGRANT GAME[1]

Social Studies

Upper Elementary Grades, Junior High School

Objectives:
>   Students will develop research skills as they gather information
>   about a specific minority group. Students will practice social
>   participation skills as they work cooperatively and compromise,
>   choosing relevant information for their game.

Activity:
>   Students will design and research a game to be played by other
>   members of their class. Each group of students using the center
>   will design a game about a different minority group. This activity
>   will consume at least ten working periods.

Materials:
>   Butcher paper to draw a game board with any desired number of
>   spaces, cardboard for chance cards, paper plate for a spinner

---

[1] Adapted from Johanna Lemlech, *Handbook for successful urban teaching*. New York: Harper
& Row, 1977, pp. 211–213.

(pointer attached with a brad and designations on spinner to read: 0, 1, 2, Chance, 3), resource materials about specific ethnic groups.

Object:

To advance from start to finish before other players; to overcome all immigrant obstacles.

Rules:

Player spins the spinner and moves or acts accordingly, moving zero to three spaces or drawing a chance card. If the player draws a chance card, he must follow its directions. Play lasts until at least one player crosses the finish line.

Procedure:

1. Students will work in teams to research the experiences and problems faced by an immigrant group. Each team studies a different group within a specified historical time period: Puerto Ricans in New York City, Irish in Boston, Mexicans in Southwest United States, freed or escaped slaves in Northern United States, Chinese in California.
2. Each team will draw a game board on butcher paper and cut out twenty-five chance cards from cardboard.
3. Each team will write on each chance card a problem or good luck experienced by the chosen immigrant group. The problems or experiences must be appropriate to the group and the historical time period.
4. After the games are constructed, students exchange games for classroom "play."

Examples of Chance Cards:

1. Your car ran out of gas and you were stopped by the Border Patrol. You did not have immigration permits. Start over.
2. You tried to rent an apartment in New York City, but the manager was afraid of "your kind." Go back three spaces.
3. Congress passes the Exclusion Act which prohibits your Chinese relatives from joining you. Go back five spaces.
4. You are a highly skilled seamstress and you have been hired to work in a clothing factory. Move ahead two spaces.

How Does the Teacher Evaluate a Game?

Debriefing is the most important aspect of gaming. In the preceding design, after students had the opportunity to exchange games and to play, the teacher should ask the following types of questions:

What problems did the (Mexicans) face?
How did you feel when these things happened to you?

Why did the (Mexicans) come to the United States?
What alternatives did they have?
In what ways did each group face similar problems?
In what ways were the problems different?

It is extremely important to remember that since gaming is
an output technique that motivates critical thinking, decision
making, and communication, there is seldom one course of action
or one answer to a problem. As in most teaching strategies the
lesson cannot be considered concluded until an evaluation (the
debriefing stage) has occurred.

CAUCUS AND DEBATE

Social Studies, Language Arts

Upper Elementary Grades, Junior High School

Objectives:
Students provide reasons or explanations for a historical act or a
point of view. Students debate the positive and negative aspects
of the act or viewpoint.

Activity:
Students choose a historical action and research the possible
alternatives. Using their notes, they debate both sides of the
question.

Materials:
Selected historical or contemporary positions and appropriate
research materials: pictures, slides, filmstrips, tapes, books.
"President Truman should have/should not have dropped the
atomic bomb." "All large cities are located next to a waterway."
"Pollution is caused by people not industry." "Cigarette smoking
in restaurants should be banned because smoking affects the
smoker and nonsmoker."

Procedures:
1. Each group chooses a debatable issue and researches the
   alternatives. When the research is concluded, the group divides
   and debates the issue. Each segment of the group draws from a
   bag to determine which side they will debate.
   OR
2. Two classroom groups research the same issue. After the
   research is concluded each group acts as a caucus to a chosen
   group spokesperson. The group must draw from a paper bag to

determine which side of the issue it will debate. The debate is
performed in front of the rest of the class.

Evaluation:
The debate itself will reveal whether or not students thought
about and researched all of the possible alternatives.

ROLES

Social Studies

Lower Grades

Objective:
Students will identify the role and function of different
occupations.

Activity:
Using a work sheet, students can match or write the occupation
and purpose for different work experiences in our society.

Materials:
Pictures of varied workers, apparel of varied workers, work sheet
for students to write on or on which to match role and function.

Procedure:
Pictures should be numbered, and they can be contained
in a "Who Am I" box. Students choose the picture, decide on
occupation and need for the pictured role. Numbers on work
sheet can correspond to numbers on pictures.

Evaluation:
Answer sheet can be available for students to self-check.
Discussion should focus on the importance of each of the
occupations.

To Extend:
Students can draw and write about their favorite careers.

ETHNIC RESTAURANTS

Social Studies, Language Arts

Upper Elementary Grades, Junior High School

Objective:
Students will construct an ethnic menu using resource materials.

Activity:
> Students will work together in small groups or teams to open a restaurant. Each restaurant must have an ethnic menu. The teams use resource materials and pictures to design their menu.

Materials:
> Pictures of food, pictures of restaurants, text material, or pencils, crayons, paints, typewriters (if available).

Evaluation:
> Each team presents its menu to the class. Evaluation discussion should focus on authenticity.

To Extend:
> Students can study their own city and find out what restaurants are available; investigate how restaurant diversity began, importance of way of life, contribution of diversity, where specialty restaurants obtain their special ingredients and foods, survey markets for ethnic specialties.

To Simplify:
> Group work will help the low achiever.

CONFLICT

Social Studies, Language Arts

Upper Elementary Grades, Junior High School

Objective:
> Students will provide a reason or explanation for the conflict and decide on ways to resolve the conflict.

Activity:
> Students will work in small groups and listen to a taped conflict or use pictures that depict a conflict or read about a conflict. As a group they will decide on the motivation for the conflict and project what will happen if not resolved. Finally they will decide on ways to alleviate the conflict.

Materials:
> Newspaper articles, pictures, tapes, paper, and pencils.

Evaluation:
> Each group shares its rationale for the conflict and system for resolution. Groups may debate the cause and the means to resolve.

To Extend:

Additional examples of the concept "conflict" can be used so that students improve their ability to think in terms of cause and effect.

To Simplify:

Group work will alleviate the problems of the low achiever.

Task Card Instructions

As a group discuss the following questions:

1. What happened?
2. Why did it happen?
3. What are the alternatives?
4. How can the conflict be resolved?

WEIGHT AND LENGTH

Science, Language Arts, Mathematics

Primary Grades

Objectives:

Students will sort objects into categories. Students will distinguish between heavy and light objects and between long and short objects. Students will extend vocabulary skills.

Activity:

Students will use a scale to weigh objects, and rulers to measure. They will categorize items into four groups: light, heavy, short, long.

Materials:

Labeled baskets, scale for weighing objects, ruler to measure, rocks, stones, marbles, discs, cotton, crayons, paint brushes, pencils, wooden figures.

Evaluation:

Observation and discussion.

To Extend:

Additional categories can be introduced: rough, smooth; hard, soft; big, small; light, dark.

To Simplify:

Use just the light and heavy category.

LIFE CYCLE

Science, Language Arts, Mathematics

Primary, Middle Grades

Objectives:

> Students observe the life cycle of plants and animals. Students sequence life-cycle events using ordinal numbers.

Activity:

> Students can observe the life cycle of plants or animals (seed to grown plants, tadpole to frog). Students can write sentences about the life-cycle events in order; students can cut out pictures and arrange them in order (pasting); students can use pictures already prepared and sequence them on a board or tray. Students can number their pictures: first, second, third, and so on.

Materials:

> Science charts depicting the growth of plants and animals; science books or pictures from *National Geographic* depicting growth; paste, crayons, scissors, pencils, actual plants at different stages of growth, tadpoles at different stages of development.

Evaluation:

> Self-evaluation. Pictures can be numbered on back. Students can use text or picture materials to "prove" their answers.

To Extend:

> Use the center as an experimental station and have students record their observations daily, describing the growth of a plant or animal. Provide an observation sheet on which students record the date, write their observation, draw a picture about it. Observation sheets should then be transferred to an individual folder.

Observation Notes

Date:
Observation:
> What did you see?

> In what ways was it different from the last time you observed?

> In what ways was it the same as the last time you observed?

> Draw a picture of your observation.

To Simplify:
> Use one event and have students sequence it and verify their observation with a prepared chart.

WEATHER STATION

Science, Language Arts

Middle and Upper Grades

Objectives:
> Students will observe temperature, air pressure, wind direction, wind velocity, and cloud forms. Students will record information and make predictions about the weather.

Activity:
> Students can use weather prediction instruments to record data about the weather and make daily predictions.

Materials:
> Mercury thermometer, alcohol thermometer, mercury barometer, wind vane, anemometer, weather maps, paper for recording information, pencils, daily newspapers, texts about the weather.

Evaluation:
> Students may compare their predictions with those of the weather bureau.

To Extend:
> Students may construct their own weather instruments and make weather maps.

To Simplify:
> Students may work in peer teams.

My Weather Chart

Name:					
	Monday	Tuesday	Wednesday	Thursday	Friday
Temperature					
Air Pressure					
Wind Direction					
Wind Velocity					
Cloud Type					

MAGNETISM

Science (Magnetism)

Lower and Middle Grades

Objectives:

> Students will discover what substances are attracted by magnets. Students will discover whether or not power can be exerted through other materials. Students will categorize the objects.

Activity:

> Students will experiment with magnets to discover what objects are attracted by magnets. Students can experiment to discover if power can be exerted through different materials by placing iron filings or pins on paper or glass and using the magnet underneath.

Materials:

> Magnets, tacks, iron filings, charcoal, soap, pins, corks, crayons, paper, glass, water, tin, rubber, erasers, chalk, paper fasteners, containers for sorting.

Evaluation:

> Observation and discussion.

To Extend:

> Students may write about what they have learned.

To Simplify:

> Peer cooperation.

MAGNETISM AND ELECTRICITY

Science (Magnetism and Electricity)

Upper Grades

Objectives:

> Students will discover ways to make work easier. Students will observe the difference between temporary magnets and permanent magnets. Students will make simple electromagnets and generalize about how to increase and decrease power.

Activities:

> Students will experiment with magnets and temporary magnets by creating an electromagnet using nails, copper wire, and dry cells. Through experimentation students will discover how to

increase or decrease the power of an electromagnet. Students will write and explain their experiments.

Materials:
Small magnets, tacks, nails, copper wire, sandpaper, dry cells, task cards, paper, pencils, simple machines.

Procedures:
Task cards should be numbered.

1. Use a magnet and test its strength by finding out how many tacks it will pick up. Test a large nail and see if it is magnetic.
2. Make an electromagnet by winding copper wire around a nail. Scrape the insulation from the ends of the wire and attach one end to a pole of the dry cell. Is the nail now a magnet? Attach both ends to the two poles of the dry cell. Have you created an electromagnet? Why?
3. Increase the number of turns of wire around the nail, then test its strength. Decrease the number of turns of wire around the nail and test its strength. Explain the difference.
4. Perform the same experiment using two dry cells. What happens? What do you have to do to make the experiment work? (A connecting wire between the two dry cells must be used; wire from the nail must travel to the opposite poles on the two dry cells.)
5. Write up your experiments explaining what you did and why you got the results you did.

Evaluation:
Students share the results of their experimentation.

To Extend:
The next two activities can be used to enrich the original experiment.

Objective: Students discover that current is needed to create an electromagnet.

Activity: 1. Students use a pushbutton to connect to the electromagnet. When the electromagnet current is complete—connecting nail, push button, and dry cells—the push button will buzz.

Materials: Nail, wire, sandpaper, dry cells, pushbutton.

Objective: Students will discover how messages can be sent using a telegraph.

Activity: 2. Students will make a simple telegraph by making an electromagnet: (a) attaching electromagnet to a

piece of wood, (b) suspending a piece of tin over
the electromagnet to make the sounder, (c) cutting
another piece of tin for a key, (d) under the key
attaching a small screw, (e) attaching wire
around the screw and attaching to a dry cell, and
(f) completing the circuit by attaching another
wire end from the electromagnet to the dry cell.
When students press the key that touches the
screw, the tin over the electromagnet should
vibrate and make a sound.

Materials: Tin, nails, wire, scissors or tin snips, sandpaper,
wood, screws, resource information about the Morse
code.

Evaluation: Observation and discussion.

WHAT IS GROWING?

Science, Health

Lower Grades

Objective:

Students will investigate different types of plant growth and
identify each.

Activity:

Seeds, mold, leaves, onions, radishes, and carrots will be
investigated using a magnifying glass. Students can decide what
kinds of plants are growing and what makes plants grow.

Materials:

Old bread (without a preservative), oranges, seeds for planting,
tinfoil pie plates, sponges.

Procedure:

The bread and oranges should be set aside on a separate dish and
observed, using the magnifying glass to determine what kind of
growth occurs. The seeds can be planted on the sponges and set
in the tinfoil pie plates. Some of the planted seeds may be stored
in a cupboard, others should receive sunshine; plants should be
watered. Students should observe and record their observations.

My Observation

Name:
1st day:
4th day:
7th day:
10th day:
14th day:

Evaluation:

Discussion about what is happening, why plants are different, and the conditions that affect growth.

To Extend:

Expect more detailed descriptions and observations.

To Simplify:

Observation with a peer.

METRICS

Mathematics

Middle Grades

Objective:

Students will practice using metric linear measures.

Activity:

Students will choose a variety of objects to practice measuring in metrics.

Materials:

Students may bring items to the center to measure. In addition: pencils, books, ice cream sticks, paper clips, pad of paper, meter stick, paper for answers.

Evaluation:

An answer sheet may be provided for some of the standard items in the center. Self-check.

To Extend:

Working with a friend, students can estimate the items to be measured, and then the measurements can be verified.

To Simplify:

Control the items to be measured so that they conform to exact measurements. Peer assistance.

Enrichment Work Sheet

	Estimate	Actual Measurement
Paper		
Card		
Book		
Pencil		

THE TOY STORE

Mathematics

Lower and Middle Grades

Objective:
Students will practice addition and subtraction facts by purchasing items at the store.

Activity:
Items at the toy store will be priced and students will be given an allowance in play money. They must decide what to purchase and how many items they can afford.

Materials:
Play money for adding and subtracting, paper, pencils, chart of items to purchase, motivating pictures.

Procedure:
Students are given coins to spend amounting to 50¢ or $1.00. They should be instructed to spend as much of their money as they can but not one penny more than they have. They must identify their purchases, how much they spend, and how much, if anything, is left over.

Example:
Chart with pictures and prices: Ball = 20¢, candy = 10¢, kite = 15¢, doll = 30¢, book = 20¢, gum = 5¢, clay = 10¢, truck = 15¢, crayons = 20¢, chalk = 15¢.

Evaluation:
Teacher must check students' work.

To Extend:
Capable students can be given constraints such as: You may purchase as many as eight items, but no fewer than six items.

To Simplify:
Use lower priced items.

HOW MUCH?

Mathematics

Lower Grades

Objective:

Students will practice number facts.

Activity:

Students will take turns reaching into a surprise box and withdrawing a problem. Students will solve the problem in different ways: using flannel board shapes, using ice cream sticks, using discs, writing the problem. Each student uses the manipulative objects first and then writes the problem using numerals and solves it.

Materials:

Box containing problems, manipulative objects, paper, pencils.

Evaluation:

Answer booklet can illustrate problem and answer. Students can self-check.

To Extend:

Students can demonstrate number families. If the problem is $4 + 5 = 9$, then students demonstrate with the manipulative objects all the possible ways to make 9.

To Simplify:

Peer assistance.

"I'M SORRY"

Music, Language Arts

Lower Grades

Objective:

Students will express feelings using instruments.

Activity:

Students use rhythm instruments to express typical feelings. Students can choose a word out of the feelings box and choose an instrument to express the word. After playing the instrument to express the word, the other students try to guess what the sound means.

Materials:

A feelings box of words, musical instruments—triangle, wood blocks, hand drum, jingle clogs, resonator bells, maracas, tambourine, sticks, cymbals, glockenspiel.

Evaluation:

Observation, listening.

To Extend:

Develop an art activity for students to make their own rhythm instruments. Use words to describe the feelings in the box: happy, bye, hello, sad, hurry, crying, angry, sorry, yippee, happy birthday, loudly, whisper.

MUSICAL JOURNEY

Music

Middle, Upper Grades, Junior High School

Objective:

Students will listen to musical compositions and decide on their place of origin.

Activity:

Students will listen to a selection of songs from different countries and identify each song's origin.

Materials:

Songs from around the world—taped or on a record, picture clues that illustrate the various songs or the countries of origin, answer sheet, pencils.

Evaluation:

Self-check with answer sheet at the learning center.

To Extend:

Students may make a musical map of the world.

TIMBRE

Music

Lower, Middle, Upper Grades, Junior High School

Objective:
> Students will listen to musical selections and differentiate among the instruments that they hear.

Activity:
> Using a work sheet that identifies the different instruments, students will listen to musical compositions and check the instruments that they are hearing.

Materials:
> Records or tapes, work sheets, pencils, pictures of instruments.

Evaluation:
> Self-check with an answer sheet.

Work Sheet Examples

1. Do you hear (a) strings, (b) woodwinds, (c) brass, (d) percussion?
2. Name the instruments that you hear.
3. Name the instrument that plays the melody.
4. Name the instrument you liked best.
5. Explain why you like that instrument.

To Extend:
> If instruments are available, have students make up a melody of their own.

FOLK MUSIC

Music

Upper Grades, Junior, Senior High School

Objectives:
> Students listen to folk music, identify historical time period, and explain meaning of lyrics.

Activity:
> Students listen to the folk music. Work songs are particularly good for this activity. Students use the time line to identify historical period. Students write several sentences to explain the meaning of the song and the probable motivation of the composer.

Materials:
> Recording, time line of historical periods, pencils, paper.

Evaluation:
> Reading and discussion about the historical events during several time periods.

To Extend:

Use just work songs, war songs, folk songs from other countries and have students conjecture about the meanings of the songs and the life of the people depicted.

To Simplify:

Students may draw pictures about the story that is told in the song instead of writing about it.

COMPOSING STATION

Music

Upper Grades

Objective:

Students will compose a three- to five-measure melody.

Activity:

Students will spin the clef and time signature spinners (made out of a paper plate, paper pointer, brad) to determine the constraints for their song. Students may work individually or with others. Using the constraints and tone bells, the students will compose a simple tune and record their tune on staff paper provided at the center.

Materials:

Clef and time signature spinners, staff paper, tone bells, pencils.

Evaluation:

Students play own and others' songs.

To Simplify:

Pair students for peer assistance.

MAKE A DESIGN

Art, Language Arts, Mathematics

Lower Grades

Objectives:

Students will create a design, will learn names for geometric shapes, and will title their design.

Activity:

Using colored paper, students will cut circles, squares, rectangles, triangles, polygons to create a design. They will arrange their shapes on a larger sheet of newsprint to create personal designs. Students will title their designs.

Materials:

Displays of geometric shapes and designs for students to see, colored paper, scissors, paste, dampened paper towels, waste receptacle, pencils.

Evaluation:

Students enjoy a creative experience.

Procedure:

Students should draw and cut their own shapes and then arrange them into a design. After the design is completed, the students can title their creation.

To Extend:

Story writing, writing poetry about their design, searching for shapes in the classroom and listing where they find them.

To Simplify:

Provide geometric shapes for students to choose or to copy.

GREETINGS

Art, Language Arts

Lower Grades

Objectives:

Students will develop small-muscle control performing arts and crafts. Students will express ideas in simple greetings.

Activity:

Students will make an original greeting card using an animal shape.

Materials:

Animal designs for tracing, colored paper, scissors, tracing paper, pencils, paste, waste receptacle, buttons, yarn, sequins.

Evaluation:

There are no wrong answers to this one!

Procedure:

A variety of animal shapes should be available for the students to trace. Students can transfer their animal shape to a piece of colored paper that has been folded in half. The shape is then cut carefully so that the greeting card will open and have a side for writing the message. The front side of the card is decorated with sequins, yarn, or whatever the student desires. On the inside the student writes a single greeting: "Hi," "Miss you," "Happy Birthday." Students will need a demonstration of the cutting procedure. They will probably need help with the message.

To Extend:

Students can design their own imaginary creatures instead of using the teacher's animals.

To Simplify:

Peer assistance.

CAN YOU RECOGNIZE ME?

Art, Language Arts

Lower, Middle Grades

Objectives:

Students will enjoy a creative experience, will express personal feelings wearing a mask, will demonstrate understanding of emotions.

Activity:

Students will make a mask, wear the mask, describe how they feel, and tell a story about themselves.

Materials:

Paper sacks, crayons, colored paper, paste, scissors, yarn, waste receptacle, dampened paper towels.

Evaluation:

Observation.

Procedure:

Students cut holes in the paper bag for eyes, nose, and mouth. They use the colored paper and other materials to decorate the mask, adding hair, eyeglasses, funny teeth, moustache, ears, and so on. After the masks are made, children put them on and tell a story about themselves or describe their feelings.

To Extend:

Students may act out parts in a play—demonstrate to others how they can change their voices and ways of speaking. (The following center is a variation of this one.)

HOW DO I FEEL?

Art, Language Arts

Lower, Middle Grades

Objective:

Students will demonstrate their understanding of emotional expressions by (1) drawing appropriate facial expressions, (2) telling how others feel, and (3) writing or dictating stories about personal feelings.

Activity:

Students will choose a card that identifies an emotion. The student will draw a facial expression to express the emotion. Students will identify how others feel; they will write stories or dictate stories about their own task card.

Materials:

Emotion cards, crayons, paper bags for drawing faces, pencils, writing paper.

Evaluation:

Observation.

Procedure:

Suggested emotion cards can include:

Sad
Happy
Crying
Hurt
Angry
Glad
Cold
Afraid
Ashamed
Embarrassed

To Extend:

Students can be encouraged to make inferences about why an individual may feel happy, sad, and so on. Capable students should be asked to give examples in their stories about the kinds of experiences that make them feel angry or hurt or ashamed.

To Simplify:

Students can dictate their stories to an aide or to an older child.

COLLAGE

Art

Primary, Middle Grades, Upper Grades

Objective:

Create a work of art.

Activity:
Students create a collage.

Materials:
Pictures from magazines, colored paper, scissors, paste, waste receptacle, wet towels for sticky hands.

Evaluation:
Self-expression, enjoyment, discussion, and collages.

Procedure:
Students can create their own pictures and shapes or cut out pictures from magazines to create an abstract, fanciful, or realistic collage.

To Extend:
Student may create three-dimensional designs using materials other than paper (wood, cardboard, cotton, buttons, etc.).

To Simplify:
Students will adapt this activity to their own ability levels naturally.

BIBLIOGRAPHY

Adams, R. S., & Biddle, B. J. (1970). *Realities of teaching: Exploration with videotape.* New York: Holt, Rinehart & Winston.

Aiello, B. (Ed.). (1975). *Making it work: Practical ideas for integrating children into regular classrooms.* Reston, VA: Council for Exceptional Children.

Anderson, L. (1984). The environment of instruction: The function of seatwork in a commercially developed curriculum. In G. Duffy, L. Roehler, & J. Mason (Eds.), *Comprehension instruction: Perspectives and suggestions* pp. 93–103. New York: Longman.

Arlin, M. (1979). Teacher transitions can disrupt time flow in classrooms. *American Educational Research Journal, 16,* 42–56.

Ausubel, D. (1963). *The psychology of meaningful verbal learning: An introduction to school learning.* New York: Grune and Stratton.

Bales, R. R. (1950). *Interaction process analysis—A method for the study of small groups.* Cambridge: Addison-Wesley.

Bandura, A. (1977). *Social learning theory.* Englewood Cliffs, NJ: Prentice-Hall.

Bandura, A., Ross, D., & Ross, S. A. (1961). Transmission of aggression through imitation of aggressive models. *Journal of Abnormal and Social Psychology, 62,* 575–582.

Bandura, A., & Walters, R. H. (1963). *Social learning and personality development.* New York: Holt, Rinehart & Winston.

Berliner, D. C., & Tikunoff, W. J. (1976). The California beginning teacher evaluation study: Overview of ethnographic study. *Journal of Teacher Education, 27,* 24–30.

Bigge, M. L. (1976). *Learning theories for teachers* (3rd ed.). New York: Harper & Row.

Birch, J. W. (1974). *Mainstreaming: Educable mentally retarded children in regular classes*. Reston, VA: Council for Exceptional Children.

Bloom, B. S. (Ed.). (1956). *Taxonomy of educational objectives: Handbook I: Cognitive domain*. New York: Longman.

Bloom, B. S. (1977). Affective outcomes of school learning. *Phi Delta Kappan, 59,* 193–198.

Bronfenbrenner, U. (1970). *Two worlds of childhood*. New York: Russell Sage Foundation.

Brooks, D. M., Silvern, S. B., & Wooten, M. (1978). The ecology of teacher-pupil verbal interaction. *Journal of Classroom Interaction, 14,* 39–45.

Brophy, J. E., & Evertson, C. M. (1976). *Learning from teaching a developmental perspective*. Boston: Allyn and Bacon.

Collins, M. L. (February, 1977) "The Effects of Training for Enthusiasm Displayed by Preservice Elementary Teachers." *Research in Education*. (ERIC Ed. 129773).

Dewey, J. (1944). *Democracy and education*. New York: The Free Press.

Dowaliby, F., & Schumer, H. (1973). Teacher-centered versus student-centered mode of college classroom instruction as related to manifest anxiety. *Journal of Educational Psychology, 64,* 125–132.

Doyle, W. (1986). Classroom organization and management. In M. C. Wittrock (Ed.), *Handbook of research on teaching* (3rd ed.). New York: Macmillan.

Doyle, W. (1984). How order is achieved in classrooms: An interim report. *Journal of Curriculum Studies, 16*(3), 259–277.

Dunn, L. M. (1967). Special education for the mildly retarded: Is much of it justifiable? *Exceptional Children, 34,* 5–22.

Erickson, F., & Mohatt, G. (1982). Cultural organization of participation structures in two classrooms of Indian students. In G. Spindler (Ed.), *Doing the ethnography of schooling*. New York: Holt, Rinehart & Winston.

Fantini, M. C. (1975). *What's best for the children?* Garden City, NY: Anchor Press.

Flavell, J. J. (1963). *The developmental psychology of Jean Piaget*. Princeton, NJ: Van Nostrand.

Fuchs, E. (1969). *Teachers talk*. Garden City, NY: Anchor Press.

Glaser, W. (1977). Ten steps to good discipline. *Today's Education, 66*(4), 61–63.

Glass, R. M., & Meckler, R. S. (1974). Preparing elementary teachers to instruct mildly handicapped children in regular classrooms: A summer workshop. In G. J. Warfield (Ed.), *Mainstream currents*. Reston, VA: Council for Exceptional Children.

Good, T. L., & Brophy, J. E. (1986). *Educational psychology* (3rd ed.). New York: Longman.

Good, T. L., & Brophy, J. E. (1987). *Looking in classrooms*. New York: Harper & Row.

Gray, W. H., & Gray, M. (November, 1985). Synthesis of research on mentoring beginning teachers. *Educational Leadership, 43*(3), 37–43.

Gump, P. V. (1982). School settings and their keeping. In D. L. Duke (Ed.), *Helping teachers manage classrooms*. Alexandria, VA: Association for Supervision Curriculum Development.

Hanes, R. C., & Mitchell, K. F. (1985). Teacher career development in Charlotte-Mecklenburg. *Educational Leadership*, 43(3), 11–13.

Harris, B. M., Bessent, W., & McIntyre, K. E. (1969). *In-service education: A guide to better practice*. Englewood Cliffs, NJ: Prentice-Hall.

Hewett, F. M., & Forness, S. R. (1977). *Education of exceptional learners* (2nd ed.). Boston: Allyn and Bacon.

Hunt, D. E. (1971). *Matching models in education*. Ontario: The Ontario Institute for Studies in Education.

Johnson, D. W. (1980). Group processes: Influences of student-student interactions on school outcomes. In J. McMillan (Ed.), *The social psychology of school learning*. New York: Academic Press.

Johnson, D. W., & Johnson, R. T. (1983). The socialization and achievement crisis: Are cooperative learning experiences the solution? In L. Bickman (Ed.), *Applied social psychology annual*. Beverly Hills, CA: Sage.

Joyce, B. R., & Weil, M. (1986). *Models of teaching*. Englewood Cliffs, NJ: Prentice-Hall.

Joyce, B. R., Hersh, R. H., & McKibbin, M. (1983). *The structure of school improvement*. New York: Longman.

Joyce, B. R., & Showers, B. (1982). The coaching of teaching. *Educational Leadership*, 40(1), 4–16.

Joyce, B. R., & Harootunian, B. (1967). *The structure of teaching*. Chicago: Science Research Associates.

King, N. (1975). *Giving form to feeling*. New York: Drama Book Specialists.

Knoblock, P. (1974). Open education for emotionally disturbed children. In G. J. Warfield (Ed.), *Mainstream Currents*. Reston, VA: Council for Exceptional Children.

Kohlberg, L. (May 1973). Moral development and the new social studies. *Social Education*, 37(5), 369–375.

Kounin, J. S. (1970). *Discipine and group management in classrooms*. New York: Holt, Rinehart & Winston.

Kounin, J. S., & Gump, P. (1974). Signal systems of lesson settings and the task related behavior of preschool children. *Journal of Educational Psychology*, 66, 554–562.

Kounin, J. S., & Sherman, L. W. (1979). School environments as behavior settings. *Theory into practise*, 18, 145–151.

Krathwohl, D. R., Bloom, B. S., & Masia, B. B. (1964). *Taxonomy of educational objectives: Handbook II: Affective domain*. New York: Longman.

Lemlech, J. K. (1984). *Curriculum and instructional methods for the elementary school*. New York: Macmillan.

Lemlech, J. K. (1977). *Handbook for successful urban teaching*. New York: Harper & Row.

Lemlech, J. K., & Marks, M. B. (1976). *The American teacher*. Bloomington: Phi Delta Kappa.

Lewin, K., Lippitt, R., & White, R. (1939). Patterns of aggressive behavior in experimentally created social climates. *Journal of Social Psychology*, 10, 271–299.

Mager, R. E. (1968). *Developing attitude toward learning*. Palo Alto: Fearon Publishers.

McKibbin, M., Weil, M., & Joyce, B. (1977). *Demonstration of alternatives.* Washington, D.C.: Association of Teacher Educators.

McLuhan, M., & Fiore, Q. (1967). *The medium is the massage.* New York: Bantam Books.

Mosston, M., & Ashworth, S. (1985). Toward a unified theory of teaching. *Educational Leadership, 42*(8), 31–34.

Newmark, G. (1976). *This school belongs to you and me.* New York: Hart Publishing.

Parsons, T. W., with Tikunoff, W. (1974). *Achieving classroom communication through self-analysis.* El Segundo: Prismatica International.

Potter, E. F. (1974). *Correlates of oral participation in classrooms.* Unpublished doctoral dissertation, University of Chicago.

Rosenshine, B. (1983). Teaching functions in instructional programs. *Elementary School Journal, 83*(4), 335–351.

Rosenshine, B. (1970). Enthusiastic teaching: A research review. *School Review, 78*, 499–514.

Rosenshine, B., & Furst, N. (1973). The use of observation to study teaching. In R. Travers (Ed.), *Second handbook of research in teaching.* Chicago: Rand McNally.

Rowe, M. B. (1974). Wait-time and rewards as instructional variables, their influence on language, logic, and fate control: Part one. Wait-time. *Journal of Research in Science Teaching, 11*, 81–94.

Rubin, L. J., & Balow, B. (1971). Learning and behavior disorders: A longitudinal study. *Exceptional Children, 38*, 293–299.

Schmuck, P., & Schmuck, R. (1977). Formal and informal aspects of classroom life: Can they be harmonized for academic learning? *The History and Social Science Teacher, 12*, 75–80.

Schrag, P. (October 4, 1986). What the test scores really mean. *The Nation*, pp. 297, 311–313.

Shepherd, C. R. (1964). *Small groups.* San Francisco: Chandler.

Silbert, J., Carnine, D., & Stein, M. (1981). *Direct instruction mathematics.* Columbus: Charles E. Merrill.

Silverstein, J. M. (1979). *Individual and environmental correlates of pupil problematic and nonproblematic classroom behavior.* Unpublished doctoral dissertation, New York University.

Stallings, J. A. (1976). How instructional processes relate to child outcomes in a national study of follow-through. *Journal of Teacher Education, 37*, 43–47.

Sweeney, R. E. (1977). *Environmental concerns the world.* New York: Harcourt Brace Jovanovich.

Thelen, H. A. (1954). *Dynamics of groups at work.* Chicago: University of Chicago Press.

Thornton, S. J. (1984). Curriculum consonance in U.S. history classrooms. Paper presented to College and University Assembly Annual Meeting of National Council for the Social Studies, Washington, D.C.

Tikunoff, W., Berliner, D., & Rist, R. (1975). An ethnographic study of the forty classrooms of the beginning teacher evaluation study. Technical Report 75-10-5. San Francisco: Far West Regional Laboratory.

Wagner, L. A. (1985). Ambiguities and possibilities in California's mentor teacher program. *Educational Leadership, 43*(3), 23–29.

Wallen, N. E. (1966). Relationship between teacher characteristics and student behavior. Part 3, Cooperative Research Project No. SAEOE 10-181. Salt Lake City: University of Utah.

Ward, B. A., & Tikunoff, W. J. (1976). The effective teacher education program: Application of selected research results and methodology to teaching. *Journal of Teacher Education, 27*, 48–53.

Weinstein, C. S. (1979). The physical environment of the school: A review of the research. *Review of Educational Research, 49*(4), 557–610.

Wilcox, K. (1982). Differential socialization in the classroom: Implications for equal opportunity. In G. Spindler (Ed.), *Doing the ethnography of schooling*. New York: Holt, Rinehart, & Winston.

Wittrock, M. C. (1986). Students' thought processes. In M. C. Wittrock (Ed.), *Handbook of research on teaching* (3rd ed.). New York: Macmillan.

Author Index

Subject Index